WHITE BOYS, WHITE NOISE:
MASCULINITIES AND 1980s INDIE GUITAR ROCK

White Boys, White Noise:
Masculinities and 1980s
Indie Guitar Rock

MATTHEW BANNISTER
Wintec, New Zealand

ASHGATE

Published by
Ashgate Publishing Limited
Gower House
Croft Road
Aldershot
Hampshire GU11 3HR
England

Ashgate Publishing Company
Suite 420
101 Cherry Street
Burlington, VT 05401-4405
USA

Ashgate website: http//www.ashgate.com

British Library Cataloguing in Publication Data
Bannister, Matthew
   White boys, white noise : masculinities and 1980s Indie
guitar rock. – (Ashgate popular and folk music series)
   1. Alternative rock music – History and criticism 2. Masculinity 3. Men, White –
Songs and music
   I. Title
   781.6'6'08909

Library of Congress Cataloging-in-Publication Data
Bannister, Matthew.
   White boys, white noise : masculinities and 1980s indie guitar rock / Matthew
Bannister
         p. cm.—(Ashgate popular and folk music series)
      ISBN 0-7546-5188-6 (hardback : alk. paper)—ISBN 0-7546-5190-8 (pbk. : alk.
paper) 1. Alternative rock music—History and criticism. 2. Masculinity in music.
I. Title. II. Series.

   ML3534.B316 2006
   781.66—dc22

                                                                                    2005026457

ISBN-13: 978-0-7546-5188-8 (HBK)
ISBN-10: 0-7546-5188-6 (HBK)
ISBN-13: 978-0-7546-5190-1 (PBK)
ISBN-10: 0-7546-5190-8 (PBK)

Printed and bound in Great Britain by MPG Books Ltd, Bodmin, Cornwall

Contents

Conclusion: … white noise 158

General Editor's Preface

The upheaval that occurred in musicology during the last two decades of the twentieth century has created a new urgency for the study of popular music alongside the development of new critical and theoretical models. A relativistic outlook has replaced the universal perspective of modernism (the international ambitions of the 12-note style); the grand narrative of the evolution and dissolution of tonality has been challenged, and emphasis has shifted to cultural context, reception and subject position. Together, these have conspired to eat away at the status of canonical composers and categories of high and low in music. A need has arisen, also, to recognize and address the emergence of crossovers, mixed and new genres, to engage in debates concerning the vexed problem of what constitutes authenticity in music and to offer a critique of musical practice as the product of free, individual expression.

Popular musicology is now a vital and exciting area of scholarship, and the *Ashgate Popular and Folk Music Series* aims to present the best research in the field. Authors will be concerned with locating musical practices, values and meanings in cultural context, and may draw upon methodologies and theories developed in cultural studies, semiotics, poststructuralism, psychology and sociology. The series will focus on popular musics of the twentieth and twenty-first centuries. It is designed to embrace the world's popular musics from Acid Jazz to Zydeco, whether high tech or low tech, commercial or non-commercial, contemporary or traditional.

Professor Derek B. Scott
Chair of Music
University of Salford

Acknowledgements

I would like to extend my thanks and love to my wife, Alice Bulmer, who read and commented on the manuscript and checked references, and my supportive family. Thanks also to Stephen Turner and Edmund King, who read some chapters, and the English Department at the University of Auckland for giving me a place to work. Nabeel Zuberi and Vicky Bogle supplied helpful ideas, suggestions and resources. Finally, I'd like to thank Michael Azerrad, for obvious reasons!

Introduction

White boys …

The words 'masculinity' and 'rock and roll' commonly conjure screaming, hip-swivelling singers, virtuosos with medallions banging on their hairy chests and an electric guitar glued to their hips, groupies, sex and drugs – the whole 1970s, decadent, Spinal Tap trip. This book is about indie guitar rock, a 1980s musical genre that eschewed many of the conventional models of rock machismo, resulting, some have claimed, in a more 'enlightened' male sexuality (DeRogatis, 1996, pp. 13–14; Gilbert, 1999, pp. 44–5; Grajeda, 2002, pp. 242–4). But I am going to argue that this is not the case.

If you're a 'straight white man' writing about (mostly) straight white masculinity, people 'tend to assume you're either gonna whomp 'em or join 'em' (Pfeil, 1995, p. viii). There is a regrettable tendency to view 'white men' as monolithic, missing the point that if gender is socially constructed, then that applies just as much to the 'dominant' group as any other. As such it would be easy for me to write a 'whomping' book about rock machismo, missing a sense of my personal investment and aspiring to an objectivity that is actually part of the problem.

The (valuable) oddness of the idea of men studying themselves is too easy to downplay in conventional academic discourse, which favours an abstract and quasi-objective lexicon. It behoves men studying masculinities not to hide behind pseudo-scientific detachment, because the implied set of power relations are the very ones which we are supposed to be questioning. The problem of subjective positioning in masculinities studies may be compounded by class differences between academics and their (usually working-class or somehow other) subjects which may result in a condescending 'gaze' that obscures the differences between 'at least two very different masculine possibilities: one physically aggressive, "macho" and overtly aggressive; the other … uptight, emotionally inhibited and fastidiously devoid of affect' (Ehrenreich, 1983, p. 133). Perhaps this latter category is a little too close for comfort, but if indie is primarily about 'young White men … aspiring to the class of salaried intellectuals … uncomfortable with the conventional gendered identities offered by the dominant strands of popular culture' (Gilbert, 1999, p. 44) then perhaps it is time to look more closely at this second model, whose modes of power and control are not mainly physical and bodily but abstract, indirect and intellectual.

I want to suggest that overemphasis on the first has tended to obscure the ways that both serve masculine hegemony in popular music. Intersecting with these themes is my account of migrating from Scotland to New Zealand, from a middle-class intellectual culture to a more 'egalitarian' and 'pragmatic' one, the resultant culture shock, playing 'indie' rock music, and the interconnections and discontinuities between different discourses of masculinity as I experienced them.

In the 1980s, I was involved in NZ alternative rock as a musician, performer and songwriter. Accordingly, I have a particular interest in musical production and musicians, an area which some suggest has been neglected in pop music studies (Toynbee, 2000a, pp. ix–x). But every musician is also a consumer and an audience, and most have a voracious appetite for pop music culture – the music press, critics, TV, radio, film and so on. Hence I have drawn extensively on such popular discourse as well as on more academic and theoretical work, believing both to be indispensable resources of ideas and possibilities. I was attending university throughout most of my band career, and have always regarded my musical and academic work as parts of a whole. As such I am equally disposed to find value in mass and high culture, a distinction I have never really recognised. Mozart or the Sex Pistols? I really wouldn't like to choose.

As regards my interest in gender, my family background is relevant. I grew up in a middle-class household in Scotland. My parents came from lower-middle- to working-class backgrounds, but had taken university degrees in science. We were an 'upwardly mobile', nuclear family, living far away from our extended families. My father, a 'scholarship boy', had few male friends, worked hard (as an academic) and left the emotional and practical management of family affairs to my mother (Hoggart, 1957, p. 238). Hence I grew up lacking contact and interaction with men, a problem exacerbated by my father's illness with cancer, which he contracted when I was seven. I poured my energies into schoolwork, and intellectual achievement became the main index of my self-esteem, soaring or plummeting according to how I did in examinations. I found more immediate pleasure and diversion in media like radio, TV and books. Unsanctioned (although not prevented) by my parents I developed an interest in pop music, initially through a couple of Beatles records they owned, which I extended into a collection through Christmas and birthday presents, and through radio and TV. At the age of 15 I bought an acoustic guitar and started learning to play. I had few male role models, but The Beatles (especially John Lennon) and the idea of rock and roll stardom were hugely important to me as a fantasy escape from my circumstances (plus I surmised, for once correctly, that rock music would improve my love life). I spent long hours in my bedroom, playing along with my record collection. In 1978 my father accepted a professorship of botany at the University of Otago in Dunedin, and after completing my higher level examinations I moved to New Zealand as a 17-year-old in 1979.

In Dunedin I combined university studies in English with playing, writing and singing in a band called Sneaky Feelings, who recorded for NZ independent Flying Nun, and were part of what was called 'the Dunedin Sound' (Mitchell, 1996, pp. 223–35; Shuker, 1998, pp. 103–4). Between 1980 and 1989 we recorded three albums and three EPs and played several hundred gigs, mostly in New Zealand, though we also toured Europe twice and released records there through

Flying Nun Europe and Normal Records in Germany. Such activities did not occur in a vacuum – bands of mostly white men playing guitars, referencing the 1960s and recording for independent labels were part of a much larger cultural movement towards 'indie' music making that was occurring throughout the Western English-speaking world (see Chapter 3 on genre).

I still play music, although I haven't released any records for some years now (the last was *Present Perfect* with my second band, Dribbling Darts of Love (1993)). As such, I have a lot of experience in popular music scenes, which could be deemed participant observation, although this implies a degree of choice and purpose that I am only constructing in retrospect. But in many ways I was also an alien – as a recent arrival to New Zealand from the UK, I was a 'stranger in a strange land'.

Gender was the locus of my alienation in my new environment. Masculinity is visibly hegemonic in 'pioneer' societies like the western USA, Canada, Australia, South Africa and New Zealand, where the 'frontier' spirit still provides a kind of national mythology, based around masculinity. In New Zealand it's 'the Kiwi bloke', a working-class, tough, pragmatic, sporty, 'matey', anti-intellectual type (Law, Campbell, Schick, 1999, p. 15; Phillips, 1987). New Zealand culture initially seemed to me to be male dominated and intellectually moribund. Women seemed to be virtually excluded from many areas of public life. Sport, especially rugby, was far more dominant than in Britain. There were few mixed-sex leisure activities. I moved from a Scottish comprehensive mixed-sex education to an NZ boys' school (which I hated). I was ill-equipped to perform the types of masculinity that seemed to be valued in NZ society. For me, music represented a potential way out of my immediate life-circumstances. However, I soon discovered that it was an unreliable means of transcendence – rather it forced me to engage more closely and painfully with the culture that I was trying to get away from. Moreover, although the local music scene resisted many aspects of the dominant culture, it also reproduced much of its 'blokey' homosociality, albeit under cover of a more bohemian style.

Craig Robertson's study of the Dunedin Sound characterises it as based around punk – not 'fashion' punk (based on appearance) but rather its DIY (do-it-yourself) ethos (1991, p. 19). The scene was marked by a 'family atmosphere', a lack of division between audience and performer, valuing 'dirty' over clean art, and simplicity over complexity (pp. 39, 35–6, 49). Bands like mine were excluded because they 'lacked the drive or energy' and were more musically complex (pp. 43–4). There was implicit ideological conflict about which values were dominant in constructions of local music. Robertson claims that the main Dunedin scene valued an extemporised approach – 'just doing it' – and devalued theoretical constructions (p. 9). This amateur, anti-intellectual approach also resonated with the local masculine pioneer ethos of egalitarianism and DIY – hence Robertson's reading may in fact be influenced by aspects of the dominant culture, something we also see in US indie scenes, discussed in Chapters 3 and 4.

Whereas in Britain there was and is a proliferation of media discourses about popular music, in 1980s New Zealand such engagement was rare in the public domain, and risked dismissal as mere 'trainspotting' (Reid, 2001). There were few music publications, and discussion of popular culture (apart from sport) risked social censure. Interest in culture was a secret you only shared with those you trusted. In itself it was not sufficient basis for friendship, and discussing it with a 'stranger' risked humiliation or being branded as eccentric, underlining how music consumption and associated activities such as collecting can be seen as 'feminis- ing' for men, especially in a strongly homosocial culture (Straw, 1997a, p. 7).

Superficially the music scene in Dunedin was slightly more sexually integrated than other aspects of New Zealand society. Women formed a substantial minority of the audience, and played in some bands, but tended to drop out as bands became better known and started touring. In our case, we fired our female bass player (see Chapter 4). There were no female bands and only a few performers in the Dunedin scene until Look Blue Go Purple in 1983–84. This male-dominated rock culture was not simply based on numerical advantage. It was also enforced ideologically. Pop music was for girls and rock music – the real stuff – was for boys. What kind of rock you liked depended on what kind of man you were: Pink Floyd, Dire Straits, the Eagles, Supertramp, Genesis and Bruce Springsteen was the 'blokey' music that was usually played by covers bands and local radio stations, while practitioners of the Dunedin Sound touted an alternative canon based on punk and its antecedents. There was no place for modern pop music or mainstream rock in the Dunedin scene:

> In a small town like Dunedin, or a small country like New Zealand, there is only room for one dominant culture and a subculture. In musical terms this meant choos- ing between Dire Straits and some kind of weird bohemian punk approach. My problem was, I didn't totally hate Dire Straits. (Bannister, 1999, p. 23)

Sneaky Feelings liked pop music, and never felt committed to the idea of an underground bohemia, or a musical avant-garde, central to many accounts of alternative music (Arnold, 1995, pp. 4–11; Azerrad, 2001, p. 3; Nehring, 1993).[1] Pop music, dancing and discos were central aspects of youth culture in Scotland, but my experience of social activities around music in New Zealand was totally different (Cavanagh, 2000, p. 24). Disco music was beyond the pale. I never saw another male musician dancing at a gig or other social function. Such behaviour would have been regarded as effeminate, and could make you the target of vio- lence (Churton, 2000, p. 79; Reynolds, 1990, p. 79). Again, this conflict between pop and rock, between mainstream and alternative ideas of music making, was also a feature of indie scenes more generally (see Chapter 3). But Sneaky Feelings did not consciously buy into any discourse of oppositional 'cool'.

Pubs were the immediate level at which rock bands had to negotiate a relation- ship with socially dominant conceptions of masculinity based around drinking and sport, and dominant ideologies of music making in relation to audiences. A measure of my naivety in this respect – I once walked into a pub and asked for a gig, wearing my school uniform. Live popular music and the brewing industry are/were closely related in New Zealand, as pubs provide the main venues and income for most popular musicians. Pub bands typically stuck to covers: chart hits or accepted classic rock like Fleetwood Mac, the Eagles or possibly heavy metal that a primarily male audience would accept, hence pub rock – loud, aggressive music played by loud aggressive men, preferably with a suitably impressive PA and lightshow.[2] The music had to be fast, loud and competent so the audience could 'rage' (drink more) and dance if they got drunk enough. Blues was the only acceptable 'ethnic' music. Pub owners initially resisted Dunedin Sound bands because of their perceived amateurism, but this diminished a little once they had been proven to attract large audiences (not usually heavy-drinking audiences, regrettably for the publicans). The alternative rock approach wasn't too far removed from pub culture: it was reasonably loud, aggressive and had plenty of fast songs – slow or 'sensitive' material was generally sneered at.

Since wimpy pop songs were what Sneaky Feelings specialised in, pubs were less than ideal venues for us. Once we had a popular record out, and played more outside Dunedin, we started to get more recognition. But we never lost the sense that we were somehow slightly eccentric, and we were always under pressure to prove ourselves. Punk veteran Chris Knox (The Enemy, Toy Love, Tall Dwarfs), as Flying Nun's self-appointed 'Jiminy Cricket' (male superego?), frequently badgered us about our musical direction (*Heavenly Pop Hits*, 2002; Bannister, 1999, pp. 67–8, 84, 100, 160–61). Also, as Flying Nun developed, it continued to be identified and evaluated in terms of a similar aesthetic to that espoused by Robertson, a sonic orthodoxy closely allied to alternative rock mores, that is, 'the Dunedin Sound'. Our most popular records (notably *Send You*, 1984) conformed closely to this punk/indie guitar rock model (Robertson, 1991, pp. 35–6, 39, 49).

In 1991 Flying Nun confirmed our paranoia by releasing a ten-year label retrospective (*Getting Older*) in which no Sneaky Feelings tracks were included. Many of the anthologised bands had also broken up, and others were pretty obscure. Moreover, I was still involved with the label with the Dribbling Darts of Love (who weren't included either). The incident ultimately motivated me to write *Positively George Street* (Bannister, 1999), the first and only book about the Dunedin Sound, but also my revisionist attempt to prevent us being written out of NZ musical history altogether. However, it wasn't just a question of our not fitting into the NZ scene – by the early 1990s Flying Nun was selling as many records overseas as at home, and was increasingly involved in the global indie scene. Sneaky Feelings did not fit into the way indie developed as a genre, because the overall trajectory was away from 'indie pop' and towards rock. While in the early 1980s there were groups like Orange Juice, The Go-Betweens and R.E.M. with whom we had something in common, they either broke up or went mainstream. We were in no position to make this jump, so we gradually got more disillusioned and sidelined.

To put it crudely, the music gradually got louder and more distorted, and bands that didn't follow this style gradually got squeezed out. Presumably such stylistic extremism was originally a way of preserving 'difference', but this very point of difference became a marketing tool with the post-Nirvana 'explosion' and prolif- eration of 'modern/alternative rock' radio, based around white boy guitar per- formers and audiences (Goodlad, 2003). Record companies are often blamed for commercialisation of local scenes, but I contend that indie's insistence on 'auton- omy', its policing of difference, its dedication to being alternative are actually part of a larger discourse of how the resistance/incorporation paradigm works to confirm hegemonic values (Carrabine and Longhurst, 1999, pp. 125–8). Rather than viewing music subcultures or countercultures only in terms of resistance then, I would see them as also reproducing dominant social structures, especially in terms of gender.

So far I've suggested some ways in which a local, dominant masculinity was reproduced and represented in the local indie music scene. However, masculinity is also part of *my* subjectivity. So it might be more apt to see the foregoing as a conflict between two different sets of cultural values – that of pakeha (white) NZ society and that of my British middle-class background – and to perhaps work into my argument the idea that indie represented more than one set of masculine possibilities.[3]

Masculinities are articulated differently in different socio-cultural contexts. Britain, like New Zealand, is a patriarchal society, but social class is a much greater preoccupation than gender. For me, class meant that the kinds of tough working-class machismo that existed in Scotland – the 'bovver boys' and 'hard men', for example – did not exert the same hegemonic force that comparable masculinities did in New Zealand. Certainly, growing up in Scotland, I was afraid of their physical and sporting prowess. But it didn't matter that much, because I was middle class and believed that in the long run society supported *my* values: my intellectual and imaginative abilities, values nurtured in my home life (aca- demic parents) and in the Scottish education system. Pakeha New Zealand clearly didn't value intellect in the same way. I was the 'New Chum': an intellectual and aesthetic young man of 'refined' sensibilities, comically incongruous in a rough pioneering society (Phillips, 1987, p. 24). Hence New Zealand is not necessarily a more masculine or patriarchal society than the UK – it simply identifies mascu- linity in different ways. For the 'Kiwi bloke', masculinity is bodily; but my mas- culinity was in my head.

In the UK there was more emphasis on music as an intellectual pursuit, but this does not mean that it was therefore less masculine. Rather it was a different kind of masculinity: activities of record collecting, debates about the composition of the 'canon'; music 'connoisseurship', exchange and hoarding of information – all provide spaces for masculine identity formation (Straw, 1997a, p. 5). My prelimi- nary suggestion here is that indie provided a space where some men could assert masculinity indirectly by participating in a kind of objective order or symbolic system of authority in which rank is determined by subjectively held notions of taste and knowledge: or as one of Nick Hornby's characters puts it, the relative importance to men of 'what you like' as opposed to 'what you're like' (Hornby, 1995, p. 222). Within this sphere of taste, allied with a certain aestheticism, some men can create a space where their subjectivity is defined through the hierarchisation and ordering of musical knowledge and experience. The kind of cultural capital they possess is relatively marginal to society as a whole – it is indeed more like subcultural capital, but it may present a potential means for long-term advancement (see Chapters 2 and 5).

Contextualising indie

To understand any cultural movement occurring in the 1980s such as indie, we need to look in some detail at the social circumstances of youth (especially male youth): political and economic hegemony; demographics – the GenX hypothesis; relevant social and intellectual change (for example, identity politics) and cultural attitudes. The 1970s had seen the gradual collapse of a long-term post-war social contract: a neo-Keynesian compact between the government, business and the unions in which state intervention was justified in terms of discourses of protectionism for local industries, tax breaks and mediation between (often compulsory) unions and business to achieve incremental pay increases tied to inflation, a period and ideology variously termed the post-war consensus in the UK (and the USA) and in NZ history 'the historic compromise' (Jesson, 1989, p. 17; Kavanagh, 1990, pp. 6–14). The increasing power of multinationals, globalisation, the oil crisis, the hegemony of international financial markets, the replacement of fixed with floating exchange rates, and balance of payments crises paved the way for massive restructuring, privatisation, budget cutting and rationalisation – Thatcherism (UK), Reaganism (USA) and Rogernomics (NZ). Cradle-to-grave socialism was now officially dead, and consensus and inclusion gave way to rampant individualism and social hierarchisation. As government subsidies and tariff fences disappeared, multinationals moved primary production to the Second World. Full-time labouring and heavy industry jobs decreased; service and information industries and labour casualisation grew (Faludi, 1999, p. 39; Rutherford, 1988, pp. 23–4).

Traditional models of 'grunt' (working-class) masculinity were looking increasingly vulnerable. Susan Faludi writes in *Stiffed* of the Long Beach shipyard, once a huge naval shipyard, employing tens of thousands, and the consequences of downsizing and privatising on its male workforce. She sees 'a social pact between the nation's men and its institutions collapsing ... masculine ideals of loyalty, productivity and service lay in shards' (1999, p. 43). US indie bands like the Minutemen, who hail from San Pedro, just around the corner from Long Beach, arose from this context – they, like many US indie musicians, came from military families, and the privatisation and restructuring of the US military industry had profound social effects (Azerrad, 2001, pp. 62–63; Faludi, 1999, pp. 51–74). Not everyone accepts Faludi's argument, however: James Heartfield

(2002) states that 'the crisis is not one of masculinity, but one of the working-class'. However, economic change did not only affect the working class. The shrinking of the state and growth of the private sector also removed traditional middle-class work, for example public service jobs. Many moved into the private sector and became 'yuppies', but others attempted to reject hegemonic values, practising 'a carefully modulated distancing from the cues and signals of ... consumer culture' (Rushkoff, 1994, p. 5). To sum up, one might say that for a significant number of people, and especially perhaps young adults, the 1980s signalled a sense of betrayal, crisis, insecurity and a worsening of their lives (Marsh, 1985, p. 1). As such, there was a tendency to either idealise the immediate past as a magical prelapsarian moment which contrasted favourably with contemporary trials and tribulations or denigrate it as a cause of present problems, and one of the main focuses was the 1960s.

Groups from all parts of the social and political spectrum lined up to take a shot at the 1960s, and especially at its most visible manifestation – the counterculture. Punk rock got in first with its denunciation of 'old hippies', a theme essentially continued in GenX's targeting of 'boomer culture'. Even 'the indie community saw what had happened to the Sixties dream ... the baby boomers' egregious sellout' (Azerrad, 2001, p. 7). But the Right also laid into the 1960s counterculture's supposed excess and moral slackness, blaming it for a culture of state hand-outs, personal narcissism and drug-addled self-indulgence, and using this to justify neo-liberal economic reform (MacDonald, 1998, pp. 1–4). The universality of this derision is nicely summed up in the figure of Neil, the pariah hippy of 1980s cult UK TV series *The Young Ones*, who is considered fair game by punks, yuppies and wide boys alike.

Geoffrey Holtz (1995, p. 2) claims that the introduction of birth control in 1960 marks a sea change in how American society viewed children, fuelled by the 'boomer' 1960s countercultural emphasis on individual and sexual freedom, and subsequent 1970s fears of population explosion. Rising rates of divorce, mothers' increased workforce participation and the commercialisation of childcare supposedly led to increased parental neglect and absence (1995, pp. 25 7, 33 7, 42 3). Accordingly, Holtz argues that the early 1970s saw a demonisation of children in popular culture, literally in films like *The Omen* and *Rosemary's Baby*, more subtly in *Bugsy Malone*, and the sexualisation of young girls (*Taxi Driver*, for example) (pp. 15, 22). Holtz suggests that the subtext was that kids were every bit as powerful and scary as adults; hence perhaps they didn't need parents to look after them. Rob Latham argues that this change in attitude towards youth is tied to the transition from Fordism to post-Fordism. Youth moved from being the ideal symbol of mass consumption towards images of youth consumption as pathological – dependence, morbidity, halted growth, aberrant reproduction: 'a symptom of a malaise of a system that conceives only one role for youth – the idleness and hedonism of consumption – but then indicts them for enacting it' (Latham, 2002, p. 74). 'In the transition to post-Fordism, the vampire proved a remarkably flexible metaphor for capturing the general cultural ambivalence regarding youth consumption' (2002, p. 70). The George Romero-directed 1976 vampire flick *Martin*, which, as the title suggests, offers a sympathetic portrait of a contemporary white male urban teen-ager (who just happens to be a vampire) 'may be seen as pioneering the figure of the slacker ... compulsive yet affectless, media-obsessed ... living in a world self-fashioned out of the scattered detritus of consumer culture' (2002, pp. 75–6).

Of course, every generation likes to imagine it has a uniquely hard childhood, and perhaps this is because of a basic truth – children have few rights and there-fore tend to become the guinea pigs of whatever ideologies and social conditions they are born into. If nothing else, Holtz's 'generation that raised itself' (1995, p. 7) has at least an equal claim to other generations. But the real problem here lies not with any one social group or subculture, but rather with broader processes of social change from modernity to post- or late modernity, from Fordism to post-Fordism: the transformation, as McLuhan (1964, p. 11) would have it, from the mechanical, industrial age of still slightly deferred gratification into the electronic, post-industrial, instantaneous present. The legacy of the 1960s is too complex to be simply dismissed or vilified, and thus Holtz's tendency to 'blame the boomers' needs some qualification. Ian MacDonald, prefacing his work on The Beatles, points out that if the ambitions of the 1960s counterculture 'had really been so irrelevant and impractical, why such resentment at [their] supposed failure to realise them?' (1998, p. 2). Gina Arnold states on behalf of the US indie commu-nity: 'we were too ashamed of the fate of hippy idealism to recognise our actual allegiance to it' (1995, p. 170). The music and ideologies of the 1960s act as key reference points for 1980s alternative music. Michael Azerrad claims in his survey of 1980s US indie rock that 'virtually every artist in this book acknowledges the influence of the Sixties musical counterculture' (2001, p. 7) because of its per-ceived idealism about music as a way of life. The other obvious point here is that any study of indie needs to be historical – the music and popular culture of the 1960s and 1970s are highly significant influences on indie, and will be examined extensively. Finally, the 1960s also offered an idealised vision of youthful inno-cence that resonated strongly with some white teenagers who perhaps felt that they had never really had the chance to be children, leading towards a considera-tion of infantilism and childlike regression in indie culture (see Chapter 6).

The Swedish authors of *In Garageland*, a study of 1980s local rock bands and society, state that 'the 1960s bought about a new phase of modernity, a radicalised, extended and deepened *late modernity* that penetrated ever deeper into the every-day life of more and more people' (Fornäs et al., 1995, p. 150). If modernity is defined in terms of a shift in the articulation of authority from direct to indirect forms (from parental authority and tradition to state intervention and the hegem-ony of mass culture, for example) then late modernity accelerates that process, leading towards the radically atomised and privatised society we live in today (Benjamin, 1978, pp. 35–6; Giddens, 1990, pp. 140–41; Weber, 1970, pp. 15–16): 'band members[' lives] ... were stamped by a new kind of uncertainty and a ...

chronic awareness of crisis' (Fornäs et al., 1995, p. 151). Typically more distanced from their families (particularly their fathers), authority and traditional values about work and sexuality, they develop identities more in engagement with school, popular culture, media and in bands, which act as a bridge between childhood and adulthood (1995, pp. 190–97, 201–6). The authors conclude that 'if identity was formerly something you grew into ... today it is something you have to acquire' (p. 207). In other words, identity is not given; it must be continuously fashioned and re-fashioned out of materials, including media.

John Lennon was my father

It is not hard for me to interpret my own upbringing in terms of such a model: a nuclear family system, pretty thoroughly disembedded from tradition and community, identification with mediated models of authority (teachers, public achievement through exams and eventually career); consumption of media: books, TV, music, a heavily mediated engagement with the world. Although I was always materially provided for, my parents were too busy working to spend a lot of time with me – basically I was entrusted to the Scottish education system, which, fortunately, was designed to coddle quiet, clever, middle-class white boys. In Nick Hornby's books, male identification with pop culture relates to a family background based around a literally or emotionally absent father and a stressed-out, emotionally overburdened mother (although my mother was certainly not ineffectual, and was a decisive influence on my own gender politics). My idea of masculinity was shaped mostly by my mediated identification with popular culture heroes (representations), but also by the sense that education and popular culture were systems in the public arena where I could 'belong', a kind of imagined community, on the one hand, but also a public space where I could potentially gain power, by 'being someone'.

Identity in modernity is no longer something we necessarily get from family, community and tradition, because our experience of them is now fragmented and disjointed. My childhood was marked by the moves undertaken as my father pursued his career, first within Scotland, and then when I was 17, to New Zealand. In such a dislocating succession of environments, my involvement with media, and especially music, provided me with a sorely needed sense of continuity, as it did for many. In the late 1970s and early 1980s then, a generation of young men came to adulthood whose primary identifications of masculinity were with mass-mediated representations of sportsmen, TV stars and pop musicians. Such identifications must contain strong elements of fantasy and instability, uncorrected by real-life interactions. Lacking a strong sense of traditional identification, but also disillusioned with the institutional alternatives (social and career opportunities), many were drifting, lacking any clear sense of a role or a future, continuing to live at home, watching reruns of 1960s TV and children's programming. This was 'dole culture' – in the UK and New Zealand, unemployment benefits offered the only stable source of income, promoting a rather self-pitying state of mind summed up in Dunedin band The Chills' 'Doledrums':

> Counting down lonely hours
> Drinking lots and taking showers
> I no longer dream about the rest of my years
> I'll check the letterbox – does anyone care?
> In the doldrums
> On the dole
> In the doldrums
> On the dole

(The Chills, 1986)

As someone who spent much of the late 1980s on benefit myself, I can attest to the authenticity of the feelings described above.

Feminism and men

The 1960s were also 'a moment when the enlargement of capitalism on a global scale simultaneously produced an immense freeing or unbinding of social energies, a prodigious release of untheorised new forces: ... ethnic forces ... the development of new and militant bearers of "surplus consciousness" in the student and women's movements, as well as in a host of struggles of other kinds' (Jameson, 1988, p. 208). One consequence of the 1960s celebration of individuality and nonconformity was that some oppressed social groups – women, gays and ethnic minorities – started organising themselves and making a claim for their right to be individuals too. Holtz (1995, p. 21) suggests that early feminism's rejection of motherhood and claiming of contraception and abortion rights reproduced this new emphasis on self-fulfilment, in which traditional roles like motherhood were seen as oppressive – 'down with childhood' (Firestone, 1970, p. 81). Basically, women were claiming the right to be like men – independent. The emphasis was reproduced in the early feminist emphasis on individual and personal rights – most specifically the right to freedom from personal oppression by male violence, coercion and sexualisation.

Feminism's critique of male power was hugely significant (after all, 'masculinities' as a subject would not exist without it), but its initial concentration on male sexual deviance and physical violence, which remains central to popular conceptions of what 'sexism' is, often had the effect of objectifying masculinity in the form of a male underclass – it was implicitly a middle-class critique of a primitive masculinity driven by base desires to control and dominate (especially sexually) (Millett, 1970). Such polemical simplification, while necessary, provided little understanding of the complexity of patriarchy. As Faludi comments on a counselling group for violent men: 'there was something almost absurd about these men struggling ... to recognise themselves as dominators when they were so clearly dominated, done in by the world' (1999, p. 9). She continues: 'the popular feminist joke that men are to blame for everything is just the flip side of the family values reactionary expectation that men should be in charge of everything' (pp. 9–10). As such, there were some strange alliances between feminists and reactionary social groups, over censorship, for example (Segal, 1990, pp. 207–8, 221–2, 226–7).

These debates were very much to the fore in the early 1980s at Otago University, forming part of the ideological context in which Dunedin Sound bands operated. Despite Robertson's claims that the Dunedin Sound distanced itself from the university, many band members were the offspring of university staff, for example myself, Martin Durrant (Sneaky Feelings), Martin Phillipps, Jane Dodd, Terry Moore (The Chills, Verlaines, Bored Games) and Jonathan Moore (Bored Games) or were students (Bruce Russell, Alister Galbraith, Graeme Downes, Kat Tyrie, David Pine) (Robertson, 1991, p. 42). The university also offered paying gigs and media exposure. Accordingly, there was an awareness of the undesirability of 'un-PC' behaviour – the stereotype of 'grunt' masculinity and its associated 'cock rock', 'sexist' or 'rockist' clichés of the type identified in contemporary texts like Frith and McRobbie's 'Rock and Sexuality' (1990, p. 373) and the *NME*. This distinction was mainly defined in class terms – Dunedin Sound bands all hailed from North Dunedin, the middle-class, university end of town. South Dunedin was the home of heavy metal, hot rods, hot dogs and 'scarfy bashers' – drunken 'hoons' and 'bodgies' who cruised the streets around the 'Varsity', looking for students to attack. Student politics and publishing at the Varsity were dominated by left-wing politicos who periodically lambasted a generally apathetic student body about sexism and racism.

Early men's movements on campus like Men Against Sexism took feminist critique to heart and largely defined masculinity in terms of a feminist view of men as violent abusers (Rutherford, 1988, pp. 25–31). NZ masculinities scholar Kai Jensen suggests, from his involvement, that such groups were primarily 'male supporters of feminism' (1996, p. 5) – as the formula suggests, a somewhat thankless task. Any preoccupation with masculinity was seen as patriarchal. The paradox was that the forms of sexism such groups addressed often had little connection with their own lived realities. This highlighted a problem with early feminist definitions of patriarchy as unchanging and ahistorical: 'The effort to identify the enemy as singular in form is a reverse-discourse that uncritically mimics the strategy of the oppressor instead of offering a different set of terms' (Butler, 2000, p. 309). What was needed was recognition that masculinity is also a social construct. My own involvement in men's groups (from the mid-1990s onwards) is detailed in Chapter 1.

Gender and writing on indie rock

Popular music has always been closely linked to changing social attitudes to sex and gender. In the 1950s, rock and roll reintroduced the male body into a culture that increasingly objectified sexuality as female. Attali claims that music has a 'prophetic' function: 'Every major social rupture has been preceded by an essential mutation in the codes of music' (1985, pp. 10–11). The glamorisation and objectification of male bodies and associated concepts of the 'New Man' now widespread in consumer culture seem to owe a big debt to popular music and associated media, especially the glamour, androgyny and self-conscious artifice of 1980s New Pop (Culture Club, ABC, Duran Duran, Human League), which, in many ways, indie rock was reacting against (Reynolds, 1985; Rutherford, 1988, pp. 32–42). New Pop discourses were mainly concerned to demonstrate how postmodernism, poststructuralism and postfeminism as manifested in MTV, Madonna, Prince and digital sampling celebrated a shiny new androgynous semiotic wonderland, where continuous self-invention through artifice and intertextual pastiche erased sexual difference, problematised authorship and created polysemic and polysexual possibilities. Rock was dead. US critics soberly marked the end of Grossberg's 'rock formation', wondering if that was a good thing (Grossberg, 1994, pp. 43–5).

Alternative guitar rock (see Chapter 3) was not much written about at the time, partly because it wasn't commercially successful, and because in the early 1980s guys with guitars were passé, even 'rockist' (Frith and Horne, 1987, pp. 177–8). But increasingly UK music weeklies were targeting a young white male demographic who saw such a retro move as the most appropriate reaction to the intensely image-conscious, status-obsessed times (Davies, 1996, pp. 125–6). More recently, there has been a small explosion of critical work on the 'genre', mainly since the success of R.E.M., Nirvana and Oasis made such projects commercially viable, but mostly concentrating on individual groups, local or, at most, national scenes. Such work can be seen to confirm narratives of local authenticity or artistic integrity, in contrast to the commercialism and cosmopolitanism of New Pop and MTV (Arnold, 1995; Azerrad, 2001; Bannister, 1999; Buckley, 2002; Cavanagh, 2000; Kruse, 2003; Nichols, 2003; Robertson, 1991; Rogan, 1992). The exceptions (for example DeRogatis, 1996; Felder, 1993; Larkin, 1995; Strong, 1999; Thompson, 2000) tend to take a basically documentary or encyclopaedic approach, offering a lot of information, but not a great deal of useful analysis or criticism. I suggest in Chapter 3, that such studies tend to be predicated on the assumption that alternative music is original, unique, different, non-conformist and independent of the dominant culture.

These commentaries have tended to avoid questions of gender and ethnic representation, partly because the genre is so clearly dominated by white males. This bias also makes the genre a little 'unsexy' for academics, who like to stress the experience of marginalised groups such as women and homosexuals. While I recognise the importance of studying oppressed groups, such studies can reify power relations in terms of a dominance/resistance model (Clawson, 1999, p. 99). Of course many accounts of indie scenes assume this model of power relations, and as such may also assume that any kind of marginal music practice opposes dominant discourses. But this is a simplification. Certainly feminism did have some significant effects on indie musical practice, but these are not reducible to a formula of resistance to the dominant order.

I have chosen to write about three examples of 1980s indie culture, in New Zealand, the USA and the UK, with the idea of demonstrating broad continuities between such globally disparate scenes. Obviously the field of indie, and even indie guitar rock, is vast, so I have concentrated on reasonably well-known artists: from the UK, The Smiths, The Jesus and Mary Chain, My Bloody Valentine and The Go-Betweens (nominally Australian); in the USA, R.E.M., The Replacements, Dinosaur Jr., Hüsker Dü and Nirvana; and from New Zealand, Flying Nun acts, including The Chills, The Clean, the Verlaines, Chris Knox, Bailter Space and The Bats. This emphasis will hopefully make the book more accessible, but it is also true to the way in which I experienced indie music at the time – on student radio, at parties, at gigs (we even supported Dinosaur Jr. in Brussels in 1988). These bands were 'the competition' – they supplied the generic context in which I was working. Moreover, they seem as typical as any of a genre which was in turn marked by a good deal of generic and stylistic similarity. I emphasise artists rather than scenes, because I think the whole idea of indie as local is questionable, given the broad continuities that I identify and how easily the local is characterised as 'autonomous' and 'resistant' (see Chapter 3). Studies of specific scenes tend to miss the way these scenes are connected. My approach also tends to highlight musical texts to a greater degree than, say, a subcultural approach – as a musician, I believe that the music is important. That said, there will be no specifically musicological analysis – the advantage being that the discussion stays within the realms of the generally comprehensible, as well as being more true to the way in which rock music is generally talked about and valued.

My concentration on the 1980s reflects my main period of involvement with indie and conforms to other studies (Arnold, Azerrad, Cavanagh, Nichols). The end of the 1970s was a watershed not only in music (the brief cosmic flare of punk, the birth of rap, the rapid proliferation of indie labels, the start of MTV) but in society more generally – the change in political climate mentioned above with the election of New Right administrations. Equally, with the collapse of Rough Trade and a number of other indie labels in the depressed economic climate of the late 1980s, the increasing incorporation of indie labels into the industry, the resultant disappearance of the UK indie chart and the crossover success of Nirvana and grunge (which in turn introduces a whole new spectrum of musical and other factors), 1991 marks the end of a chapter in the indie story – as well as the virtual end of my own involvement in indie scenes as a musician (Arnold, 1995, pp. 4–6; Azerrad, 2001, p. 3; Bannister, 1999; Hesmondhalgh, 1999, p. 39; Lazell, 1997, p. 1). However, I have written about Nirvana, because they sum up many of the concerns addressed herein.

Indie guitar rock largely anticipated most of today's white alternative mainstream: the little boys' rock of Blink 182 or Green Day; the tortured 'artistic' posturing and 'high seriousness' of quasi-progressive bands like Metallica or Radiohead (Keightley, 2001, p. 129); the heavy metal pop of the Foo Fighters; and, of course, Britpop and grunge, although perhaps its spirit is most tellingly evoked by the garage rock revival of the last few years: The Strokes, The White Stripes, The Hives and D4. It seems relevant to enquire as to how such a supposedly marginal genre has become institutionalised. It is often suggested that indie is now a commodity; its 'purity' defiled by sellouts, buyouts and mergers (Arnold, 1995, pp. 168–71; Azerrad, 2001, pp. 493–501; Harrington, 2002, p. 475; Hesmondhalgh, 1999, p. 40). However, in what sense was indie 'pure' to begin with?

An overview

So far I've suggested that indie guitar rock is a musical genre that eschewed many of the conventional models of rock machismo. As a white heterosexual male indie musician in 1980s New Zealand, but also a middle-class intellectual and recent immigrant (from the UK) I found that the experience of playing in a rock band in a homosocial culture both confirmed and challenged the above model. As a 'soft' male, I and many of my peers rejected 'rockist' machismo (see Chapter 1), but in other ways the local indie scene was quite hard and homosocial, policing musical style, demanding fidelity to a 'punk' version of authenticity marked by rough sound, amateurism, minimalism and purity. Initially my response was to critique and reject this culture (as it had critiqued and rejected me) but I eventually realised that my own, more intellectual assumptions about music and gender were, in their own way, equally masculine (my class conditioning had tended to obviate the gendered implications). I now realise the importance of my own subjective positioning as a man, critiquing other men; how it problematises any simplistic notion of a 'top-down' patriarchal oppression and necessarily leads towards a more careful consideration of indie masculinities as marked by internal division, stratification and multiplicity, and as produced by particular sets of historical and social circumstances. At the same time, I still perceive broad continuities between indie scenes and their representations of masculinity across the Western world – and here it is relevant to outline significant social and economic changes in the Western cultural landscape – feminism, identity politics, generational tensions, economic recession, the growth of the New Right and how these affected representations of (male) youth in 1970s and 1980s popular culture.

Chapter 1 surveys writing on masculinities, focusing on problematic binaries and dichotomies between observed and observer and masculine and feminine, present in sociological and psychological theorisations of gender but persisting even in poststructural critiques of subjectivity. I argue that masculinities have often been reified as other to the subjectivities of researchers and writers, as a rough working-class, deviant 'other', through a middle-class gaze that disavows the involvement of the observer. The Frankfurt School offers a psycho-social theorisation of such controlling, observational masculinities as rational, controlling superego, increasingly in modernity associated with 'indirect' forms of authority – surveillance, discipline, objectivity and rationalisation (Foucault, 1978, pp. 135–45). The foregoing indicates in a preliminary way how masculinities are articulated through 'splitting' (in the case of masculinities into 'primitive' id and rational, controlling superego). Intersubjective theory offers a way of mediating between and resolving such binary oppositions, by suggesting that Freud's intrapsychic model needs to be placed in a wider frame of reference, of relationships between subjectivities (Benjamin, 1988, 1998).

Chapter 2 argues that masculine hegemony in culture is articulated through the splitting of high and low culture and the processes of distinction that operate to uphold it: purification and aestheticisation (Bourdieu, 1984), and Adorno's insistence on the autonomy of high culture (Adorno, 1973, 1990). As Andrew Ross observes, the history of popular culture is not just of the people but of 'experts in culture whose traditional business is to define what is popular and what is legitimate, who patrol the ... borders of ... taste' (1989, p. 5). In terms of the gender specificity of this model, the argument is not so much that high and low correspond to masculine and feminine, but that they correspond to the Freudian split between superego and id, and the implied model of repressive power relations. Popular cultural aesthetics take up differing positions within this system – sometimes the feminine or vulgar is elevated and idealised, as in Ross's formulations of the camp 'trash aesthetic', sometimes it is low or 'primitive' culture, for example black 'hipness' (folk discourse), but while such approaches may serve to 'negate' the system, they do not challenge its basic polarities. In the folk discourse, production is idealised, but in camp, there is a corresponding idealisation of consumption as a form of production through the 'innocent eye' of a 'passive' audience of cultural 'dupes'. I argue that Warhol and the Velvet Underground (camp) offered a Foucauldian critique of the Freudian repressive hypothesis by rejecting its binary of activity and passivity and instead showing how power can be asserted through passivity and the gaze. The case study here is the emergence of a gendered rock aesthetic, proceeding from high cultural modernism, through 'folk' discourses of authenticity (and 'body' and sexuality, through identification with black culture) towards the emergence of art rock and punk, leading towards alternative rock. This demonstrates how high cultural categories of purity and aestheticisation, applied to popular culture, work to confirm patriarchal power.

In Chapter 3 I discuss indie guitar rock as a genre. This serves two purposes: first, by focusing on transnational continuities of sound, performance style, lyrical concerns, production practices and gender, it refutes the idea of indie as primarily 'local' (and the degree to which the local can be read as 'folk' authenticity). Second, theorising genre not as a list of fixed qualities but rather as deriving

'identity' from its difference to other genres emphasises the importance of 'negation' – what is absent is as important as 'what is there' (Toynbee, 2000b; Nehring,
1997, p. 51). This is especially relevant in genres that define themselves as 'alternative'. In the early 1980s, indie was in a process of becoming a genre, defining
its relationships to other genres and styles, as well as wider cultural and social
processes. This process of definition involved a flirtation with the 'others' of pop,
femininity, ethnicity, the 1960s. Indie guitar rock, which became arguably the
dominant form of indie, was marked eventually by a rejection of such alternative
narratives and a hardening of style towards a purist, 'white noise' autonomy. This
move parallels Adorno's pronouncements (1973) about the function of art in
modern society (and can be similarly critiqued).

Having argued against homosociality as a reification of 'machismo' or 'men
behaving badly', in Chapter 4 I suggest how it functions on a more abstract level
as a mode of policing, of rejection of alternative narratives of identity and influence (as was implied in Chapter 3). Moreover, the often reified homosocial solidarity of rock (theorised here in terms of 'kinship') is more usefully viewed as an
ongoing hegemonic process of readjustment and limitation of the feminising possibilities that are inherent in the presence of the male body to an audience. This
objectification or commodification of masculinity in rock is directly in conflict
with its homosociality, because in the former the male body becomes subject to a
gaze that it traditionally arrogated to itself. The presence of an audience also highlights subjectivity and disavowed emotionality within homosociality, thus interfer-
ing with its supposedly instrumental orientation. Accordingly I look at homosociality
as it works in discourses around musical style, in terms of audience/band relationships and in intra-band relations.

Chapter 5 examines media technologies and gender in indie. Initially I focus
mainly on 'hard' technologies but later on 'soft' systems of information control
and organisation such as archivalism and canonism. Indie masculinities are positioned ambivalently between the traditional association of hard technology with
masculinity, classical discourse, which naturalises technology, and the folk discourse of technological dystopianism, but negotiate between these positions
through ideologies of incompetence and non-intentionality (represented by Lester
Bangs and Brian Eno). They employ technological means but with an implied lack
of control about the outcome, thus escaping the charges of instrumentality and
direct authorship. Yet ironically such an approach produces not diversity, but
rather a homogenous indie sound, a 'white noise'. This leads towards a consideration of sound as an indirect means of control in indie, with special reference to the
'wall of sound' or characteristic indie 'drone' and how they reconcile discourses
of technological modernity and primitivism while also 'masking' authorship.

Canonism, archivalism and connoisseurship are both 'soft' technologies and
indirect forms of power, central to cultural legitimation in popular as well as high
culture. I suggest re-envisioning indie as a history of record collectors – the importance of rock tradition to indie, of male rock 'intellectuals' and secondhand record

shops; a narrative suppressed because of the normative emphasis on rock as a folk discourse, spontaneous, instinctual, closely allied to a 'natural' masculinity. I also consider such activities as models of rational organisation; offering points of symbolic identification with a masculinised and intellectualised public sphere.

Chapter 6 argues the connections between melancholy (indie rock's predominant affect) and white masculinities, by situating indie in a tradition of negative or alternative aesthetics that is deeply beholden to Cartesian dualism. This pessimistic but also patriarchal worldview is incarnated in the Romantic figure of the suffering artist. Caught within patriarchal dualisms of masculine/feminine, aggressor/victim, rational/irrational, self/other, male indie 'stars' like Morrissey and Kurt Cobain display a schizoid oscillation between mutually exclusive subject positions. I argue for the importance of a more relational or reflexive model of subjectivity in which the opposing terms are seen in a mutually constitutive relationship. Only in this way can the problem of male depression (which indie music anticipates and describes very well) be overcome.

In the conclusion, I return to a reconsider the terms of the book's title – the importance of indie 'white noise' for white boys, using Attali's definition of noise as possibility and novelty, and examining how indie white noise fails to realise the promise of Attali's theory, but instead tends to reiterate existing subject positions and gender discourses. I look at more positive and non-schizophrenic possibilities for indie masculinities, that highlight the importance of relationship – for example the presence of dialogue within music (The Go-Betweens, R.E.M., Hüsker Dü, Minutemen), the presence of multiple voices or perspectives, or in terms of musical performance as a process rather than product oriented-practice, thus defeating commodification.

Notes

1. Ironically, this populism was based on alienation – unlike the other Dunedin bands, which arose from specific groups of friends who had gone to school together, and who had some investment in the punk scene, Sneaky Feelings were more like a disparate collection of individuals with a common interest in music (partly as a way of overcoming isolation). This also meant that we didn't have a hard-core audience of friends, arguably another factor in our difficulties. But it was also based on the fact that, for us, punk rock was not an ideal, and 1977 was not 'Year Zero'.
2. NZ pub rock was more like Australian pub rock than the 'revivalist' UK version (Churton, 2000, p. 241; Dix, 1988, pp. 178–94; Johnson, 1992, pp. 130–35).
3. NZ cultural historian Michael King (1999, p. 10) states that the term 'pakeha' derived from the Maori word 'pakepakeha', which means 'fair-skinned folk'. The relationship between the UK, New Zealand and white masculine hegemony is actually rather complex. See Bannister (2005).

Chapter 1

Reviewing theories and representations of masculinities

White men in Western society, historically, have not theorised themselves, but assumed that masculinity is a universal norm – 'mankind' (Easthope, 1986, pp. 1–2; Rutherford, 1988, p. 23; Seidler, 1989, pp. 3–4, 14). Moreover, discourses of scientific objectivity and rationality, legacies of the Enlightenment, Descartes and Newton, have perpetuated patriarchal hegemony through insistence on detached objectivity and their consequent reduction of the world to an object outside the mind (Brennan, 2004, pp. 4, 94; Horkheimer, 1994, p. vii). Rational analysis, proceeding by an 'either/or' method (the same as used in binary code) performs an analytical splitting of the world into dichotomies – subject and object, feeling and reason, feminine or masculine: 'Abstract masculinity ... is a mode of conceptualisation that emphasises mutually exclusive dualities' (Humm, 1995, p. 163; see also Hartsock, 1983).

The detached, scientific mode of observation artificially splits off the consciousness and subjectivity of the researcher from the 'object' of study. But increasingly, commentators suggest that observation reveals the truth not only of the thing observed, but also of the observing subject.[1] 'Most of what has been perceived as universal in the observed system (gender or sex) may in fact have been part of the observing system' (Holter, 1995, p. 102). Social structures, according to Bourdieu (Bourdieu and Wacquant, 1992, p. 7), lead a 'double life' and both objective and subjective (observers' and actors') perspectives are part of their totality, so an absolute separation between observer and observed is epistemologically problematic, especially in the social sciences, which are, after all, about people studying other people. In arguing for the interconnection of subject and object, Bourdieu implicitly suggests that we are not obliged to choose one as 'better' than the other, but rather to listen to both. Any theorisation of masculinities has to take into account the way in which taken-for-granted empirical epistemologies and methodologies may reproduce existing models of power relations. I contend that studies of masculine behaviour are in turn limited to the degree that they adopt a scientific/empirical or binary approach. Masculinity is reproduced through epistemology, not just through 'male bonding'.

Binary systems are not timeless and ahistorical because hegemony is never an established fact. There is continuous renegotiation of boundaries as circumstances change, and some terms may be prioritised over others. For example, Mulvey (1989) posits a primary identification of spectatorship with masculinity and of spectacle with femininity. But today male bodies are also objectified and eroti- cised: masculinity is also becoming an object of the gaze (Faludi, 1999, pp. 34–40; Rutherford, 1988, pp. 38–9). This complicates the gender positioning of the spec- tator, and shows us how binary boundaries can shift over time. However, I would argue that the constant here is the gaze itself and the consequent process of objec- tification. Behind the shifting gender positions of the binary there is a meta- discourse – and it is thoroughly masculinised – the idea of the gaze itself as a way of looking at the world. The salient characteristic of the gaze is the split between the subject and the object – and it is in this area that gender is most often natural- ised, especially in intellectual discourse.

Masculinity is not just one half of this binary system, it is also present in the binary 'mode of conceptualisation' itself; it is not an essence, but rather a hegem- onic position, a powerful way of seeing or describing the world (Hartsock, 1983, pp. 130–32; Humm, 1995, p. 163). As such, it is often not directly observable by empirical methods – rather it is in the way such accounts are constructed, and the implicit theories of representation at work in them. As such, there is also a femi- nine position, in which such splits can be re-envisaged in terms of a continuum or relationship. My central concern is the role played by subjectivity in theoretical approaches to masculinities; particularly the subjectivity of the researcher or writer. It is customary to identify subjectivity with the merely personal and unveri- fiable, but I argue that it is not possible to separate subjective and objective modes of knowledge. As I indicated in the introduction, acknowledging my subjectivity in my research on New Zealand masculinities helped me move away from finger- pointing dualism towards a more inclusive and progressive approach.

This theorisation of subjectivity may be used to critique each of the main approaches to gender study: sociology, psychology and social construction (dis- course theory). Sociological theories and studies, it has been argued, historically suffer from the problem that they centre on public and male-defined domains and ignore the private, for example Marxism's stress on economics as excluding domestic, unpaid and usually feminine labour (Hearn, 1992, pp. 25–7, 80; Morgan, 1992, pp. 60–2). They are often about men, but this does not mean that gender is theorised; rather it is assumed (Morgan, 1992, p. 19). Moreover, the groups studied are often constructed as subordinate or oppressed. As such, researchers tend to identify with them (Hebdige, 1979), which can lead to simplification of power relations, or against them, in which case we are left with the impression that the subjectivity of those researched is simply 'wrong', 'false consciousness' (Hills, 2002, p. 64). Whatever the case, they are objectified in a way that does not expose the practices of the observers, leading to the question of whether socially dominant groups are really observable, a point particularly relevant to masculini- ties research (Shumway, 2001). We will see examples of this in sociological and subcultural studies of masculine groups below. Similarly, psychological approaches to masculinity are based on Freud, who explicitly identifies masculinity with objectivity and reason, thereby removing it from analysis. A critique of Freudian dualism is required. Finally, social constructionist approaches to gender, which typically proceed by problematising the very notion of the subject, are limited if they simply replace the masculine, autonomous self with a fragmented, feminine subject. I try to resolve this dualism by introducing Jessica Benjamin's concept of intersubjectivity, which asserts that 'shared' subjectivities can constitute a form of reality which is not reducible to an objective/subjective binary (not to be confused with Habermas's use of the term) (Benjamin, 1988, pp. 19–24; Habermas, 1970).

Straw men

R.W. Connell is a prominent masculinities scholar who uses sociological methods and approaches. He argues against a psychologising or universalising approach, and cites recent close-focus, ethnographic research on masculinities, emphasising the plurality and hierarchy of masculinities and their collective and dynamic character (Connell, 2000, p. 23). Connell has made many valuable contributions to the field (1987, 1995), but I want to focus on a recent work that highlights some problems in his assertion that gender is basically 'an empirical question, not one to be settled in advance by theory' (2000, p. 23).

In his account of 'Aussie iron man' Steve Donoghue, Connell demonstrates some of the contradictions of being a 'poster boy' for hegemonic masculinity, for although Steve has 'realised a schoolboy dream' by making a living out of sport, his training regime is 'like being in jail' (2000, p. 71). Being a male role model means denying himself sport-associated masculine social pleasures like drinking, sparring, womanising and carousing (p. 73). Ironically, one of his major sponsors is a brand of beer (p. 85). Indeed, he doesn't even really have time for a girlfriend (p. 72). So Connell establishes how Steve's public performance of ideal masculinity involves renouncing many of the pleasures of the 'patriarchal dividend' (p. 35).

Throughout, Steve's body is the focus – his physical size as a child, his involvement in swimming and the development of his body through discipline and practice, so that this 'natural' physical endowment is shown to be instrumental: 'The magnificent machine of Steve's physique has meaning only when subordinated to the will to win' (2000, p. 85). To keep earning, Steve has to keep winning; thus sport, far from being a natural propensity for participation in organised physical activity, is presented as part of a larger capital- and media-fuelled engine of economic production. In other words, he is being exploited. The final implication drawn is his immaturity – shielded from adult responsibilities by his highly specialised lifestyle, his success and his coach, he remains rather childlike, with 'a severely constricted social world and an impoverished cultural world'. Steve 'confirms' this by his predictable responses to questions about feminists, homosexuality and politics (pp. 78–9). Connell summarises: 'Steve certainly enacts in his own life some of the main patterns of contemporary hegemonic masculinity: the subordination of women, the marginalization of gay men, and the connecting of masculinity to toughness and competitiveness. He has … been celebrated as a hero [and] … is being … constructed as a media exemplar of masculinity by the advertisers who are sponsoring him' (p. 84).

Steve may be an iron man, but he's a soft target. What disturbs me about this account is the way it is structured around a mind/body dichotomy, which invisibly connects Steve's body with his 'false consciousness'. In the same way that mass culture critique connects feminine body with lack of talent or intellect, it is implied that Steve's inarticulacy needs to be interpreted by a superior, intellectual awareness. We have to ask 'How valid would we find ethnographic discourse about others if it were used to describe ourselves?' (Rosaldo, 1993, p. 107). A degree of connection between researcher and researched is needed for ethnography to be successful – this is lacking in Connell's study. Connection may introduce new issues of personal bias, but the inclusion of the researcher's subjectivity in the discussion is clearly relevant, especially when the subject is something both parties share.

Instead, Connell identifies masculinities in terms of a working-class model of physical strength and inarticulacy: 'masculinity refers to male bodies' (2000, p. 29). 'Exemplary masculinities in Western society are typically defined by a specific body-reflexive practice: sport, violence, heterosexual performance, bodybuilding' (p. 86). This view confirms the superiority of the observers (Donaldson, 2003, pp. 158–9). But many men don't imagine their masculinity mainly in terms of their bodies. My masculinity is largely in my head; that is, in my pride in my intellectual and creative abilities. Writing about masculinities in terms of the body is a way for male intellectuals to avoid considering themselves as masculine (Morgan, 1992, p. 4). It elides all the apparently ungendered ways in which masculinity is articulated – intellectual ability, creativity, reason and objectivity – and how these link to practices of power.

Ethnographic and subcultural studies of rock

Sociological methods have been hugely influential on popular music studies, mainly via the Birmingham School's 1970s investigations into youth and working-class subcultures as 'resistance' to mass culture. Popular music provides some spectacular examples, such as Paul Willis's rockers, and Dick Hebdige's punks. However, the power/resistance paradigm can lead to simplifications, especially about rock, masculinity and the working class (Hebdige, 1979; Willis, 1978).

Paul Willis's study of British working-class biker culture suggests that 'the touchstones of this world were manliness, toughness and directness of interpersonal contact ... they lived in the unreified world of the present and its immediate relations' (1978, p. 13). Willis connects masculinity with an ideal of 'unreified' existence, a working-class reality that represents an implicit left-wing critique of the 'straight', capitalist world: 'This absolute security of identity was characteristically expressed through a distinctive style. There was a rumbustious extroversion, a rough bonhomie, sometimes a bravado ... their sense of security was enacted through an essentially masculine style' (1978, p. 18). This sense of 'ontological security' is maintained at least partially by attacking other social groups as 'feminine', including women but also blacks, 'Pakis', mods, hippies and even subordinate members of the group: 'if there were other ways of living, then there were other ways of being masculine' (p. 33). Willis defends these attitudes by claiming they are preferable to 'bloodless humanism': the rockers' sexism and racism is more honest than an intellectually correct but abstract worldview (pp. 34–5).

Willis relates the bikers' lifestyle to their preferred music – 1950s and 1960s rock and roll – by the concept of homology: 'the loud, strident tones of the music symbolically held and generated all the important values – movement, noise, confidence' – fast, 'driving' rock and roll simulates the adrenalin rush one gets from rapid acceleration (1978, p. 36). 'The music did have a distinctiveness, a unity of construction, a special and consistent use of techniques, a freshness and conviction of personal delivery, a sense of the "golden" age which could parallel, hold and develop the security, authenticity and masculinity of the bike culture' (p. 63). Their listening is selective, preferring the 'golden greats' of the first rock and roll boom and some 1960s British groups, as long as they perform in an authentically rock and roll style: they distinguish between early Beatles (good), their psychedelic period ('daft') and their later returns to a more roots style (good again) (p. 65). Clearly considerations of style are valued above unquestioning allegiance to one artist. Willis's observations on the musical practices of the group suggest that the rockers' musical canon is as closely guarded as their masculine identity as a group: the bikers' cultural choices consistently re-enact their social practice: no women, no blacks, a rigorous policing of the remainder for stylistic correctness and authenticity. Other aspects of their musical practice, such as the preference for singles over albums, are explained in terms of the need for 'action'. LPs encourage passivity and ennui; besides, one no longer 'controls' the music (p. 64). This could also be read in terms of gender.

Willis understands masculinity in terms of a working-class paradigm of toughness, which has nothing to do with his identity as a social researcher. But at the same time, as a left-wing intellectual, Willis wants to see 'hope in the proles' (glamour) but can't help projecting on to them the qualities that he feels he (the middle class) lacks (fear). But this view of the bikers as 'noble savages' raises the question of why Willis is studying them; as Angela McRobbie suggests, for '(male) sociologists ... to admit how their own experience has influenced their choice of subject matter ... seems more or less taboo' (McRobbie, 1990, p. 68). In contrast, his complementary study of hippy culture doesn't mention masculinity at all, although almost all the participants are male (Willis, 1978, pp. 83–169). Perhaps because of his closer class identification with them, Willis doesn't 'see' them as masculine.

Dick Hebdige's *Subculture* (1979) follows and expands Willis's approach, analysing the behaviour and apparel of youth groups – punks, mods, skins, Rastas – and their formulation in signifying practices as style. His study is based on men, but like Willis, masculinity as such is not theorised (McRobbie, 1990, p. 73). Instead, their fandom is envisioned as 'resistance' – creating styles and using commodities in their own ways, unlike the 'masses' who passively consume 'vacuous disco-bounce and sugary ballads' (Hebdige, 1979, p. 60; see also Clarke, 1990, p. 85). Hebdige takes punk's dismissal of 'pop' at face value, but we should be more critical of this implicitly gendered identification (Thornton, 1995, p. 95). Moreover, his concentration on leisure activities in the public domain, or, in rock parlance, 'the street', means the domestic sphere is excluded, along with the institutional sites of hegemony (school, work, home), opening the text to charges of being self-referential and apolitical (McRobbie, 1990, p. 69).

The focus on the UK raises the question of how far these subcultures exist overseas – even in the British context the book was criticised as being London-centred (Clarke, 1990, p. 86; McRobbie, 1990, p. 75). Is it possible to generalise about punk without including the USA, for example (Gendron, 2002, pp. 264–5)? But this would compromise the purity and originality of the scene, and Hebdige's highly selective account of its influences. His insistence on its autonomy is masculinist. Music, while it is the organising principle of the subcultures Hebdige discusses, is curiously absent from the text, which leads to false generalisations: 'judging punk as a reaction to glam rock ... This is simply wrong' (Clarke, 1990, p. 88). But in homosocial terms, it makes perfect sense – the 'foppishness' of glam rock alienated youth who formulated the 'scruffiness and earthiness' of punk as a reaction (Hebdige, 1979, p. 63). Hebdige highlights the extent to which social practices around popular music are often typed as masculine, and this doesn't extend only to 'macho' behaviour. He also implicitly demonstrates how subcultures offer a specific kind of identity, security or subcultural capital, which appears to be important to male self-definition.

Subcultural studies represented rock masculinities as working-class, physical, expressive, aggressive and resistant. Pop music journalism, especially in the UK, incorporated many aspects of the subcultural approach, and punk provided a phenomenon amenable to such interpretation. However, rock journalists' commitment to punk meant that, like Hebdige, they tended to downplay its more misogynistic aspects, which were projected onto unfashionable musical genres: 'The Blues had a grandson ... a malformed idiot thing that stays chained up in the cellar ... it gibbers and hoots, flexing its muscles and masturbating frantically ... it brags incessantly of its strength and masculinity ... this thing's name is heavy metal' (Murray, 1992, p. 604). Heavy metal became a male scapegoat, a caricature of rock – suitable for comic treatment, as in *This is Spinal Tap* (1983; Chambers, 1985, pp. 122–4; Hebdige, 1979, p. 155). For UK punk and post-punk critics, metal was an example of 'rockism', which incarnated all the perceived excesses of 1970s rock – commercialism, supposed self-indulgence and distance from the audience, 'cock rock' machismo and drug excess (Christgau, 1990; Frith and McRobbie, 1990, p. 374; Woods, 2001).

The second way in which UK pop journalists distanced themselves from the contradictions of rock masculinity's supposed proletarianism was by placing it in US rock, hence Jon Savage's dismissal of Bruce Springsteen as 'a reassertion of "traditional" masculine virtues' (Savage, 1997, p. 174). Masculinity correlates to old-fashioned, essentialist ideologies of rockism (Frith, 1988, pp. 98–101; Laing, 1997, pp. 117–18). Michael Azerrad notes how Seattle indie Sub Pop exploited UK projections about masculinity and Americana, when in March 1989, label owners Bruce Pavitt and Jonathan Poneman flew *Melody Maker* journalist Everett True over to write up the burgeoning grunge scene. 'Pavitt's hunch that Sub Pop's "white trash" aesthetic would win over the English panned out just as he'd hoped ... The UK press believed that such raw rock & roll could only be played by Neanderthals, and Sub Pop obligingly played to their preconceptions. "Our bands are all lumberjacks," Poneman declared. "Or they painted bridges." And if they didn't, Sub Pop made it seem like they did' (Azerrad, 2001, pp. 441–2). So UK projections about American masculinity were double-edged: on the one hand, they deplored it but, on the other, they tacitly acknowledged that it embodied the essential 'authentic' spirit of rock and roll. This approach seems complementary to Willis's projected masculine other as both 'scary' and 'glamorous'.

In turn, US rock critics have often taken the complementary line – that UK music is 'faggy' or effete, as in Dave Marsh's disdain for 'art rock' (1999, pp. 391–2). Marsh sees rock as a specifically American form of expression, oozing a vitality that British groups can never emulate: 'These English guys will never really get it ... except as a pose' because they are 'living ... in a place where blues and country are fascinating affectations and purist obsessions rather than essential parts of the musical landscape' (Marsh, 1985, p. 12). Underlying this is an organic argument about place, identity and tradition – the English lack the popular tradition. The subtext is that if you are white and non-American, you can't really 'get' rock and roll (with a few glorious exceptions: The Beatles, the Rolling Stones and so on). These preoccupations continue into indie – for example Joe Carducci champions a homosocial 'working-class' masculinity as central to rock, and heaps scorn on pop, women musicians and gender-bending UK stars like David Bowie (Christgau, 1991; Gelling, 1999). Carducci's extensive involvement with US indie SST makes him an invaluable source for gender and indie in the USA (see Chapter 4). The main point, however, is that both UK and US critics reproduced a similarly tough, working-class, marginalised masculinity (although they viewed it differently).

Recent studies of masculinities in rock continue to reproduce the de facto association of rockist genres like metal and machismo with masculinity, for example Robert Walser's *Running with the Devil*. Given the author's experience as a musician, it is surprising that his discussion of metal masculinity focuses on videos, which would be surely less likely to buck the stereotypes than his own observations (Walser, 1993, pp. 108–36). One wonders why Walser's subjectivity as a male metal musician does not inform the discussion. Perhaps it is because, like earlier researchers, he sees masculinity as being other to his own experience. Walser discusses metal musicians' use of classical music, which might lend itself to a gendered reading (see Chapter 2) but would also imply a more intellectual construction of masculinity. Masculinity is more than a 'performance' – indeed I will argue that indie masculinities are characterised by a tradition of 'non-performance' (Walser 1993, pp. 109–10; Zanes, 2002, p. 308).

As a counter-discourse to the conventional model of rock machismo, Simon Reynolds' and Joy Press' *The Sex Revolts* posits male passivity and ego liberation through psychedelic music: 'rock lost its hardness, became a medium in which the listener is suspended and *enwombed*' – the 'psychedelic mother's boys' (1995, pp. 184, xii). They claim that psychedelia was a feminisation of rock, expressing 'a longing to *come home*, to return to the womb' (p. xii). The authors identify 'psychedelic mummy's boys' as initiating a tradition of male passivity in rock, from the 1960s through to indie guitar music of the 1980s. This passivity is linked to the supposed effects of psychedelic music, which, like LSD, is supposed to 'destroy' the superego. Therefore some have argued that it can represent a more 'enlightened' male sexuality (DeRogatis, 1996, pp. 13–14). This claim is discussed in Chapter 2.

Similarly, Sarah Cohen's ethnographic studies of indie music making in Liverpool highlight some non-macho performance styles: 'The lead singer of Cast … holds his guitar tight up to his chest … in a manner that conveys a youthful fragility and earnestness … enhanced by the clarity of his voice and the way he stretches up his neck to the microphone' (1997, p. 26). Lyrical themes include deceit, lack of control, uncertainty, loss and a wistful dreaminess involving numerous references to the sky and space – blocking out or escaping from the world. 'The sounds produced by bands like Cast, Space and the Lightning Seeds suggest a masculinity that is rather soft, vulnerable and less macho, aggressive and assertive, less threatening and explicit than that promoted by many styles of heavy rock or metal, rap or funk.' The lyrics suggest 'fragile masculinity – men who are lost, confused and betrayed' (p. 29). However, Cohen claims gender cannot be read off the music alone (as Reynolds and Press do); rather the scene is 'produced as male through the everyday activities that comprise the scene; sensual, emotional aspects … and through systems of ideas … including the contested concept of the "scene" itself' (p. 17). Most bands 'comprise four or five musicians on drums, bass guitar, lead guitar and sometimes keyboards, most of whom are white, working-class men in their 20s and 30s' (p. 18), as are their audience, playing in grimy pubs (a further disincentive for women). Similarly the economy around the scene is mainly male, from music and record shops to recording studios, and there is a recognisably masculine style of banter (Cohen, 1997, p. 22; Easthope, 1986, p. 88). Cohen concludes: 'the precarious position of male rock music-makers in Liverpool may make their efforts to dominate the scene and exclude women … more urgent … in order to achieve status' (1997, p. 32). However, 'within the safety of that position … music enables these men to nevertheless express feelings of powerlessness and frustration … through musical performance within the scene … expressed in a manner that is discouraged in other public events and settings or through everyday conversation' (pp. 33–4).

The value of Cohen's study is that it theorises rock masculinities in a specific socio-cultural context, and relates cultural activities to the social matrix of everyday life. What it suggests is the basically subordinate nature of the subjects – their lack of cultural capital, and their efforts to create it by excluding others from participation in the scene. There are many similarities with other indie scenes: its apparently 'insular' and regional nature, homosociality, and its rather traditional musical style, instrumentation and lyrical concerns (Arnold, 1995, pp. 10, 163–5; Hesmondhalgh, 1999, pp. 46–7; Kitts et al., 1998, pp. 2–3; Kruse, 2003, pp. 1, 138–44; Straw, 1997b, pp. 496–7). The contrast between the homosociality of the scene and the relatively childish or vulnerable personae of some of the performers recurs in other indie scenes (Kitts et al., 1998, p. 4).

The shortcoming of the study is that like many ethnographic studies it simplifies the forces acting on its subjects by trying to explain social behaviours in terms of an observational model. Cohen's investment in the scene is not sufficiently theorised, and her dispassionate stance raises as many questions as it answers (Thornton, 1995, pp. 105–7). Moreover, looking at one 'scene' in isolation does not give a sense of the interconnectedness of indie musical practice. Cohen (1997, pp. 24–8) explains the music purely in terms of its local environment (Liverpool), when surely its continuities with other indie scenes are equally significant. However, Cohen's distinction between rock masculinities in performance and in everyday life is important, as it suggests that 'vulnerable' onstage male personae do not necessarily challenge homosociality and patriarchy. The stage is a special place where gender roles are not as fixed as in everyday life, but this is because it is also a place of power – licence to play with gender presumes a privileged position. It is worth keeping this in mind when reviewing some of the more extravagant claims made for indie music and gender by other writers.

I suggest that viewing masculinities in rock music purely in terms of representations of masculinity (that is, the characteristics of male performers and audiences) and reading their music as homologous with their practice will only take us so far. In Foucault's terms, what matters most is not so much what is 'in' the discourses (representations) or who 'authors' them, but the overall 'economy' of discourses: 'their intrinsic technology ... this, and not a system of representations, determines what they have to say' (Foucault, 1978, pp. 68–9; 1991). In the case of rock masculinities, clearly music is an example of such an 'economy'.

Subcultural studies tend to type subcultural production as resistant 're-appropriation' of existing products by 'active' audiences. Such an account is incomplete, because production of music is more than just a manifestation of audience resistance. Lack of discussion of music is a key problem of Hebdige's account. An account of musical production complicates the classic subcultural model, because it means that subcultures can no longer be viewed in isolation from, for example, media, the importance of which to subcultural production has also been underestimated (Thornton, 1995, p. 119). It complicates the notion of audience to breaking point. The subcultural approach can also tend to produce a top-down model of power, which overlooks how power works within subcultural groups: 'comparatively little attention ... has been paid to the hierarchies *within* popular culture' (Thornton, 1995, p. 7).

In summary, ethnographic and subcultural approaches tend to be dominated by middle-class academics observing working-class or otherwise marginal subjects (Morgan, 1992, p. 4). The classic subjects of masculinity studies are well-recognised categories of some form of 'deviance' (violence, crime, working-class machismo, homosexuals), repression (the military, police, prisons), difference (masculinities in other societies), physicality (sport, health, representation of male bodies) or children (boys' schools, problem youth).[2] The researchers remain invisible, while certain other groups or themes become objectified as masculine. If the subcultural emphasis on power/resistance is retained, there is a tendency to assume that power comes primarily from above, but this ignores how power functions within the group. Moreover, the relation of researcher and researched is already a power relation.

Connell himself recognises this need for a broader perspective and, by implication, the limitations of many ethnographic and local studies: 'Ultimately, the large historical context, the big picture, is essential for understanding ... ethnographic detail' (2000, p. 39). 'We must pay attention to very large scale structures ... the world gender order ... hegemony ... connected with patterns of trade, investment and communication, and a transnational business masculinity, institutionally based in multinational corporations and global finance markets' (2000, pp. 40–1); these in turn are historically related to Western imperialist expansion (Wallerstein, 1974). 'The "individual" of neo-liberal theory has the attributes and interests of a male entrepreneur ... a person who has no commitments, except to the idea of accumulation' (Connell, 2000, pp. 51–2). Such masculinities 'do not require bodily force, since the patriarchal dividend ... is accumulated by impersonal, institutional means' (p. 52). I think these are important insights, but it is unclear how far Connell's avowed commitment to empiricism allows him to pursue them. Jeff Hearn similarly points out how institutions reproduce hegemonic masculinity as much as individual men: 'Their individual power accrues from the general, that is a social structural, relation of men to women, in the public domain and elsewhere' (1992, p. 3). The implication is that individual men and their behaviour may be ultimately superfluous to the production and reproduction of patriarchies, which are not about the direct agency of men but are produced through structures and institutions operating in the public domain, which is, in turn, already gendered. The Frankfurt School (see below) offers important insights into how gender is implicated in the production of modern institutions.

In my discussion of sociological approaches to masculinities, I have frequently used psychological terminology to critique sociological concepts, so it is timely to examine psychological theories of gender and masculinity – I will introduce Freud, and then assess the Frankfurt School's attempt to combine psychology and social structure.

Gender and psychology

Most psychological accounts of gender follow Freud in placing its formation in early childhood. The infant is 'polymorphously perverse' – with no fixed sexual orientation (Freud, 1953–74, vol. 3, pp. 214–15). Freud's insistence on our fundamental bisexuality refutes the idea that physiological sex determines gender: 'All human individuals ... combine ... masculine and feminine characteristics, so that pure masculinity and femininity remain theoretical constructions of uncertain content' (Freud, vol. 19, p. 258). But according to Connell (1995, p. 9), Freud goes on to argue that socialisation (the Oedipus complex) largely and presumably in his view, necessarily, entails the repression of such ambiguities of personal gender identity. The Oedipus complex is Freud's account of how gender formation occurs: the male infant has an incestuous desire (springing from the id) for the mother's love and the elimination of the father (Freud, 1953–74, vol. 7, pp. 216–17; Segal, 1990, p. 71). The successful resolution of the complex involves identification with, rather than desire for, the same-sex parent (the homosexual taboo) and the introjection of the threat it represents as a prohibition (the incest taboo) in the nascent superego.

Freud's model is all about domination and submission, desire and denial, as if in a hostile world, characterised by violent struggle between self and other, it is only by being punished that we learn. This is the Freudian concept of internalisation, or 'how individuals transform themselves by doing to themselves what has been done to them' through the creation of a censorious superego which 'embodies the external prohibition (morality)' (Benjamin, 1978, p. 39). This superego is identified with the father, and 'social reality'. 'While Freud acknowledges that the restrictions of culture are painful, he also believes that they protect us from the dangers of nature ... that the rule of authority is preferable to the war of all against all' (Benjamin, 1988, p. 4). Men, according to Freud, are by nature sadistic, active and desiring, but they learn to repress themselves (Benjamin, 1988, p. 3). Identity and masculinity are closely linked – the achievement of autonomy (individuality) means internalising the father's authority and rejecting 'attachment' to the mother, thereby achieving a form of self-mastery (of the id) (Benjamin, 1978, pp. 38–9). The mother's work is not valued and theorised in Freud, because it upsets the emphasis on the production of an autonomous self (dependence is 'regressive'): 'In the classic psychoanalytic emphasis on the father, the mother's work in maintaining and producing life was taken for granted, rather than represented, and so the alienation of the subject from that which created and maintained "his" life was reproduced' (Benjamin, 1998, p. xv). By the same token, Freud is unable to satisfactorily explain feminine gender formation, except as an inversion of the sadistic male drive. For example, he defines male masochism as a perversion (thereby suggesting that it is 'natural' in women) (Silverman, 1992, p. 189).

Freud's interpretation of the Oedipus narrative omits the way it is set in motion by the father (Laius)'s attempt to murder the infant Oedipus (Benjamin, 1988, p. 142). This suggests that the father, far from representing social reality (the repression of desire), has in fact his own desires, and is not as noble and disinterested as Freud makes him sound: 'the sovereignty of the father is a fact of social origin, which Freud fails to account for' (Beauvoir, 1972, p. 74). The disavowal of the subjectivity of the father can be viewed more generally as a reification of masculinity as authority and reality, or of the phallus, which everyone, apparently, desires. It also relates to Freud's own status as a scientist, determined to establish the objective truth of the phenomena he saw. The Cartesian scientific worldview assumes an essential, knowing self which is separate from the world (Descartes, 1968, p. 47; Benjamin, 1988, pp. 179–80). Freud challenged this view in one respect by showing the importance of the unconscious, but continued to assume a basic opposition between self and world, individual and society.

> The classic psychoanalytic viewpoint did not see differentiation as a balance, but as a process of disentanglement. Thus it casts experiences of union, merger, and self–other harmony as regressive opposites … Merging was a dangerous form of undif-ferentiation, a sinking back into the sea of oneness – 'the oceanic feeling' that Freud … couldn't relate to … In its most extreme version, this view of differentiation pathologized the sensation of love: relaxing the boundaries of the self in communion with others threatened the identity of the isolate self. Yet this oneness was seen as the ultimate pleasure, eclipsing the pleasure of difference. (Benjamin, 1988, p. 47)

Freud, then, is a case study in patriarchal psychology, although one impossible to conduct without the tools he provided. His theories mainly work to describe/symptomatise a masculine experience. By the same token, what Freud wrote about femininity clearly also refers to men. To sum up, patriarchy in Freudian psychology is represented in the father (and the phallus), but also more broadly in its understanding of subjectivity and identity as separation. The object of classical psychoanalysis is the production of the rational Cartesian autonomous self, unburdened by neurosis (regressive attachments) – in other words, someone very like the analyst himself. This paradigm has come under increasing attack: 'Feminist theory has ... exposed the mystification inherent in the ideal of the autonomous individual ... based on the paternal ideal of separation and denial of dependency' (Benjamin, 1988, p. 187). By envisaging the subject in isolation, Freud was forced towards a pessimistic view of it as in endless conflict with Nature and civilisation, and within itself (id and superego). This individualistic gloom is everywhere in Western culture of the last century, nowhere more than in the work of male indie artists, such as Kurt Cobain and Morrissey (see Chapter 6). It occurs because of the way in which the subject is always envisaged as in conflict with the other: that is, as a 'failure of relationship'. But this malady of the self is not correctable using traditional Freudian psychology, which is part of the problem rather than the solution. Chiefly I mean here the way in which Freud's intra-psychic model needs to be contextualised – the Frankfurt School provides an example of such an endeavour, although it is not successful.

Masculinity and the Frankfurt School

The Frankfurt School took Freud's account of identity and applied it to the social world. In doing so, it offered the first extensive theorisation of masculinity and culture in modernity, combining a Freudian perspective on identity with a Marxist/ Weberian emphasis on social structure, combining psychological and sociological perspectives (Benjamin, 1978, pp. 37–38). Many of the School's assumptions have passed into commonsense popular discourse about culture. Our ways of judging culture are still beholden to its high-modernist binary worldview (Frith, 1996, p. 66). Like Freud, it also offers deep insights into how Western white hegemonic masculinity works, especially in the public sphere (institutionally and culturally), revealing strategies of intellectual masculinities.

It can be argued that, like Freud, the Frankfurt School operates on the assumption that 'within a patriarchal society our understanding of the nature of ... authority is tied up with our sense of the position of the father within the family' (Seidler, 1988, pp. 272, 277–84; see also Horkheimer, 2002, pp. 97–128). Industrialisation absents the father from the home, and his place is taken by mediated interventions from the state or mass media. This threatens the Freudian process of individuation, because children do not internalise paternal authority, but manifest only a blind subservience to abstract systems of authority and communication (leading to totalitarianism). They do not individuate but remain infantile, pacified by the 'false' gratifications of mass culture. They lose their ability to resist (Benjamin, 1978, pp. 35–6). Resistance presupposes internalisa-

tion of the strong qualities of the Freudian father. Having been one of those children myself, I would baulk at this stark assessment; on the other hand, the idea
that modern mass media may to some extent 'stand in' for formative relationships does not seem totally implausible, especially in an age where electronic
media may act to some degree as surrogate parents (Benjamin, 1978, p. 42).

Power in Western industrialised society increasingly 'expresses itself not
directly as authority but indirectly as the transformation of all relationships into
objective, instrumental, depersonalised forms' (Weber, 1970, pp. 15–16; see also
Benjamin, 1978, pp. 35–6). There is a shift from power as specific and personal –
God, the monarch or the father – and from direct forms like violence or coercion,
towards impersonality: surveillance and regulation, bureaucratic and legal process,
technology and ideologies of efficiency and instrumental rationality (Benjamin,
1978, p. 36; Weber, 1970). This allows 'the technical apparatus and the social
groups which administer it a disproportionate superiority to the rest of the population' (Adorno and Horkheimer, 1994, p. xiv). This domination is associated with
patriarchy: 'the concordance between the mind of man and the nature of things …
is patriarchal: the human mind, which overcomes superstition, is to hold sway
over a disenchanted nature' (Adorno and Horkheimer, 1994, p. 4; see also Hearn,
1992, p. 168; Morgan, 1992, p. 57). Such a theorisation of power no longer
depends on a visible authority figure; hence modern Western society has been
termed 'patriarchy without the father' (Benjamin, 1978, p. 36). Patriarchy works
impersonally, through rational systems.

The Frankfurt School argued that rationality had become a new form of domination, in that science, technology and industrial progress, based on reason, were
threatening human individuality and values (Aronowitz, 2002, pp. xiii–xv). Max
Weber (Frankfurt School, but influential on its thought) identified a new ideology
of 'instrumental' rationality, which valued efficient process and systematisation
above and beyond any social end, unlike the traditional, substantive reason
(Benjamin, 1978, p. 36). His main example was Western capitalism – 'an economic system based, not on custom or tradition, but on the deliberate and systematic adjustment of economic means to the attainment of … profit' (Tawney, 1970,
p. 1e). Its lack of any direct reference to moral values meant that its benefits for
society were problematic (enter Adam Smith's 'invisible hand') (Giddens, 1991,
p. 20).

From the Marxist perspective, capitalism enforces alienation – as producers
become divorced from the products of their labour, and employers from the
process that produces profit, so they become alienated from themselves (Rius,
1994, pp. 78–80). They take an instrumental relation to themselves and others,
using them 'purely as a means to an end, instead of enjoying the relation or
process for its own sake … The victory of instrumental reason is a victory
against nature – the world of objects becomes a field of resistance or an empty
reflection of the subject's will to dominate' (Benjamin, 1978, pp. 36, 40). Jeff
Hearn states that 'although not spelt out by Weber, the rationalization thesis

seems to have ... major implications for men and masculinities: it is mostly men who manage the introduction of rational method; men and masculinities are affected by the progressive introduction of rational method; and what is understood by rational method will be reciprocally related to men and masculinities' (1992, p. 168).

The Frankfurt School provides a useful model of how patriarchal authority can become institutionalised as the voice of reason and truth, and how, in modernity, it has got out of control. However, the School could not solve the problems it raised, except through applying more reason, either 'greater self-awareness on the mind's own tendency towards domination' or regression to traditional forms of rationality and masculinity, as in the (more recent) cultural critique of Christopher Lasch or Allan Bloom (Benjamin, 1988, pp. 137–9, 191; Bloom, 1988; Lasch, 1978). The patriarchal dualism of Frankfurt School theory leads to an impasse – rationality can only be overcome by an appeal to other, purer or more objective kinds of rationality, resulting in circularity.

To put it another way, because the Frankfurt School (and Freud) see autonomy as the ultimate goal of human development, this entails separation from and mastery of nature – domination. Autonomy is a form of self-domination, and thereby of others. Thus all human relationships become forms of domination or submission. This explains why Frankfurt School theories of culture are generally viewed as allowing too little space for individual agency and subjectivity. Femininity, for example, is not theorised other than as a negation or inversion of masculinity – again demonstrating how rational dualisms lead to essentialisation of the other.

Jessica Benjamin comments:

> The idea of rationalization forms a bridge between intellectual history and the history of social and economic relations. It describes the essence of modern social practice and thought. It is, in Foucault's sense, a discourse. My argument is that it is a *gendered* discourse, that the instrumental orientation and impersonality that govern modern social organization and thought should be understood as masculine ... Thus regardless of woman's increasing participation in the public, productive sphere ... it remains ... a man's world. (1988, p. 187).

The implication is that masculinity in modernity has ceased to be only about the behaviour of men – through its association with discourses of instrumental rationality, it has become apparently objective and universal:

> Rationalization, at the societal level, sets the stage for a form of domination that appears to be gender-neutral, indeed to have no subject at all ... It is precisely this objective character, with its indifference to personal need, that is recognized as the hallmark of masculine power ... apparent gender neutrality is a mystification, like ... commodity fetishism – an illusion created by the social relations themselves. (Benjamin, 1988, p. 184)

Michel Foucault supplies perhaps the clearest examples of how 'invisible' discourses of authority work in modern society, describing how systems of rationality have replaced immanent or intrinsic value with 'objective' systems of
surveillance, standardisation, exchange and discipline. 'We are valued for how
closely we approximate an imposed system', of measurement, for example
(Foucault, 1979, p. 183; see also Starhawk, 1987, p. 73). Such systems might
seem remote from the world of popular culture, but when we consider how popular
media encourage conformity to an abstract standard, feminine beauty or 'ideal
body weight' for example, it becomes clearer that 'discipline' is not only a matter
of juridical authority, but is imposed through 'abstract systems' (Giddens, 1990,
pp. 83–8).[3] This could lead towards a consideration of such systems in pop culture:
lists of top bands and albums, for example – canonism, connoisseurship and
archivalism (see Chapter 5). Alternatively, the centrality of the gaze in Foucault
(1984, pp. 206–13) suggests a reading of how alternative rock culture polices
musical style in terms of surveillance (of sexuality especially, which is central to
both the Foucauldian and the rock music worldviews) (see Chapter 2). Foucault
might object that the concept of hegemonic masculinities simplifies relations of
power to a dominance/resistance model (that masculinities or other powerful
groups simply impose their will on the weak (1980, p. 59)). But Foucault's models
of power relations, while more complex and reflexive than the models so far
examined, still employ a rhetoric of division, domination and submission: 'The
subject is either divided inside himself or divided from others. This process objec-
tivizes him. Examples are the mad and the sane, the sick and the healthy, the criminals and the "good boys"' (Foucault, 1983, p. 208). Cameron Duff (1999)
comments that '[t]hrough such practices, power creates a series of binary identifications which the subject is compelled to observe'. Commentators have further
suggested that his emphasis on the inevitability of power in human relations is
basically masculinist: 'the agonistic model cannot account for, much less articulate, processes of empowerment' (McCarthy, 1994, pp. 246–7; see also Butler,
1990, p. x; Deveaux, 1994).

The rationalistic, Cartesian worldview produces a split between object and
subject that is potentially schizophrenic. Relations with the other are reduced to
binary possibilities of domination and submission. The idea that masculine possibilities are similarly split between victim and aggressor positions relates to the
objectification of masculinity as working-class deviance or bodily violence (or in
Freud as id), leading to a dichotomised sense of it as either dangerous or revolu-
tionary. This becomes particularly clear in Chapter 2, where describe how the
objectification of black masculinity meant it could only be seen in terms of threat
or idealised possibility – the 'noble savage'. It is also discussed in Chapter 6 as a
melancholic or misery-making structure.

Psychoanalytic Freudian revisionists like Jessica Benjamin and R.D. Laing
demonstrate how agonistic discourses of rationality, objectivity, autonomy and

separation deny the importance of human relationship, which is essential not only to psychoanalytic practice, but also to the formation of human subjectivities per se. For example, Laing's key criticism of Freud is that 'we take a single man in isolation and conceptualize the various aspects into "the ego", "the superego", and the "id"' (1965, p. 19). But for Laing there is no such thing as a self in isolation from the world; it is constituted through its relations with others. 'Each and every man [*sic*] is at the same time separate from his fellows and related to them. Such separateness and relatedness are mutually necessary postulates ... Here we have the paradox ... potentially tragic ... that our relatedness to others is an essential aspect of our *being*, as is our separateness, but any particular person is not a necessary part of our being' (Laing, 1965, p. 26; see also Merleau-Ponty, 2003, p. 416). In this sense the self is neither a subjective nor an objective entity; rather it is 'intersubjective'. It thus becomes possible to say, contra social constructionism, that there is an 'essential' being or identity, but that it is not a unified object (contra rationalism). Rather it is (ideally) an equilibrium: 'Balance within the self depends on mutual recognition between self and other' (Benjamin, 1988, p. 53). This formulation presents a clear departure from Freud, in which each subject is basically driven by his own desire, and any check to that desire is perceived as hostile and repressive.

The paradox of power/control is that it represses not only the other but also the subject. Jessica Benjamin analyses it in terms of Hegel's master/slave dialectic:

> the slave did the work that mediated the master's enjoyment of the object, without having enjoyment himself, while the master who had enjoyment, had no direct contact with the object of desire. Thus the two aspects of subjectivity – transforming the object and enjoying the desire for it – were split, and neither subject could own their desire. To transpose this psychoanalytically: only when the mother has her own enjoyment as a subject of desire, and when the (formerly) male subject does his own work of representing and holding desire, is this split overcome. (1998, pp. xv–xvi)

Gender and social construction

The critique of the autonomous rational self has become a focus of modern thought. Such a 'united' self is often identified with patriarchal values. Typically, commentary on identity has moved to the opposite pole – if the autonomous self is 'false', therefore it follows that identity is a fiction, or a patriarchal construct. Relevant here is the post-structuralist line that identities are constituted through discourse, that selves are defined through language, through situation in a structure of difference: '"self" is the residue that results from the intertwining of multiple drives that, while seeming to speak with a more or less unified voice, are actually anonymous' (Bortle, 2001). It is a construct of Oedipus, the dominant discourse of order (Deleuze and Guattari, 1983). It is easy to see how this concept

could be employed in gender analysis. For many social constructionists, if the
concept of autonomous self is basically patriarchal, then a broken-down, decon-
structed, fragmented self is therefore feminine (Massumi, 1992, pp. 86–9;
Reynolds, 1990, pp. 137–8).[4] But this is too simple, because it assumes (like
Freud) that feminine is simply the opposite of masculine.

Some have seen social construction/discourse theory as overdeterministic, limiting the possibilities for change (Connell, 1995, pp. 51, 71). If we are always/
already constructed by discourse, then it is hard to see how we can 'step outside
it'. Rock music academic Neil Nehring (1997, p. 11) argues that this leads to resignation and pessimism, by problematising identity at the precise moment when
repressed voices such as those of women and ethnic minorities are struggling to
articulate themselves. Change, Nehring argues, is based on strong feeling, but
post-structuralism undervalues emotion because it undervalues the subject
(p. xvii). Carole Vance argues that 'to the extent that social constructionist theory
grants that sexual acts, identities and even desire are mediated by cultural and historical factors, the object of the study ... threatens to disappear' (1989, p. 21). The
body becomes 'a field on which social determination runs riot' (Connell, 1995,
p. 50).[5] The body is not simply a passive object to be 'written' upon; rather,
'[b]odily experience gives perception a meaning beyond that established simply
by thought. Thus, Descartes' cogito ("I think, therefore I am") does not account
for how consciousness is influenced by the spatiality of a person's own body'
(Scott, 2002).

For psychotherapist R.D. Laing (1965, pp. 65–9), body represents 'my being in
the world' – that part of me that is present to others and which mediates my interaction with them. To be embodied (to be in my body) is to be not just physically
but emotionally present in a social situation. The opposite is disembodiment
('unembodiment' in Laing), which implies that 'I' am no longer identical with the
body which I inhabit, that I am somehow cut off from it, and that I am similarly
cut off from social interaction, a situation which Laing would describe as potentially schizophrenic. In such a situation, my body becomes an aspect of a false self
– that is, that which exists for others, but does not exist for me. Body exists to the
degree that I feel subjectively real, and that the actions of my body correspond
with what I feel to be subjectively real.

This probably sounds a bit essentialist – feminist social constructionists like
Judith Butler would say that there is no 'I' to magically confer identity, but
rather that identity and gender are aspects of performativity, not essence:
'gender is always a doing, though not a doing by a subject who might be said
to preexist the deed' (1990, p. 25). For Butler, the gendered subject is a construction, and gender is always a performance: 'the notion that there might be
a "truth" of sex, as Foucault ironically terms it, is produced precisely through
the regulatory practices that generate coherent identities through the matrix of
coherent gender norms' (1990, p. 17). For social constructionists, the other,
like identity, is an effect of discourse. 'Irigaray argues that both the subject and

the Other are masculine mainstays of a closed phallogocentric signifying economy that achieves its totalizing goal through the exclusion of the feminine' (Butler, 1990, p. 9).

However, Jessica Benjamin argues, 'identity is not self ... we can say that a self can be nonidentical, and yet contain a state, express a feeling, identify with or assume a position. The critique of identity does not prevent us from postulating a psychic subjectivity that takes up various positions through identification, a kind of "identifier behind the identification"' (1998, p. 87). Benjamin suggests, like Laing, that the subject is constituted through its relations with others, but that there is a difference between our fantasy (personal or collective) of the other and the subjectivity of the other. It is the negotiating of this difference that constitutes the ongoing work of identity. The keyword here is 'relations' because it assumes that the subject is not simply constituted by outside forces, but rather it assumes some kind of reciprocity or mutuality with others. While social constructionism would argue that these subjects are simply more effects of discourse, even if this is true, the relations between them are (or can be) real, for in those fundamental relations we have (hopefully) with family, lovers and close friends.

Butler and other related theorists have to introduce some such notion of a fundamental relation with the (usually maternal) other for their theories to work, but at the same time this assumes a reality to the subjectivity of the other which is self-contradictory, in terms of their theory. For example, Butler claims,

> the masculine subject only *appears* to originate meanings ... His seemingly self-grounded autonomy attempts to conceal the repression which is both its ground and the perpetual possibility of its own ungrounding ... this dependency, although denied, is also *pursued* by the masculine subject, for the woman as reassuring sign *is* the displaced maternal body, the vain but persistent promise of the recovery of pre-individuated *jouissance*. (1990, p. 45)

To both this and Irigaray the same objection can be raised – what exactly is this feminine body? Isn't it in some sense 'real'? Doesn't Butler presume a time 'before' the Law – which elsewhere she describes as an illusion (Butler, 1990, p. 46)? The exposure of the illusion of the 'phallogocentric economy' depends on the contrast with a feminine that is 'real' (in Lacan's terminology, the 'real' is that which cannot be represented – the maternal feminine) (Benjamin, 1998, pp. xvi, 46, 47–8). But the problem is not whether the feminine can be represented in a phallogocentric economy (clearly it cannot) but that theorists seeking to find a way out of the impasse are limited by the very binary terms of the Cartesian, Freudian, masculinist worldview that assumes an absolute schism or split between subject and object, between illusion and real. In its place, Benjamin proposes an 'intersubjective' approach.

Subjective realities

The real and the subject are not mutually exclusive. The self has subjective reality
– we believe in it, whether or not it is an illusion (Benjamin, 1998, pp. xvii–xviii).
But this sense of self is not autonomous – rather it develops from our relations
with other subjectivities. Being is relational, but this does not mean it is only a set
of relations. In order to be real to ourselves we have to be real for another. We have
to experience love. Love is not simply reducible to a sexual drive, as in the Freudian
world. Benjamin's concept of desire is more complex because it recognises the
importance of relationship: 'the experience of *being with* the other cannot be
reduced to the experience of *being regulated* by an other' (1988, p. 46).

Revising Freud's drive model, Benjamin proposes, rather than a simple yes/no
model in which desire either achieves its aim or is frustrated, holding out for a
third position, which she identifies with the parent (usually mother)/child relationship (1988, pp. 12–15; 1998, p. xv). At some point the infant becomes aware that
the parent is a separate being, with its own subjectivity (clearly, the parent will not
always act in a way that gratifies the child's desire and vice versa). The argument
is that this 'loss' of unity can be endured as long as the child has had the prior
experience of being in a loving relation with the other, and that the parent can
survive the attack of the frustrated child (can contain its rage, rather than capitulat-
ing to it or raging back – this presumes that the parent has a basic level of ontological security) (Benjamin, 1988, pp. 25–9, 34–6, 43–4). A successful transition
depends on the child having had a prior experience of being recognised and confirmed in its own identity. The child's desire, while it cannot always be granted,
can be contained and represented by the parent effectively saying 'I know/
understand how you feel' – that is, recognising the desire. This recognition is a
two-way process, because in it the child learns that while, no, he can't have what
he wants, at least his desire for it is acknowledged: 'a degree of imperfection "rati-
fies" the existence of the world' (Benjamin, 1988, p. 47). This (usually mother's)
work of containing and representing desire is crucial to the formation of subjectivity and identity, because it encourages us to recognise that human relationships
can recompense us for failed gratification. But it is also largely unrecognised – in
terms of the theories we have examined so far, this 'women's work' is invisible.

Men's groups

Since 1995, I have participated in a men's group. It meets monthly in members'
homes and has a small but consistent membership varying from five to eight, with
ages varying from the early thirties to the mid-fifties. Most are from middle-class,
white backgrounds. Some are married with children or in a relationship; some are
solo. Most have jobs or careers. Two of the founding members have experience in

counselling and mental health, but the group has no affiliation with any institution. The purpose of the group, as I understand it, is on becoming better men, specifically by 'getting in touch' with emotions and with each other. Many of the customary forms of homosocial interaction within New Zealand society – work, sport – do not allow participants to express feelings or be responsible for them. Instead they tend to require acting out certain socially accepted ideas of masculinity, which are not necessarily in the best long-term interests of participants.

The group never meets with a set agenda. Its primary purpose is not intellectual – there is no required reading. There are few set rules on behaviour, although members are expected to turn up on time and stay for the duration (usually about two and a half hours), not to consume drugs or alcohol during that time, and not to discuss what occurs there outside the group. We usually start with a 'round', in which each member focuses on how they feel about their lives at that moment. This 'check-in' establishes a sense of trust and rapport. During the round, we are encouraged to listen without interrupting, interpreting or offering advice. Instead, we 'mirror' – responding empathically to what others are saying, searching our feelings and experiences for correspondences to what is described.

Members are encouraged to speak for themselves and not on behalf of others – the use of 'I think (feel)' is preferred to generalisations or formulae like 'you/we think' or 'he feels' because such statements are often disingenuous. Part of the purpose of the group is to 'hold' emotions, and these may include deep depression or aggression. Recognition is the key – we name and recognise feelings (both our own and those of others), without necessarily trying to explain or justify them. These techniques are of course widely used in counselling, psychotherapy and other men's groups (Seidler, 1991, pp. ix–xiv).

Sometimes the round takes up the whole meeting, or sometimes a member will have a particularly urgent need to speak, but usually a topic or theme emerges: parents, relationships with partners, pornography, sex, work, depression, but most frequently relations between members. We are encouraged to reflect on our interaction, rather than scoring points or coming to a conclusion. Basically the group is there to emotionally support its members where possible, but this does not mean that criticism, arguments or disputes do not occur; on at least one occasion a member has voluntarily left the group for a period. Ironically, bad feeling and projection on the part of a group member – 'acting out', breaking the rules – is often healthy for the group, leading to a more lively interaction.

New members usually come by invitation – in my case, I expressed interest and was invited. There is no formal process of induction and the group does not advertise. Some members are friends outside the group and also interact informally. I joined because I wanted to interact with men and come to a better understanding of what masculinity meant. Since the band had broken up, I had worked in female-dominated workplaces and had few male friends. My family background was marked by difficulties (on my side, at any rate) relating to my father and brother. I was unsatisfied with the male–male relationships that I had. I was also depressed.

Initially I used the group mainly to get things off my chest – confessing my shameful secrets, and feelings of loneliness and sadness. There were things that I could never have discussed with my partner – pornography, for example. Over time I began to realise that the group was more than just a confession box, but that it could also offer me a new understanding of how to relate to other people. I learned to stop living so much in my head – disentangling my fantasy of others from 'reality' (not in the sense of 'objective reality' but in the sense of recognising the subjectivity of others and not confusing it with my own).

The trust and rapport I have built with men in the group is a useful standard by which to judge my interactions with others in the outside world, especially other men. It has helped me cope with academics, whose intellectual perspicacity is sometimes not matched by a similar level of emotional 'savvy'. I get on better with my father because I have learned to see him as a human being rather than to expect him to behave 'like a father should'. I have started to replace my fantasy of him with a recognition. The group has allowed me to perceive positive qualities in other men, without idealising or denigrating them, something I was previously unable to do. It also helps me cope with others' aggression and sadness (again because I have learned how to recognise others' feelings and distinguish them from my own). I have a stronger sense of my agency.

I increasingly find my group experience informing my academic work, especially that focusing on gender. I now seek out writing and theory that corroborate and expand my group experience, for example relational psychology. I think that the group, while not theoretical or intellectual, has helped build a more stable foundation for my ideas about gender. Although some have characterised the men's movement as being essentialist or anti-feminist, my experience is otherwise. The importance of interpersonal interaction, and of recognising and tolerating both our difference from and similarity to others (mutuality) is, I think, one of the most powerful and profound lessons of feminism, and one that men can only benefit from.

I think it is reasonably clear how Benjamin's theories relate to my experience in the men's group. The group is about coming into relationship, recognising the subjectivity of others and adjusting our own expectations accordingly. In a patriarchal society, such processes have generally been denigrated as 'women's work'. The very existence of the group acknowledges that such work is of fundamental significance to a sense of well-being and connection with the world. At the same time, men are discouraged from taking on this role themselves, which is both their and everyone's loss, because the institutionalisation of the disavowal and disparagement of subjectivity is life-destroying. The social constructionist view of gender as performance may have some validity at the social and institutional levels, and in media and culture, but my experience in the group suggests that there is more to male subjectivities than an endless performance of masculine positions, and that some men want to break out of the circle.

Conclusions

The study of masculinities is about more than simply observing men. Patriarchy cannot be reduced to a model of how men behave, because as the dominant social group they are not available for investigation in the same way as other groups, and because the very tools of such an investigation – the terms, the mode of observation, the types of interaction, the necessity of detachment – are already gendered. Moreover, masculinities are often invisible, or operate indirectly through discourses of rationality.

How might all this apply to the study of rock masculinities? Musical cultures or scenes may define themselves (or be defined by academics) in opposition to the 'mainstream' or dominant culture, but this is a simplification, especially in relation to gender discourses. For although rock cultures may be viewed to some degree as providing opportunities for repressed classes and ethnicities to assert themselves, this licence is seldom extended as far as gender. Representations of indie as anti-macho or resistant need to be interpreted in a larger social and ideological context. This approach is also continuous with Foucault's understanding of resistance as part of, rather than in opposition to, the overall 'system' (1984, pp. 377–8). I have shown that post-structural approaches to gender which produce a fragmented subject do not necessarily challenge the binary logic of patriarchy. Accordingly, we must be suspicious of facile equations of postmodern fragmentation with deconstruction of masculine autonomy.

Notes

1. However, since 'sight ... is the sense that separates', such visual metaphors, typical of scientific discourse, may be misleading (Brennan, 2004, pp. 10–11).
2. For example, in *Men and Masculinities*, over a five-year period (1998–2003), the main subject areas in descending order of frequency are: ethnic masculinities; technology, work and the working class; violence; the male body; sport; media representations; military institutions; schooling; and male fashion. There is very little associating masculinity with intellectualism, art or the middle classes.
3. Abstract systems deal in information rather than material goods, like currency, the phone network or the stock exchange.
4. Nehring (1997) provides a book-length critique of postmodernism's disdain for the subject and its implications for gender.

5. For Foucault, 'the aim of disciplinary technology … is to forge a docile body that may be subjected, used, transformed and improved' (1979, p. 198).

Chapter 2

Powerless power: masculine intellectualism and aesthetics

Nothing more infallibly classifies, than taste in music.
(Bourdieu, 1984, p. 18)

To understand masculine power in culture we need a broad critique of how masculinity is articulated not as physical presence or through representation, but as an intellectual, ideological and even spiritual force – that is, the extent to which culture or art's very valuation is bound up with masculinity. Central here is the question of how we attribute value to some kinds of culture over others – apparently gender-neutral discourses of merit, excellence, authenticity, artistic value and so forth. Taste is a form of cultural power, and judgments about taste are often justified by recourse to intellectual criteria. It is the (gendered) ways in which this expertise is constructed that are my concern here.

In this chapter I look at how hegemonic masculinities exert control over culture, looking first at their naturalisation in high culture and how this continues into the domain of the popular through practices of aestheticisation or 'purification' of mass culture. I argue that any aesthetic that depends on mutually opposing categories of high and low culture repeats patriarchal dualism. This also applies to inversions of the system where the low is represented as high, as in the idealisation of a 'pure' folk culture or ironic advocacy for 'trash' culture. Sarah Thornton (1995, pp. 7–14) has demonstrated how such techniques are employed within popular culture to demonstrate 'uniqueness'. In line with Chapter 1, I argue that hegemonic masculinities work through not representing themselves directly, but through controlling, policing or appropriating the economies of representation. This process is first examined in relation to high culture and classical music, but also occurs in aesthetics of the popular: folk discourse, originally identified with black music's influence on rock, latterly more through discourses of liveness, amateurism and authenticity, but also increasingly 'camp' (emulating femininity, utilising an ironic 'high' awareness). Andrew Ross argues that '"hip", "camp", "bad" or "sick" taste, and, most recently, postmodernist "fun" … are opportunities for intellectuals to sample the emotional charge of popular culture while guaranteeing their immunity from its power to constitute social identities that are in some way marked as subordinate' (1989, p. 5). Operating in tandem with these cultural distinctions is a psychological discourse: the Freudian insistence on the superego/id split, initially in high culture's insistence on overall intellectual control as key to how we understand masculinity in classical music in terms of autonomy and a mind/body split. Rock culture was initially theorised in opposition to high cultural superego – as repressed, primitive, instinctive id, related to 'black' culture, as in Mailer's *The White Negro* and the counterculture's insistence on 'ego death' through psychedelia (more recently imagined in postmodern accounts as feminised *jouissance*). The more self-conscious camp aesthetic of art rock (Warhol, The Velvet Underground) critiqued this 'repressive hypothesis', rejecting the essentialist identification of rock culture with 'freedom from repression', but also resurrected 'primitivism' in the form of an idealised representation of the mass cultural consumer as dupe or innocent eye. The essence of the argument, then, is that the high/low distinction works along the same lines as the Freudian split between superego and id as a means of perpetuating patriarchal power.

This does not mean that such strategies only confirm masculine hegemony: according to Ross, they are characteristically double-edged, both 'strategies of containment' and essential to 'civil rights and the gay liberation movements' (1989, p. 5). That is, the intellectualisation of the popular can be both a way of reaffirming the 'powerless power' of the (usually male) intellectual, and a force for social change (p. 11). But my concentration here will be on the ways in which white masculine artists and intellectuals appropriate subordinate masculinities (camp, black). Through this flirtation with otherness they enhance their subcultural capital, giving rise to the apparent paradox that 'gender-bending' male rock stars may perpetuate, rather than challenge, patriarchal values.

This brings me to my second point: how high culture (classical music especially), idealised by the Frankfurt School, is only meaningful in relation to its 'low' opposite – they are mutually dependent. Thus the 'trash' aesthetic represents an inversion of mass-culture critique. It does not transcend the binary terms of the system, but rather associates true art with 'junk' on the one hand, and also with an idealisation of the mass-culture consumer, as a passive, anonymous, ignorant, childlike dupe – as a Romantic 'innocent' – thus smuggling in high culture Romanticism through the back door. Accordingly 'passive' masculinities – linked to psychedelia, the 1960s underground and the countercultural ideal of ego obliteration – which take up a 'feminised' position, do not challenge the binary logic of patriarchy (Gilbert, 1999; Reynolds and Press, 1995). Warhol demonstrates how passivity – passive aggression, disembodiment and aestheticisation through surveillance – can be powerful, and how campness and irony can be employed for hegemonic ends.

In apparent opposition to this high culture approach is the 'folk' discourse, which associates value in popular culture with its affiliation to marginalised social groups and subcultures, setting the communal, shared, authentic or resistant values of a culture in opposition to the dominant, commercialised mainstream. 'Authentic folk music is presented as an "Other" with which pop music can be adversely contrasted; or its values are seen as surviving ... within certain favoured forms of popular music, usually ... associated with specified groups or subcultures'

(Middleton, 1990, p. 129). The 'folk' aspects of indie include locality, 'liveness', a DIY, amateur approach, technological dystopianism and understated performance style as marks of authenticity (see Chapter 3). As we saw in Chapter 1, Reynolds and other UK critics were critical of this approach, but reintroduced 'purity' at a high cultural or aesthetic level. UK critics were more likely to use an aesthetic rather than a folk concept of purity, with the reverse applying in the USA.

But although each approach locates 'art' in a different place, both are based on a similarly stratified view of society and culture (canonism, for example, is central to both). The folk/high opposition may be more apparent than real, because, as Middleton (1990, p. 127) points out, both high art and folk culture share a Romantic lineage. Both depend on an idea of purity or autonomy from the mass or commercial mainstream as a measure of value. High cultural autonomy is reimagined as folk authenticity. Thus both end up (in different ways) confirming patriarchy. Particularly relevant here are white appropriations of black 'hipness', which were so central to defining 1960s rock, and which imagined black culture as the supreme example of a 'pure' folk culture (Keightley, 2001, pp. 121, 126–7). This explicit identification with blackness was gradually relinquished in rock, becoming more like a general identification with marginality. This development was carried furthest in art rock, perhaps the key influence on indie music, in the way that it progressively problematised bodily presence in performance as a guarantor of rock 'authenticity' and authorship. Starting with Phil Spector, moving through Warhol and the Velvets to the shifting personae of Bowie and 1970s glam rock, the body of the performer becomes more and more instrumental to the overall masculinised intellectual control of the artist/composer, producing a body/mind split. Of course such a discourse did not originate in popular music – it can also be discerned in classical music and more generally in modernism. Similarly, art rock's scorn for 'folk' authenticity functioned as an embourgeoisment of rock values. A bodily masculinity was gradually replaced by a disembodied, controlling mind. However, 'folk' purity also returned in the form of indie's much-vaunted 'locality' and more broadly a fascination with amateurism and 'innocence', which again tends to conflate artistic value with naivety (cue again the 'psychedelic mummy's boys'). Keir Keightley writes that 'this privileging of a symbolic childhood ... became an ongoing feature of rock culture, seen subsequently in the alternative rock community's celebration of the deliberately "amateur", "naive" or "twee"' (2001, p. 124).

To reframe the foregoing in psychoanalytic terms, the folk or low/high opposition corresponds closely to Freud's model of the relation of id and superego. So black culture was imagined as bodily instinctive force, as id, attacking the repressed white superego, breaking it down, through the sensual power of music and drugs – 'ego death'. But the Freudian model is incapable of understanding such breakdown other than as a return to pre-Oedipal infantile omnipotence, social anarchy and chaos. It does not offer a realistic agenda for social change. Similarly camp's reification of consumption apparently reproduced the Frankfurt School's passive, narcissistic consumer who has failed to develop a superego. But power is reasserted through voyeurism. The Freudian passive/active split fails to take account of how intellectual control is not the same as activity. Later, I will discuss Warhol's Pop Art aesthetic as an example of how high cultural values of purity, mediated through 'camp', become central to masculine hegemony in art rock and alternative rock (Bourdieu, 1984, pp. 3–4).

Classical discourse

I want to begin by critiquing Adorno's conception of the place of high culture, that is 'art', in modernity. Adorno, as part of the Frankfurt School, suggests that in modern society it is increasingly difficult to reconcile individuality in art with an increasingly repressive social structure. He emphasises negation: modern art, to be authentic and 'objective', must declare its autonomy from a social structure that represses individual freedom (Adorno, 1973, pp. 19–21; Subotnik, 1976, pp. 247, 251). The author can no longer simply 'express himself' in his work, because this would be false consciousness – it would imply a freedom that is not borne out in reality. Hence he has to disappear from the work in an act of self-negation (Subotnik, 1976, pp. 253–4).

> The musical subject ... had to yield to and assimilate the formal features of objective reality to a far greater extent than ever before; Subotnik writes that 'by increasing the explicitly formal character of music, the subjective could acknowledge its own underlying dependence on a foreign source of authority, objectivity, without ever going beyond the autonomous processes of musical construction' (1976, 256). To put it simply, the musical subject had to disappear from the music; and Adorno accordingly claims that in the late Beethoven corpus it almost never appears directly. Henceforth, 'the very absence of a subject from a musical configuration necessarily constituted an integral component of that configuration' (1976, 256), and Adorno believes that the subject in Beethoven's third period maintained its identity exactly through its own negation. In this way, both autonomy and heteronomy are comprised at the same time. (Verster, 1995)

This objectivity is established through the removal of expressive elements from the music and the substitution of formal, logical elements – avant-garde moves such as serialism and repetition. The result is a music of indeterminacy, atonality, difficulty and emotional reserve which expresses the alienation of modern life. Beethoven's career, for Adorno, is prophetic of the trajectory of classical music in a modernising society. The composer's presence in his own work is radically reduced – he has become a spectator to the spectacle of modernity. Similarly in modernist literature, indifference has become the mark of genius: the artist, 'like the God of the creation, remains within or behind or beyond or above his handiwork, invisible, refined out of existence, indifferent, paring his fingernails'

(Joyce, 1921, p. 252). This tendency becomes most clearly expressed in avant-garde art.

Alternative rock aesthetics (Warhol, art rock, punk) are similarly structured around the concept of negation: we find a similar removal of the author occurring (self-negation); the music is declared autonomous from the mainstream, and negative and critical in character. Alternative rock thus to some degree shares Adorno's profoundly dystopian worldview (Subotnik, 1976, pp. 269–70). Popular music engaged, in a foreshortened form, with similar aesthetic struggles to those Adorno identifies in classical music. Ideas of the artist's investment in his work changed, but the ways in which these changes were envisioned were governed by a patriarchal logic, given that Adorno's modernist aesthetic was, as we have already established, dominated by binary splits. Indifference becomes supreme power. 'The production of an "open work", intrinsically and deliberately polysemic, can ... be understood as the final stage in the conquest of artistic autonomy ... To assert the autonomy of production is to give primacy to that of which the artist is master, i.e. form, manner, style rather than "subject" ... which involves subordination to functions ... of representing, signifying, saying something' (Bourdieu, 1984, p. 3).

Adorno's attribution of superior status to classical music on the basis of its individual, autonomous nature effectively stymied criticism of classical music in terms of the kinds of values and social conditions it reflected (Green, 1988, pp. 6–11; Huyssen, 1986; Small, 1987). Many commentators since Adorno have stressed that high cultural autonomy as expressed in classical music is not a negation but a confirmation of Western discourses of rationalisation and domination of mind over body, from the machine-like subordination of the orchestra to the composer/conductor, to the ban on spontaneity and expressions of community or physical participation. High culture is historically specific – its representation of Western post-Renaissance culture is not universal or supreme. The general implication is that the creation of a special category for high culture, as articulated in classical music, represents a logical extension of capitalist ideology:

> The ideological aspects of this art give the appearance that capitalist society, having once established itself, is thereafter eternal and inevitable, that its parts are autonomous and fragmented, and that we are all therefore impotent to make any fundamental changes to it ... The material world is thus justified, in that a better society is made to appear not merely unattainable, but superfluous, by virtue of a superior spiritual world that is held to be open to everyone. (Green, 1988, p. 111)

> The attribution of universal subjective validity to art has become common sense ... this ideology is fundamentally individualist because it leaves the individual to discover art's message and raise 'himself' above immediate reality. At the same time it denies the possibility of such an alternative experience in the real material world, alternative to establishment ideas ... It de-socialises not only the work, but also the attitude and understanding of the listener. (Green, 1988, p. 115)

Hence the Romantic ideology which emphasises subjective response and the 'special' place of art is complicit with hegemony, in its reinforcement of a scheme of mutually exclusive dualities which effectively divorce art from society (Leach, 2001, p. 143). Moreover, its emphasis on individualism suggests how art viewed in this way becomes a profoundly private experience, not associated with any form of community.

Classical music and masculinity

In *Music, Gender, Education* (1997), Lucy Green considers how classical music posits an implicitly male subject or creator. Green argues that femininity (actual, as opposed to ideal) is usually seen as disruptive in relation to music. Starting off with performance, she notes how the looking/being-looked-at dichotomy – the performer becoming the object of a gaze – is historically constructed as gendered male/female (Green, 1997, pp. 22–6; Mulvey, 1989, p. 20). Male classical musicians avoid the gaze, minimising display and mediating through technology, which minimises bodily presence – women musicians, by contrast, are often highlighted, emphasising their singularity and sexuality. Historically, in musical performance, some female delineations have been more acceptable – the singer or the solo performer – whereas men are acceptable in most performance contexts (Green, 1997, pp. 27–30, 60–62). The singer is acceptable because she presents a 'natural' ability that is already gendered (it is easy to tell sex from a voice) and because singing is seen as deriving from the body rather than from technology. The solo performer is acceptable because she presents an exceptional spectacle. The more the female performer departs from these traditional positions, the more disruptive she becomes. For instance, a woman instrumentalist no longer connects music with the body but mediates through technology: 'The woman player is clearly capable of at least attempting to control an alienated man-made object … The interruptive power of the instrument seriously detracts from the fullness of the intention to display … the sex-life of the woman instrumentalist is less suspect, and her display less susceptible to interpretation as a sexual invitation' (Green, 1997, p. 53). Green argues that men's sexuality is not seen as an obstacle to musical performance:

> Those very qualities which for the female player are interruptive of her femininity are for the male player relatively affirmative of his masculinity. For male instrumentalists throughout history, the delineation of gender has been nearly always metaphorically transparent: it is there, but we do not see it, we see through it … we do not hear it, we hear through it. (1997, p. 54)

That is, there is a 'natural' association between masculinity and the technology which is central to classical music performance. As such, it renders the technology invisible – rather we listen through it to hear the 'author' speaking:

> ... with composition it is a metaphorical display of the mind of the composer which enters into delineation ... Whilst we listen to music, it is not just the inherent meanings that occupy our attention, but also our idea of the composer's mental processes. (Green, 1997, pp. 84–5)

> The masculine delineation of music is articulated through ... the cerebral control of knowledge and technique which is implicit in the notion of composition. (Green, 1997, p. 216)

The Romantic conception of the genius, is, Green argues, masculinised by its association with controlling mind and with the privatisation of experience. The array of music and musical practices open to women is already circumscribed both by musical meaning and by musical experience. Similarly, in rock music, few female performers highlight their femininity unless they are appearing in a traditionally feminine role: a singer, or a singer/songwriter who accompanies herself acoustically. Chrissie Hynde or Patti Smith would be unlikely to appear in a dress, as this would highlight their disparity with the medium. The more attractive a woman is, or the more she chooses to display herself onstage, the more her technical competence will be questioned (Green, 1997, pp. 72–9).

Green (1997, p. 185) goes on to explore how gendered practices and assumptions affect girls' participation in music at school, arguing that despite the provisos laid out above, girls still find classical music more accommodating because the autonomous ideology of classical music professes to reduce the display and objectification that is a feature of popular music. Hence girls can participate in classical music without feeling their gender is such an issue. However, in important fields like composition, they lack confidence and Green argues that this is because of the inherited ideology of creation as a masculine practice. Boys' failure to do well in music was figured by all parties as due to laziness or carelessness, hence identifying the possibility that they 'couldn't be bothered' (Green, 1997, pp. 198, 213). Some boys stated that their failure was their own choice, because they were tested, in their view, on the 'wrong' music (that is, not the music they were interested in) (p. 212). Their ability is identified as extra-curricular. 'The boys' deviance and refusal ... thus turn ... into an assertion of their real, closely guarded musical superiority' (p. 191). Ineptitude becomes deviance:

> The disruptive boy who is in this position can display characteristics of madness which only feed the similitude of genius ... This similitude and the harnessing of misbehaviour to creativity is denied to girls. Their music, unlike that of the boys, is largely associated with being good or conformist ... Only exceptional talent ... can overcome this problem. (pp. 190–91)

Masculine deviance is subsumed within the larger patriarchal discourse: 'It is *because* boys play wrong notes that they achieve pleasing results' (p. 200): 'music itself has come to imply a male creator, and, through him, masculinity. This causes all music, at some usually sublimated level, to delineate masculinity: not "machismo", but masculinity in the vast complexity of its understandings and construction' (p. 133).

Andreas Huyssen suggests that the identification of femininity with mass culture implies an equally strong identification of high culture with masculinity: 'The powerful masculinist mystique which is explicit in modernists … has to be somehow related to the persistent gendering of mass culture as feminine' (1986, p. 198; see also Adorno, 1990, p. 313). But this connection of masculinity with high culture is not as immediate or self-evident as the association of femininity and mass culture. High cultural values are typically represented as universal truths, either by recourse to scientific proof or by conferral of art status. Thornton (1995, p. 13) ranks gender second only to age as an apparatus of social distinction in music subcultures.

High cultural discourse is also routinely employed within popular culture to establish hierarchies and enforce cultural and social distinctions. Punk and high modernism make a particularly good match, as demonstrated in Flying Nun style-policeman Chris Knox's review of the New Zealand Top 10: 'Seduced by sugary hooks and blatantly obvious rhythm tracks, you wander blindly through the stunning mediocrity of it all until someone of objectively immaculate taste, such as myself, opens your poor sagging eyes and shows you the light' (1986, p. 54). Knox identifies Top 10 pop as 'product', contaminated by sensual, compromising, commercial and implicitly feminine elements; hence his puritanical dismissal of it as sugary mediocrity. Rather he takes a modernist 'form follows function' approach: 'Music should be unadorned so as to communicate directly with the audience … the fewer steps between performer and audience the better' (Knox, 1991). He argues that 'true' beauty can only be found in an unflinching perception of the 'ugly truth' – ugliness (masculinity) is the guarantor of authenticity (Knox, 1989b). This reproduces an Adornoesque emphasis on negation. His 'extremely narrow and perverse' tastes come close to a Frankfurt School-style elitism, while also reproducing a bourgeois critique of low or vulgar art (Bourdieu, 1984, p. 486).

Sarah Thornton points out how 'studies of popular culture have tended to embrace anthropological notions of culture as *a way of life* but have spurned art-oriented definitions of culture which relate to *standards of excellence*' (1995, p. 8). For example, Thornton (1995, p. 5) argues that academics have tended to uncritically accept the binary notions of mainstream, dominant, feminised versus marginal, authentic, masculinised subculture used within subcultures, but we should recognise the binary formulations used by subculture followers as a strategy rather than a fact. She notes that '[f]eminist analyses are a general exception to this rule, but they tend to restrict their enquiry to criticizing the devaluation of the feminine and … the subordinate position of girls … They have not extended this insight to a general examination of the way youth cultures are stratified within themselves' (1995, pp. 7–8). That is, feminist approaches can also tend to perpetuate the dominance/resistance binary, and thus reify masculinity as simply dominant. Thornton suggests that popular cultures produce systems of social and cultural distinctions, just like the rest of society. Adapting Bourdieu's 'cultural capital', the 'linchpin of a system of distinction in which cultural hierarchies correspond to social ones', Thornton proposes the term 'subcultural capital' (basically 'hipness') to describe operations of 'distinction' within popular culture (1995, pp. 10–14).

Cultural capital is both objective (consisting in material objects) and embodied (style, knowledge). While Bourdieu maps out a hierarchical society, in which material capital and access to power and resources (for example through class) broadly correspond to social and cultural capital, subcultural capital is initially specific to subordinate social groups. Class origins and material resources are less important than embodied capital ('cool') (which may improve one's prospects of long-term material and social gain – a 'hip' band has at least in theory the opportunity for career advancement). Subcultures reproduce dominant discourses in an inverted form – so, subcultural capital represents a kind of negation or inversion of the dominant culture, a reversal, but not elimination of hierarchy.

Rock aesthetics – folk and black culture

In terms of cultural capital, Kier Keightley (2001, p. 120) argues that the early 1960s folk protest movement's use of mass culture critique was central to defining the difference and ideological grounding of an emergent rock aesthetic. Folk music performed many of the functions that high culture did for the Frankfurt School – seriousness, political critique, an anti-mass, individualised, marginalised expression which was organically connected to a community, rather than being industrial product. Black culture represented the paradigmatic instance of this folk authenticity (Cutler, 1991, p. 51; Keightley, 2001, p. 125). For example, the 1970s US rock 'authenticity' critics emphasised popular music's African-American roots, implicitly rejecting European bourgeois high art traditions (Shuker, 1998, p. 20). Robert Christgau (1973, p. 4) speaks of writing out of a desire to redress what he perceived as a critical inattention to black music. Dave Marsh (1985, p. 12; 1999) sets up a canon of authentic 'rock and soul', and argues for rock as an organically American form of expression. In turn, black masculinity is usually regarded as having some kind of parental role in the production of rock: 'Buried deep in the collective unconscious of rock and roll there's a simple figure drawn from real life: One man, one guitar, singing the blues. But he's not any man. He's black, southern, poor and … dreaming' (Marsh, 1999, p. 2, discussing Chuck Berry's 'Johnny B Goode').

No one would deny the importance of black culture to rock music. But equally, few would deny that black culture has often been misrepresented. Its association with folk authenticity (and sexuality) tells us more about the attitudes of the observer than of the observed: 'more evidence of the confusion at the heart of the dominant ideal of masculinity: heterosexual, white' (Segal, 1990, p. 169). Frith argues that white audiences have historically demanded that black performers conform to their expectations of an exotic blackness: 'that they embody sensuality, spontaneity, and gritty soulfulness' (1996, p. 131). This 'savagery', favourably reinterpreted as 'naturalness', becomes the hope of a new Eden, and hence an idea of an authentic folk culture, a mystical place of creativity that is outside modern society and beyond normal social relations. Closely connected is the discourse of rock's freedom from sexual repression, symbolically represented through the equation of electric guitar and penis, and the assumption that 'the primitive stands for the African-American influence upon electric guitar performance' (Waksman, 1999, p. 4). Since feminism, the specifically masculine character of this sexuality has been emphasised (Whiteley, 1997, p. xvii). Sexuality is fundamental to rock culture's 'difference' but also the basis for its critique – assertions of black 'sensuality' can equally be employed by conservative groups who want to denounce 'jungle' music (Frith, 1996, pp. 127–9; Street, 1986, p. 15). The fact that both pro- and anti-rock'n'roll factions viewed the black contribution similarly – in terms of a natural sexuality – should make us consider how accurate it really is.

Keightley suggests envisioning African-American influence primarily as a 'folk' discourse which authenticates rock, rather than as a real engagement with black culture: 'rock historians have misinterpreted … taste for African American music … as overt "political" statements. Instead, white youth … adopt this music as a sign of youth's own, privileged difference, expressing … their refusal of the mainstream' (2001, p. 125). Blackness functions as a kind of symbolic marginality, which allows young whites to imagine themselves as an oppressed minority. Similarly, Andrew Ross (1989, pp. 70–1, 93–4) argues that while jazz was central to the development of black 'consciousness' on both sides of the colour barrier, it only became politicised as the voice of the people when it became bebop (at the precise moment it ceased to be a popular form). Its acceptability depended on its being seen as a 'pure' folk/art culture, magically divorced from commerce. In the long run, the earlier identification with ethnicity was replaced by a 'youthful' rebellious white masculinity. 'By the end of the 60s, to be white and hip no longer meant a wholesale identification with black culture … By then, hip had become the distinctive possession of an ideological community – the predominantly white counterculture – bound together by a set of "alternative" taste codes fashioned in opposition to the straight world' (Ross, 1989, p. 96).

To understand this movement in psychoanalytic terms, I want to look at an influential example of 1950s white masculinities' response to black culture: Mailer's *The White Negro*. Mailer analysed a new figure on the US cultural stage: the hipster or beatnik. 'For Mailer, the hipster – whom he assumes to be both male and white – rebels against a society that guarantees "a slow death by conformity," and, abjuring his race and class privilege, voluntarily takes up a "Negro" positionality' (Savran, 1998, pp. 4–5). The 'Negro' for Mailer is a personification of id, of natural force and instinct, who

> could rarely afford the sophisticated inhibitions of civilization, and so he kept for his survival the art of the primitive …. he subsisted for Saturday night kicks, relinquishing the pleasures of the mind for the more obligatory pleasures of the body, and in

his music he gave voice to the character and quality of his existence, to his rage and
the infinite variations of joy, lust, languor, growl, cramp, pitch, scream and despair
of his orgasm. (1957, p. 5)

Mailer constructs 'black' as primitive body, both 'noble' and 'beastly'. David
Savran (1998, pp. 4–5) argues that this began with Beat writers' meditations on
black masculinity, and how it might provide a hip alternative to contemporary
white American masculinity (see also Segal, 1990, p. 179). Mailer offers a classic
illustration of the Freudian concept of the repressive hypothesis (Foucault, 1978,
pp. 1–49) of human 'instinct' against civilised values, arguing that such values are
no longer tenable, given the horrors (war, the atomic bomb) they have created.
Black culture offers an alternative, but necessarily (given his use of Freud) a rather
ambivalent one, because, like the psychopath, the White Negro is a creature
devoted to the 'immediate satisfaction' of his every desire (Mailer, 1957, p. 5). 'To
"encourage the psychopath in oneself" was not to trust in History ... but to exploit
the libertarian possibilities of free enterprise with one's most violent fantasies and
desires' (Ross, 1989, p. 87) – a rejection of the past in favour of continuous present
encouraged by bomb culture.

This ambivalence is expressed through the use of dichotomies – the black
'body' and its associated sexuality can be read as both masculine (in his potency
and potential for violence) and feminine (because he is identified with his body).
This allows Mailer to sympathise with blackness as the object of racist violence,
but also to suggest that the day of reckoning may be close at hand. So Mailer
identifies two opposite positions in the same persona – a feminised victim (to be
'beat' by definition is to lose) who can also be psychopathically violent and
misogynist – 'Mailer's celebration of virility ... fed the macho obsession that was
later to draw endless fire from the woman's movement' (Ross, 1989, p. 88). The
implications are several – that ethnicity is a key discourse in defining white masculinities, that black masculinities represent a new set of possibilities for white
culture (the recognition that black culture was becoming a powerful force in the
USA) – but these possibilities are necessarily disruptive to the existing social
order. This in turn is explicable in terms of a Freudian model of repression – blackness expresses a state of pre-Oedipal infant omniscience that implies both a childlike pleasure in immediacy and also a total disregard for civilised values. However,
Savran argues that this model is less important for what it says about black culture
than for what it reveals about white male anxieties and projections: it constructs a
white masculinity split between Freud's feminine and masculine positions (see
Chapter 6 for a discussion of this sadistic/masochistic opposition in terms of masculine 'schizophrenia'). In other words, white identification with blackness allows
white masculinities to take up a 'victim' position, and this in turn generates the
fantastic identification with blackness that is so central to white musical subcultures. So this psychological model does not seem to contradict Keightley's argument about folk purity.

Rock and high art

Discussions of popular music are peppered with the language and ideology of high culture: terms like genius, classic, art and so on. 'The popular music industry has drawn on this conventional language of genius ... which in turn is how modern society continues to understand the role of the artist' (McRobbie, 1999, p. 40). Rock music's elevation to the pantheon occurred in the 1960s – 'In three short years [1964–67] rock'n'roll had gone from ... vulgar entertainment ... to being hailed as the most important musical breakthrough of the decade' (Gendron, 2002, p. 1). Rock and roll had become rock, a new musical 'avant-garde', set apart from pop, although sharing, paradoxically, its mass popularity (Chambers, 1985, pp. 115–22). Contrasting rock with rock and roll, Jon Landau states: 'of the two, rock is a music of far greater surface seriousness and lyric complexity. It is the product of a more self-aware and self-conscious group of musicians. It is far more a middle-class music' (1972, p. 21). Some have argued that 1960s rock was invented by a small and elite coterie of white middle-class musicians, working in the studio in relative isolation from audiences, whose newfound fame and fortune allowed them increasing freedom to play the role of artist, relatively autonomous from the demands of the market (Keightley, 2001, p. 119; Moore, 2001, p. 65). Again, the connection to classical ideas of musical artistry is not so far-fetched.

Paul Théberge (1989, p. 106) describes how the multi-track studio can produce and reproduce a hierarchical model of labour relations, in which technological and aesthetic expertise are combined in the producer or musician/producer's manipulation of individual parts and players (see also Toynbee, 2000a, p. 69). The studio becomes to the rock artist/producer as an orchestra is to a composer, with each multi-track channel becoming an individually scored part. 'This "rock elite" of aesthetically *and* technically competent music makers was reinforced in its position by the onward development of technology ... In effect the record industry had ceded control to a coterie of established rock-masters' (Toynbee, 2000a, p. 93). Such practices also gave a new status to the 'technological expert', the usually faceless technologist whose knowledge of complex technology and 'abstract systems' is essential to the maintenance of production – in the case of rock, the 'producer'. Théberge's model is a bit reductive, but it does highlight the importance of the producer, who, to some extent, combines the roles of conductor and composer in assuming responsibility for the overall sound of the record, without actually appearing in the finished work (Thompson, 2004, p. 22; Toynbee, 2000a, p. 97). Finally, emergent rock was densely packed with high cultural references – from The Beatles' use of classical instruments, to Dylan's use of 'poetic language' and namedropping.

Of course, it was these very paradigms – rock as progressive, as art, as 'sterile' studio perfectionism – which punk and post-punk music was reacting against with its 'back to basics' approach. However, such an approach could easily blend into existing ideologies of artistic distinction; for example, the post-punk musician could be represented as being relatively autonomous from market demands, and thereby more of an artist. Alternatively, by adopting an avant-garde aesthetic and by other practices (particularly archivalism) such musics ultimately bought back into the traditional high art/mass culture binary aesthetic.

Art rock

Historically the term art rock has been used to describe at least two related, but distinct, types of rock music, arising in the late 1960s. The first, progressive rock, arose mainly from UK psychedelia and emulates European classical tradition: extended pieces, orchestration, complex harmonies and rhythms, and 'grand concepts' – Yes, Genesis, later Pink Floyd (Moore, 2001, p. 65). This was the 'boring hippy music' that punk rockers hated, and was not a particularly great influence on indie (apart from Pink Floyd). However, more 'pop' offshoots of psychedelia – the later Beatles, the later Beach Boys, The Byrds, early Pink Floyd, Love – continued to have a strong influence on indie rock. This is approximately the grouping denoted by the 'psychedelic mummy's boys', a 'tradition' well described by Jim DeRogatis's *Kaleidoscope Eyes* (1996) and in Reynolds and Press's *The Sex Revolts* (1995). This group is discussed below under the heading 'Psychedelia and ego death'.

On the other hand, art rock was also used to describe groups and artists who rejected psychedelia and the hippy counterculture and followed the more 'radical' path blazed by The Velvet Underground, which identified not so much with classical as with avant-garde and used techniques such as collage, *musique concrete*, irony and parody – in other words, a modernist avant-garde approach – and the glam rock of David Bowie, Roxy Music and Lou Reed, which 'offered an aesthetic perspective that was markedly different from that of progressive music. Its "artistry" went beyond traditional European aesthetic canons, and, like "Pop Art", looked to … modern industrial life and its continual reproducibility' (Chambers, 1985, p. 114). In the 1960s, UK art schools had been key sites at which popular music and discourses of art intertwined, producing musicians and audiences who thought of themselves as artists, or who applied art terminology and ideology to music as part of an overall bohemian lifestyle. Frith and Horne describe well their influence on glam, 1970s art rock and punk. But also increasingly important was the American influence, from Warhol and Pop Art (Frith and Horne, 1987, pp. 108–16). Writing of the latter, Ellen Willis states:

> From the early sixties … there was a counter-tradition in rock and roll that had much more in common with high art – in particular avant-garde art – than the ballyhooed art-rock synthesis [progressive rock]; it involved more or less consciously using the basic formal canons of rock and roll as material (much as pop artists used mass art in general) and refining, elaborating, playing off that material to produce … rock-and-roll art. While art rock was implicitly based on the claim that rock and roll was

or could be as worthy as more established art forms, rock-and-roll art came out of an obsessive commitment to the language of rock and roll and an equally obsessive disdain for those who rejected that language or wanted it watered down, made easier ... the new wave has inherited the counter-tradition. (1996, p. 73)

Art rock took the popular as its 'material', apparently collapsing traditional distinctions between high and low culture; and between Romantic, classical or modernist ideologies of art as autonomous and intellectual and the bodily pleasures of mass culture. However, although the materials of the artist changed, the artist's attitude towards them remained in important ways the same – distanced (Bourdieu, 1984, pp. 53–5). A common criticism is that art rock 'relates to rock and roll not organically but intellectually, what is most striking about art rock is that it isn't very sexy' (Christgau, 1973, p. 285; see also Landau, 1972, pp. 129, 134). This mind/body dichotomy, it is argued, belongs to high culture.

The first figure in this tradition is Phil Spector (Willis, 1996, p. 73). Spector made music which aspired to classical grandiosity, but was popular in its materials, forms and audience. He is also important as the first star producer of popular music and its first 'auteur'. He 'created a new concept; the producer as overall director of the creative process, from beginning to end. He took control of everything, he picked the artists, wrote or chose the material, supervised the arrangements, told the singers how to phrase, masterminded all phases of the recording process with the most painful attention to detail, and released the result on his own label' (Williams, 2003, pp. 15–16). Musically, Spector made his most significant contribution in the studio, drilling huge rock orchestras of top session musicians, shaping the sound from the mixing desk and adding a cavernous echo that swamped the individual instruments and turned the sound into a massive, oceanic roar: his trademark 'Wall of Sound'. Spector 'changed pop music from a performing art ... into an art which could sometimes exist only in the recording studio ... this immense conceptual shift paved the way for art rock' (Williams, 2003, p. 18). While not exactly conforming to the multi-track model of the producer, Spector nevertheless was the Svengali-like, shaping force behind the sound and style, orchestrating and managing a multiplicity of elements and players (Toynbee, 2000a, pp. 87–9). He was a new kind of rock and roll artist, one who did not perform (except as a conductor) and produced only finished works, like a painter, composer or film director, a long-haired, dandified genius (Williams, 2003, pp. 46–7).

Although Spector favoured black performers, his aesthetic did not foreground the body of the performer in the way that is commonly identified with rock music (in contrast, cultivation of personal style and 'expressivity' is much more formalised in classical music) (Frith, 1996, pp. 191–5, 210; Gracyk, 1996, pp. 19, 32). The performers on Spector's records are almost obliterated by the Wall of Sound, especially on later records like 'River Deep Mountain High' (Spector, 1991), where Tina Turner is almost literally screaming to be heard above the surrounding din. Similarly, the increasing use of reverberation obscures the rhythmic impetus, with its connotations of danceability. We could say that the body in Spector is threatening to disappear. Sometimes the artists *did* 'vanish', as when Spector released records bearing the name of artists who did not perform on them, such as The Crystals' 'He's a Rebel'. When the record came out, the 'real' Crystals were on the road, and had to quickly learn 'their' hit (Thompson, 2004, p. 74; Williams, 2003, p. 69). Stars, personalities and bodies were instrumental to Spector's obsessive overall control and vision, paralleling the auteur theory of cinema, or the centrality of the composer in classical tradition. Spector's example and sound proved influential on Brian Wilson of The Beach Boys, for example, hailed as another proto-rock genius, a studio master. This studio-bound eremiticism continues into indie through figures like Kevin Shields of My Bloody Valentine and the Reid Brothers of The Jesus and Mary Chain, whose soundscapes in turn owe a lot to these 1960s precedents. The importance of 'sound', as opposed to a performer, marked a movement towards a classical tradition of impersonality, or rather personality as mediated and transformed into a specifically art discourse, for example The Byrds (see Chapter 5).

Spector and Wilson are known as eremitic studio obsessives who laboriously produced fantastical and arguably monomaniacal soundscapes through their mastery of technology; forms of grandiosity compensating for disengagement from external realities (Cohn, 1980; Miller, 1996, pp. 46–7; Siegal, 1997).[1] Both habitually absented themselves from their own work – disavowing their own physical presence, treating individual musicians and group members as interchangeable, associating instead with an overall intellectual mastery of the sound (Green, 1997, pp. 84–5, 216).

The contrast commonly drawn in rock criticism is between the personal insignificance and instability of these producers and the vastness and resonance of the work – Spector was described as 'an infant in charge of Armageddon' (Cohn, 1980, p. 153). There is an ongoing association between these types of sounds, cultural texts and male 'nerds' who dream of fulfilment through music, reproduced as a mind/body dichotomy: physical weakness equals aesthetic strength; disembodiment equals power. More broadly, the category of 'producer' foregrounds themes of intellectual control and detachment that seem a long way from rock's supposed emphasis on the body.

> Spector was reclusive enough to know all about the obsessive possibilities of rock; and like Brian Wilson ... he refined his ... fantasies to the point of implosion. His records gradually became more intricate, more convoluted, more garbled ... and when an audience could no longer give him the gratification of admiring the sounds inside his head, he simply stopped ... For the self-satisfied hermit, rock is not really about sex or dancing or living dangerously, but instead about daydreaming ... The narcissistic rocker lives life at one remove, and perceives it through a filter of unthreatening stereotypes. Phil Spector might have never felt at ease making love or dancing or having fun ... but in those fantastic miniatures ... he was free to create

his own utopia of love, dance and fun, a world where he was in complete control.
(Miller, 1996, pp. 46–7)

This emphasis on narcissism and vicarious living is continued in Andy Warhol
and The Velvet Underground.

Art rock and camp

Andy Warhol took Spector's combination of the disembodiment, 'distance' and
refinement of high culture with the 'immediacy' of mass cultural forms like rock
and roll several stages further. There are striking similarities between the two –
both were small, nerdy guys with bad self-images, routinely bullied and consequently obsessive about their personal safety, who found in popular culture a
means of escape by creating larger-than-life personae. Both were entrepreneurs,
and liked to let other, more glamorous types stand in or do their work for them
(Moon, 1996, pp. 80–81; Watney, 1996, pp. 22–3; Williams, 2003, pp. 27–8).
Both were 'camp' and had reputations as dandies, and reverenced stardom, fame
and glamour. Both used low materials for high ends, and they shared a fascination
with surface – literally for Warhol, while for Spector it was a fascination with
'pure' sound. But Warhol's aesthetic was more thoroughly worked out than
Spector's, which represented a transitional phase between old-fashioned auteur-
ism and the thoroughly postmodern, detached tenets of pop art.

Warhol apparently did away with the Romantic concept of the artist altogether
(Morse Peckham, cited in Frith and Horne, 1987, p. 110). He certainly revised
some of the Romantic tenets: the division between high art and mass culture, the
idea of the artist as author – a strong, autonomous individual who produced 'original work'. Indeed many of his works involved minimal participation by their
author (Smith, 1988, pp. 61, 88, 122, 183, 221, 294). Warhol's whole modus oper-
andi opposed intentionality – 'doing things because you believed in them' or commitment was directly counter to his ethos (Bourdieu, 1984, p. 54; Smith, 1988,
p. 255). In person, Warhol was usually described as 'simple', non-verbal, childlike
and helpless, even 'catatonic' (Smith, 1988, p. 122). This persona of a 'blank' or
faux naif suggested that Warhol was somehow incapable of doing anything except
watching (Smith, 1988, pp. 8, 20, 25, 34, 44, 53, 59, 88, 100, 105, 122–5, 188,
193). It was a powerful form of blankness, however, because it created a public
space for others to perform – the Factory. His blank gaze created multiple personae, a succession of media 'stars', who were, like Warhol, famous not for what
they did, but for their very visibility.

Warhol envisioned the artist as his mass cultural 'opposite' – the audience/
consumer/fan: 'his famous mute withdrawal is a devoted fan's attention to his
culture … a conscious equalisation of everything' (Smith, 1988, p. 292). His
worship of glamour and stardom demonstrated how fans and stars produced each

other, just as commerce and art were inseparable (Smith, 1988, p. 295). The prec-edent for Warhol's combination of artist and fan is the late Romantic aesthete dandy, as described by Wilde and Baudelaire. 'A man who lives only through an image of himself' (Koch, 1974, p. 114), the dandy exists as he is perceived by others. He aestheticises his life and commodifies himself; and in a commodified world, this makes sense – because for Warhol 'stars' and mass culture were more real than life. In Warhol's aesthetic, art was a transcendence of life – life was only bearable if experienced as art. In a sense, then, his position was not so different from that of the Romantic artist – the materials changed, but the attitude towards them did not. Indeed, Warhol did aspire to be taken seriously as an artist, and that is the main way in which his work and life are understood today (Smith, 1988).

Warhol's debt to Duchamp and the Dadaists reflects the paradoxes of his mass culture aestheticism, most obviously through art works that simply recontextual-ised mass-produced objects ('ready-mades'), forcing the audience to analyse the shaping nature of their response to their perception of art (Koch, 1974, pp. 56–7; Smith, 1988, p. 2). This exposes the fiction that art is independent of an audience, but at the same time it may cultivate another fiction – that art is only created by the spectator's gaze, which is central to understanding Warhol's combination of artist and fan personae.

Warhol used mediation both to create a public persona and also to keep people at a distance – he would take tape recorders and cameras to parties, 'the clicking of the shutter … retrieving the distance his feelings have threatened' (Koch, 1974, p. 28). Much of his art has this sense of real-time immediacy. (For a more recent example of this approach, we might think of Steven Soderbergh's 1989 film *Sex, Lies, and Videotape*, in which the main character, played by James Spader, simi-larly uses mediation as a way of avoiding intimacy.) Warhol's identity was highly invested in media, almost to the point of his real-life existence being questionable: '[he] doesn't exist in a way. He's like a white hole' (Danny Fields, quoted in Smith, 1988, p. 288). This could also be expressed in the formula 'famous for being famous'. Koch implies that for Warhol, 'fame is … the resolution of a conundrum of existence and inexistence, that, under the conditions of so proud a pathological withdrawal, fame alone presents the terms under which life is worth living' (1974, p. 27) (Morrissey provides an obvious counterpoint here.)

Existence is dependent on the perception of others – in turn Warhol's aesthetic is based around the metaphor of voyeurism, or looking at others: he 'has managed to discover a certain kind of immediacy in his removal from things. We might call it the immediacy of the unobstructed view' (Koch, 1974, p. 28). The voyeur '*is a man who absents himself* … the impulse to conceal himself becomes more … intense as more … is revealed' (Koch, 1974, p. 41). The dandy presents himself as a spectacle for the gaze of others. Warhol was both: 'He has joined the dandy's strategy with that of the voyeur, and elevated the conjunction to a principle of being'; someone 'who makes people come to him and do their thing while he deigns or deigns not to look' (Koch, 1974, p. 120; see also Smith, 1988, pp. 41, 106, 190, 297).

Gay readings of Warhol tend to see his 'shyness' as linked to his homosexuality – as such they may oversimplify if they read Warhol's passivity as an identification with femininity (Sedgwick, 1996). Flatley argues that 'the defining condition of voyeurism – "repetitive looking at unsuspecting people" is precluded' (1996, p. 126), because Warhol's subjects were perfectly aware of being watched, but this is to assume that voyeurism is only defined by the unawareness of the performer, rather than by the gaze of the spectator, and clearly this is not so (in pornography, for example).

Commenting on the Factory scene, Koch claims that although Warhol presented himself as a 'blank', he was in fact also a controller, 'defended by the force field of an intense passive energy' (1974, p. 26). (When feminist activist Valerie Solanas shot Warhol in 1968 her explanation was, 'He had too much control over my life' (quoted in Frank, 1996, p. 210).) This power was not demonstrated overtly, but through the highly controlled, indeed obsessive strictures around contact with others.[2] To touch Warhol was the ultimate faux pas: 'to exert the slightest pressure of any kind promptly gives one the creepy feeling of committing an inexcusable act of aggression' (Koch, 1974, p. 26; see also Smith, 1988, p. 366). His sexual life seems to have been minimal (Smith, 1988, pp. 93–4, 106, 129, 295). Rather, he relied on others to act out for him: 'as the ultimate voyeur, Warhol has surrounded himself with exhibitionists. His strategy is far more successful … than theirs. By making himself the prime witness of (their) pathetic dream of autonomy, Warhol has achieved his own airtight image of autonomy … a master of passive power' (Koch, 1974, pp. 120–21). He is 'one who is seen because he sees, one present because he is absent, a star who is in fact a stargazer' (Koch, 1974, p. 122). He used people without directing them, 'intelligently using their needs to exploit themselves' (Tally Brown quoted in Smith, 1988, p. 258). For example, his *Screen Tests* (1964–66) use the blankness of the camera's gaze and the lack of directorial input and interaction as ways of 'cracking' their subjects – few people can keep up their 'cool' under such circumstances. This process acted as an initiation rite for induction into the Factory circle (Ross, 1989, p. 168; Sargeant, 2002, pp. 90–92; Smith, 1988, pp. 298–300).

Warhol was notorious for his indifference to human tragedy. 'When he heard that Fred Herko had jumped out of the window, his famous remark was "What a shame we didn't run down there with a camera and film it"' (Tavel, quoted in Smith, 1988, p. 301). The condition of Warhol's aestheticisation of life was withdrawal from direct emotional contact with others, and the removal of emotional affect from his work (Smith, 1988, pp. 88, 291–2). 'He thinks of himself as being inhuman … a robot' (Tavel, quoted in Smith, 1988, p. 300). Clearly this idea of the artist as absent voyeur is immensely important. It represents Warhol's response to Adorno's problem of how the artist could continue to create in an inhuman, mechanised world. Adorno argued that the artist (subject) had to disappear from his work (object). Warhol accomplished this by removing his intention from the artistic process, creating the work through his perception, his 'vision'. Warhol ironised and problematised the relationship of performer to author – but, as Ross states, this ambiguity 'was neither exactly complicit or dissenting, since it was based on an outright refusal of the act of judgment ... an attitude of pure *indifference*' (1989, p. 150).

This apparent suspension of judgment is double-edged: its noncommital passivity is also its claim to superiority; it is 'above these things', as in Bourdieu's 'distance from necessity' (1984, p. 5). It is also a commentary on bourgeois art, as in Bourdieu's 'pure taste': 'a systematic refusal of all that is "human" ... the passions, emotions and feelings which *ordinary* people put into their *ordinary* existence (1984, pp. 31–2). It does not necessarily imply a free-for-all polysemy; rather categories of camp and bad taste became institutionalised in a burgeoning alternative rock discourse, as its 'pseudo-artistocratic patrilineage' (Ross, 1989, p. 145).

Like Spector, Warhol exists not as presence, but as a controlling or organising principle behind and beneath the surfaces of media. Both vastly successful commercial artists, and both simultaneously absent and present in their own creations, they join a tradition of American narcissists like Orson Welles and Howard Hughes, beings whose entire existence seems to be in the public arena, as a 'brand'. Comparison can also be made to Walt Disney: not so much a personality or an artist as a commodity, a condition to which Warhol clearly aspired (Smith, 1988, pp. 95, 171, 361). This branding process was also developed in 1970s art rock, from the avant-garde (The Residents) to the mainstream (Pink Floyd) – bands who were cults of 'unpersonality' (Cutler, 1991, p. 73; Jones, 1996, p. 6).

Warhol demonstrates how passivity can be powerful. The passive voyeur uses his gaze to control and incite others to act. This calls into question any simple binary division of masculine activity and female passivity, opening new possibilities for masculine self-presentation in rock music – crucially how men onstage could appear physically passive, homosexual and even childlike without renouncing their artistic control, how discourses of amateurism and repetition could be annexed, so that pasty-faced white boys could present themselves as credible rock artists without having to 'perform', physically or technically (there is an analogy here with 'punk' acting, see Chambers, 1985, pp. 133–4; Doyle et al., 1996, p. 15). But however 'deviant' such representations appeared, they were mainly employed by white men – there was little corresponding growth in possibilities, however perverse, for feminine or ethnic representation.

Warhol also anticipated the characteristic slacker pose of disengagement: 'Our apparent and oft-condemned apathy is actually a carefully modulated distancing from the cues and signals of the boomers' consumer culture – an appraiser's sideways glance at the efforts of our elders to capture what's left of our hearts, minds and wallets ... an ability to derive meaning from the random juxtaposing of TV commercials, candy wrappers, childhood memories and breakfast treats' (Rushkoff, 1994, pp. 5–7). Important here is the idea of the subject as disengaged, as 'accepting' the flow of media (but also 'controlling' its meaning) and this seems pretty close to Warhol. But the price of this approach is a profound cynicism about the value of 'real' life (Smith, 1988, p. 255). Warhol's aesthetic is, at base, not a lot of fun – or, rather, it depends on an idea of 'fun' that is based on spectatorship rather than participation. Although appearing to challenge Western individualism, its insistence on disembodiment is in fact continuous with that tradition. Both Spector and Warhol reduce the world to an object for their delectation, but the price they pay for this is that they can no longer participate in it meaningfully.

Warhol's approach reverberates throughout art rock, most obviously in his stance of distance and disengagement. His infamous blankness is echoed in the cool detachment of The Velvet Underground, and thus the characteristic impassivity of the male indie rock star, 'cultured and autistic' (Arnold, 1995, p. 163). His famously non-existent sex life became symbolic of a kind of renunciation of the body for the higher end of worldly fame, and his 'naive' celebration of mass culture was taken up by artists such as Jonathan Richman. But equally it also articulated Warhol's commentary on the idea that mass culture was itself infantile or infantilising – the simplistic automatism of his works says a 'a child could do this. Or a machine'. But a childlike view of the world is not necessarily innocent – indeed it could equally express an autistic numbness incapable of emotional relation.

I'll be your mirror – The Velvet Underground

The Velvet Underground's influence recurs from the 1970s onwards and in indie scenes all over the world, from New York to what is now the Czech Republic, from England to Australia and, of course, Dunedin (Bannister, 1999, pp. 14–15, 102; Mitchell, 1996, p. 102; Szemere, 2001, pp. 31, 63, 124). No other band exerted the same grip on the minds of 1970s/1980s art/alternative rock artists, writers and audiences: 'From savagery and darkness to limpid beauty, there is no body of work in "rock" that comes within a bone's throw of the Velvet Underground' (Knox, 1985a). 'Modern music begins with the Velvets' (Bangs, quoted in Heylin, 1993, p. 3), who 'became the model for an avant-garde within rock'n'roll, the source of a self-conscious, intellectual trash aesthetic' (Frith and Horne, 1987, p. 112) and 'the first important rock-and-roll artists who had no real chance of attracting a mass audience' (Willis, 1996, p. 74).

Warhol was the group's major initial patron, including them in his Exploding Plastic Inevitable. Willis argues that they shared Warhol's simultaneous and paradoxical valorisation of art and mass culture: 'insofar as it incorporates the elite, formalist values of the avant garde, the very idea of rock'n'roll art rests on a contradiction', that of creating a form of elite mass culture, 'anti-art art made by anti-elite elitists' (1996, p. 74). The trash aesthetic functions not so much as a democratisation of culture as a testament to the superior taste of a discerning elite who can find sublimity in abjection.

The Velvets' appeal is usually defined in terms of white middle-class bohemian groups, to whom 'art' is a central ideology: 'middle class adolescents (temporarily) excluded from … power [who] express their distance from the bourgeois world … by a refusal of complicity whose most refined expression is a propensity towards aesthetics and aestheticism' (Bourdieu, 1984, p. 55; see also Gilbert, 1999, p. 44). As a university student, Gilbert notes: 'liking the Velvets was something to have in common with Spanish students as much as other provincial English kids' (1999, p. 36). Finally they represented 'Thin White Boys' (Gilbert, 1999, p. 31) a specific type of masculinity he associates with alternative rock worldwide: 'young White men coming from or aspiring to the class of salaried intellectuals … with all of the ambiguity of class identity which that implies … uncomfortable with the conventional gendered identities offered by the dominant strands of popular culture, but unable … to fully embrace gay culture' (Gilbert, 1999, p. 44). They were hugely influential on aspiring artists and musicians: 'Mark E. Smith … Siouxsie (and the Banshees) and Ian Curtis … might have all hated each other's music … but would certainly have known all the words to "Heroin", just as could be said of Ian McCullough [sic], Bobbie Gillespie [sic] or Johnny Marr' (Gilbert, 1999, p. 36).

Commonly dismissed in their time as a 'fag' band (Bangs, 1987, p. 373), the 'perversities' the Velvets catalogued gave rise to new sexually ambiguous stars like Bowie (Chambers, 1985, pp. 132–5). That is, they established 'camp' as a rock category, as a possible subject position. This is not to say that they promoted homosexuality as a lifestyle or as a politics of difference, however. Homosexuality and androgyny were, for Bowie and the other glam rockers, personae that could be employed, but also taken off again. As Andrew Ross (1989, pp. 146–7) points out, camp is a strategy – a way for intellectuals to get a 'taste' of low pop culture while simultaneously maintaining a critical distance from it.

Warhol and the Velvets' campness could be more accurately described as an aesthetic of disembodiment. If embodiment meant playing out a version of black heterosexuality, then art rock bands refused this approach, treating the body as purely instrumental to delivering whatever persona the artist adopted (as with Bowie). As the glam, performative element was increasingly absorbed into the mainstream (New Pop), what was left was a kind of autistic blankness, exemplified in punk and continued in indie. That is, by problematising their onstage presence, indie rock masculinities were not just refusing normative heterosexuality – they were identifying with dominant discourses of power.

The Velvets emulated Warhol's art/pop synthesis. The repetitive minimalism of their music echoed Warhol's emphasis on simplicity – and like him, they ignored the conventional hierarchies of artistic representation (Frith and Horne, 1987, p. 117). They integrated an aesthetic of chance and non-intentionality into their music making, and a presentational 'blankness' into their performance personae. Like Warhol, then, they challenged traditional ideas of the Romantic artist expressing himself though his work. Voyeurism is also central – many Velvet songs are visions of decadence and excess, but rather than celebrate excess (as in hippy culture), the Velvets' approach was to stare blankly at it – responding to

mass cultural critique by confirming it – implying that, yes, they were discon-
nected and numbed by mass media, and, no, they really didn't care. Like punks,
the Velvets proclaimed their unshockability – their supreme indifference to the
human spectacle unravelling before them, which is in turn to some degree incited
by their very presence and gaze. There is a profound asceticism in their litany of
human vanity, akin to monasticism. At the same time, because there is no God,
there is no recourse to any external reality outside the world of the image and the
gaze. To paraphrase the song which gives this section its title, in reflecting what
we are, they disavow their own subjectivity.

White hole

Warhol showed a way for white masculinities to assert their cultural authority
over popular culture by aestheticisation – the cultivation of distance, refinement
and a disengagement from the body, and the gradual replacement of bodily performance with an ideal of mental control, the artist not as performer but as critical observer, as gazer or voyeur, replacing a 'black' countercultural identity with
a white one. As such, the Velvets' approach sharply contrasted with the hippy
counterculture: their aim was to 'express uptightness and make the audience
uptight' (Frith and Horne, 1987, p. 112) – joy became sorrow, collectivity isolation, liberation enslavement, love sadomasochism, acid visions of utopia a junkie
vision of decay. They debunked the myth of black sexuality and cultural authenticity in rock with a chilly blast of European hauteur by the Foucauldian technique of emphasising that sex is not expressive, but repressive, not freedom but
enslavement, not heterosexual but queer.[3] Perhaps the best example is 'I'm
Waiting for the Man' (1967), a telling rejoinder to the Summer of Love and a
demythologisation of its projections – turning a fantasy of blackness into a much
more concrete description of a real-life interaction, in which the power positions
of black and white are reversed. The first reversal is in the title itself – traditionally 'the man' was white – he was the boss, as in 'working for the man'. But here
'the man' is a black dealer. In the song, the narrator is trying to score in a black
neighbourhood, and has to endure the taunts of black men who question his right
to be there. They call him 'boy' and he calls them 'sir', thus reversing the traditional assumptions of white supremacy. They also accuse him of chasing their
women, another ironic inversion. The narrator's relationship to 'the man' is
totally dependent – indeed in the song Reed actually sings the sexually sugges-
tive 'waiting for my man'. There is a clear parallel between his quest for the
needle and his 'awe' at black manhood. In the final verse, however, the narrator,
having presumably got his fix, now takes the position of mastery attributed to the
man. His mastery of the moment reproduces the instinctual assumed nature
of blackness (but of course it is also a part of the high). Tomorrow he will
have to go back to the black 'source' to score again. We can see here an endless

oscillation (part of the junkie's lot) between highs and lows, passivity and mastery, whiteness and blackness that is characteristic of masculinity as described by Savran (1998). This tension is there in the music, a self-consciously simplistic stomp which is both 'primitive' and extremely self-aware. The text also reproduces an ironic historical account of perceived white male inadequacy in popular music – always dependent on the black injection for a life-giving fix. Aptly, Lou Reed later wrote his own version of Mailer's 'White Negro' in 'I Wanna Be Black' (*Street Hassle*, 1978) (Werner, 2000, p. 212).

The Velvets also marked a new 'explicitness' about sex and desire in rock and roll. Whereas most rock and pop music had been mostly vaguely utopian or euphemistic about sex and drugs, the Velvets were a specific catalogue of 'perversities': sadomasochism ('Venus in Furs' and 'Femme Fatale', 1967), homosexuality ('Sister Ray', 1968), transvestitism ('Candy Says' and 'Some Kinda Love', 1969) and so on. Many songs were 'confessions' – 'Heroin' (1967), for example. However, this specificity has the effect of demystifying and thus ultimately desexualising the songs. They're about sex, but the sex in them is not fun; it's about power, pain and numbness. This numbness is echoed in the characteristic narrative perspective of Reed's writing: he maintains a cool, almost clinical distance, as if he is handling laboratory specimens. Although the Velvets write about a New York demi-monde, 'the symbolic identification of both the Velvets and their fans is not with the junkie, the paranoiac, the hustler or the freak, but with an idealised image of the detached observer who can walk through this urban twilight and ... make it into something beautiful' (Gilbert, 1999, p. 39). They do not offer the 'wild life' but rather a tour of it – a walk on the wild side. This voyeuristic detachment is echoed in the accompanying music, which is harsh, sometimes dissonant, rhythmically leaden and largely stripped of black influences. Formerly rock's primitivism was inscribed precisely in its linkage to black American culture – its dance rhythms, its textural pleasures, its expressivity through the use of blues and gospel. The Velvets devised ways of expressing primitivism that referred back mainly to the white European classical avant-garde – minimalism, purity and the drone, an aural and rhythmic attack that was assaultive and grating (Willis, 1996, p. 75).

The 'truth of sex', then, for the Velvets is that sex is not a refuge from or resistance to power – it is power (literally in the way they write about sadomasochism). Of course the Velvets' interest in S&M is continued in punk rock, but the more general point is that they envisioned sexuality away from the body and towards the eye that observes it – surveillance. But this objective, journalistic eye can only watch – it cannot participate. This dualism is also echoed in Reed's writing, which oscillates between visions of lurid excess and primitive child-like purity ('Jesus', 'I'm Set Free' and 'Pale Blue Eyes', 1969). While this is often ironic ('Beginning to See the Light', 1969), the recurrence of quasi-religious imagery suggests patriarchal Christian mind–body dualism in which renunciation of the body represents the only path to salvation.

The difference of the Velvets is in what Gilbert terms 'the gaze *of* the Velvet Underground' (1999, p. 39). They changed rock by the way they viewed it – not as expressing an inner essence, but rather as material they could arrange as they saw fit; again, this is close to Bourdieu's 'pure gaze' (1984, pp. 31–2). At the same time, they actively sought, as Warhol did, to minimise their own involvement with that process – to question themselves as authors by problematising their own presence. Warhol's emphasis on naivety allowed him to smuggle in an intellectual aesthetic in the face of the anti-intellectualism of US society. Given that rock is also avowedly anti-intellectual, such a strategy might work as a way for aspiring rock musicians to appear artistic and serious without saying as much in their performance. To control without appearing to be in control – this goes to the heart of Warhol's use of the gaze as a mode of invisible organisation. Warhol and the Velvets suggested a way forward for masculinities in rock. Act like you don't know you're on stage, appear infantile or naive, a gormless 'fan'. Be a victim. But such self-deprecation is necessarily ironic – if you're 'not all there', then where is the rest of you? The implication is that you 'know' better.

Jonathan Richman, another Velvets acolyte, pioneered such a brand of straight, geeky masculinity which functioned as an almost puritanical commentary on countercultural excess.

> Armed with [the Velvets'] inspiration Jonathan began to write songs informed by his own startlingly iconoclastic perspective … which railed against the close minded cool of the counter culture. The era in question was late '60s early '70s, by which time it was simply accepted that you wore flares, had long hair, hated your parents, laid as many chicks as would let you, and ingested as many different mind altering substances as possible. Bands were stretching out and jamming, placing greater and greater emphasis on musical prowess and insipid pseudo mystical lyrics. The 'oh wow man, heavy' and 'don't bum my trip' set was in full bloom. Into this bathetic milieu steps Jonathan with minimal singing and playing ability, a clean cut kid, with short hair, button down shirt, straight leg pants, and a plastic Harley Davidson jacket. (Crain, 2002)

The 'purification' of rock and roll that the Velvets initiated is expressed through Richman's adoption of a straight, naive persona. Later he seemed to regress to childhood entirely on songs like 'Hey There Little Insect' and 'Ice-cream Man' (1977). Richman anticipates rockism by several years by presenting himself as sexually naive – an implicit critique of hippy sexism. This was a persona later employed by David Byrne of Talking Heads – professing ignorance of the more sleazy or self-indulgent aspects of 1970s rock, presenting himself as a wide-eyed innocent, or even as an 'organisation man', as on 'Don't Worry About the Government' (1977). Clearly such an approach invites speculation as to the degree that it endorses 'straight' white masculine values. Richman's influence on punk/ indie is well documented (Alberti, 1999, p. 173; Azerrad, 2001, p. 464; Cavanagh, 2000, p. 25; Harrington, 2002, p. 337; Nichols, 2003, p. 88).

The paradoxical impassivity of the 'straight man' is a key strategy for indie masculinities, because it distances performers from the problematics of sexuality and allows them to distance themselves from a fixed meaning. One can't tell whether the performer 'means' what he does or says (and therefore one can't condemn him). By not offering the audience any kind of emotional cue or simple identification, he can thus hold himself apart, and perhaps imply a rational detachment or intellectual superiority from the spectacle: 'I am here but not necessarily part of this' (Eminem's Slim Shady persona is a more recent example). So while this approach denies authentic masculinity, it rearticulates masculinity by virtue of its (superior) disengagement from social and performance interaction. To relate it back to ethnicity, it represents a polar opposition to the traditional association of rock with physical expression and performance. But Richman's 'rock and roll simpleton' persona also arguably smuggles in an ethnic stereotype through the back door – for was not his stance of innocent fun very close to the idea of the folk culture as a gentler, simpler place, inhabited by pre-sexual primitives? The ongoing significance of Richman as a prophet of a 'new' victimised white masculinity is confirmed by his presence in the Farrelly Bros film *There's Something about Mary* (1998).

Punk

Punk elevated this sense of self-reflexive awareness combined with bodily disengagement to the level of an overall aesthetic: 'one of the things that makes the punk stance unique is how it seems to assume substance or at least style by the *abdication* of power: *Look at me! I'm a cretinous little wretch! And proud of it!*' (Bangs, 1987, p. 273). All the punk really had over the hippy was a superior awareness of his own marginality and insubstantiality. The price paid for this superior awareness was ascetic renunciation: 'While the original primal impulse of rock and roll was to celebrate the body … [Lou] Reed's temperament was not only cerebral but ascetic … the self-conscious formalism of his music … was an attempt to purify rock and roll, to purge it of all association with material goodies and erotic good times' (Willis, 1996, p. 75). Most obviously this was expressed in the renunciation of physical expression, dancing, on-stage moves and instrumental competence. Rather, the body's presence could only be affirmed by acts of violence – self-mutilation (Iggy Pop, Chris Knox, Henry Rollins) or the use of excessive volume as bodily assault (as described in Chapter 5) and by lyrics that increasingly replaced sex with violence or regressed into a pre-sexual childhood fantasy land.

Warhol aimed not to emulate the forms of high culture, but rather its attitude – intellectual, distanced, ascetic, refined. This clearly connects to the formation of cultural capital within rock culture, and the ironic elitism of punk. More specifically one could say that attitude was what mattered – rock and roll was no longer about what you did, but how you regarded it. The Velvets were central to this

shifting towards more self-reflexive personae. This is replicated in the recurrent
and all-pervasive irony of alternative rock discourse:

> The peculiar astringency of the Ramones' style – Joey's insistence on keeping the 'I'
> in his vocals separate from himself ... The Rolling Stones depended ... on that kind
> of relativism ... which is why a cut like 'Out of Time' sounds as up-to-date as ever,
> while the Beach Boys and a lot of the early Beatles ... sound ... incomplete: you
> have to forget a little of what you know to enter into that world completely. (Carson,
> 1996, p. 115)

In the old model of authenticity, performers 'meant what they said'. In post-punk,
the whole point was that they didn't. Or that you couldn't tell, as with Jonathan
Richman. Punk critics challenged 'authenticity' by implying the superiority of an
ironic, relative sensibility, which has become part of the alternative rock worldview (DeCurtis, 1999, p. 32). But was this an advance in terms of gender, or simply
the replacement of one kind of male hegemony with another? Perhaps in punk and
alternative rock, 'this ironic distance of the performative mode, in a strange way
... requires a rather secure, a priori sense of identity' (Zanes,1999, p. 39). Punk's
dictum was 'we don't care' (the Sex Pistols' 'Pretty Vacant', 1977). Like that of
Warhol, this was an act of disavowal of the 'straight' world, which is a Cartesian
epistemological stance: that by denying emotional engagement or direct involvement in the world, one becomes free of illusion and can see things as they 'really'
are (Descartes, 1968, p. 47; Benjamin, 1988, pp. 179–80). This disavowal of sensuality and emotion can also be interpreted, when used by men, as a mode of
control. The result is 'affirmation of a peculiarly joyless sort, for the new wave's
minimalist conception of rock and roll tends to exclude not only sensual pleasure
but the entire range of positive human emotions' (Willis, 1996, p. 77).

The music in turn was regulated by a 'code of sonic requirements' – it had to
be loud, fast and raucous and it had to signal its own refusal of the mass. The
Ramones' style was so narrowly defined as to exclude the possibility of any diversity in rock. As Jerry Harrison of Talking Heads notes: 'they had like a manifesto
... every time they'd stray from that basic premise they lessened the impact of
their original thing ... we saw the danger in that immediately' (quoted in Gans,
1985, p. 37). The ways in which such an aesthetic was justified drew heavily on
the language and ideologies of high modernism: real art should be difficult (so as
to resist commodification) and autonomous and pure, and it is marked off from its
mass cultural commodification, individualism. The Ramones 'defined the music
in its purest terms: a return to the basics that was both deliberately primitive and
revisionist at the same time, a musical and lyrical bluntness of approach which
concealed a wealth of complex, disengaging ironies beneath. It was zero-based
rock'n'roll, and the conquest was so streamlined that the smallest shifts in nuance
... had enormous implicit resonance' (Carson, 1996, p. 108).

Carson illustrates how the punk aesthetic references high modernist values –
autonomy, purity, primitivism, aggression and minimalism – but with the implication

of a kind of ironic self-effacement (from Warhol) as if the surface of the music conceals an inner complexity and intellectuality.

Punk and ethnicity

Lester Bangs suggests that punk rock had 'outgrown' the African-American model: 'white hippies and beatniks before them would never have existed had there not been a whole generational subculture with a gnawing yearning to be nothing less than the downest baddest *niggers* they could possibly be' (1987, p. 146) but 'there's an evolution of sound rhythm and stance running from the Velvets through The Stooges to the Ramones and their children that takes us farther and farther from the black stud postures that Mick Jagger, Lou Reed and Iggy partake in but Joey Ramone doesn't … at the sacrifice of a whole passel of macho defenses' (p. 278). Remarkably, the latter passage comes from an article ('The New White Noise Supremacists') about racism in punk, so Bangs quickly recants, but it's hard to avoid the conclusion that his punk (incompetent, foolish, unsexy, alienated) was an ironic white inversion of an equally idealised representation of black manhood. In other words, Bangs is complicit in the racism he decries: he, by helping create punk, helped create the 'New White Noise Supremacists' (racist punks) – a point which he acknowledges, although in relation to his personal conduct rather than his ideological outlook (pp. 276, 280–81).

Bangs, like Richman, was deeply suspicious of hippy culture and imagined punk as a return to more honest values, and this included a reconsideration of rock masculinity. He reversed the equation that associated rock masculinity with power and sexuality, moving towards Savran's masochistic opposite position – the loser, the victim, indeed 'the punk' (in the original sense of the word, a catamite). Rock creativity (mojo) moves from discourses of power and mastery (the 1970s prog rock musical 'virtuosity' that Bangs despised) back towards a Romantic ideology of 'innocent' untutored creativity combined with a voracious appetite for pop culture, junk food and drugs. This updated 'white negro' anticipates the figure of the slacker.

What emerges in the 1970s and the punk rock aesthetic is a new kind of rock masculinity – the loser who invites aggression. Richman's 'geek' persona enraged his hippy audiences; punks incited aggression by their mere appearance. This allowed them to imagine themselves as 'victims', demonstrating Foucault's thesis (1978, p. 45) that there is pleasure and some power in being victimised. It is usual to imagine that passivity and aggression are opposite – but in this chapter we have seen how they function as complementary, each producing the other within white masculinities. The characters of Richard Linklater' film *Slacker* (1991) demonstrate this well, in their perverse refusal of action and possibility, alternating with sudden acts of pointless violence or lurid fascinations with assassinations and serial killers. The 'slacker' is passive-aggressive – resistant 'to the demands by

others for adequate performance'. The passive-aggressive typically denies authorship of the very real social effects that he/she creates, disavowing aggression and
projecting it on to others (Corsini and Auerbach, 1996, p. 653). One can see how
feminism might have encouraged such masculine avoidance strategies: 'it's not
real acceptable to prattle on about killing bitches … it's got to go underground'
(Sutton, 1997, p. 531). Aggression is rearticulated indirectly through technology
(see Chapter 5). In turn, passivity plays a role in creating aggression, as in Warhol's
'passive power'.

Psychedelia and ego death

Though they are usually seen as opposite, there were important parallels between
the 1960s hippy counterculture and the Factory scene. Both were seeking a kind
of ego death, with clear implications for masculinity as controlling superego. They
aimed to be 'mind-blowing' and this is central to their claims to be progressive, in
gender and other fields. Both advocated transcendence of the everyday through
aesthetic style (immediacy, repetition, machine noise, feedback), uninhibited sexuality, Oriental mysticism and drugs (Heylin, 1993, p. 11). Lester Bangs noted
that both the Grateful Dead and the Velvets were pioneering a new sort of music,
'utilising the possibilities of feedback and distortion … both claimed to be the
avatars of the psychedelic multimedia trend' (1987, p. 42). However, the Velvets
did it better, claims Bangs, because they had the avant-garde intellectual background which the Dead lacked (1987, p. 42). Hippy psychedelia was supposed to
be about joyful release, but the ego death initiated by Warhol and the Velvets
emphasised rather the act of destruction, without the utopian associations of
renewal: 'all-admired theories attacking the "ego" as the root of all evil and unhap-
piness had become for the *avant-garde* the grounds for a deeply engaged metaphor of sexual sadism, for "blowing the mind", assaulting the senses …
"obliteration" of the ego was not … liberation … but an act of compulsive revenge
and *resentment*' (Koch, 1974, pp. 71–2). To put it slightly differently, the counterculture saw 'ego death' in rock as a Freudian release from repression, but art rock
took a more Foucauldian approach, emphasising the perverse pleasures of submission to repression. We can see, then, in hippy culture and the Warhol/Velvets
proto-punk tradition two opposite attitudes to the 1960s dream of liberation and
release – one utopian and one profoundly dystopian.

However, when we look at writing on psychedelia, masculinity and music, we
see that these two distinct approaches have been conflated and presented as one.
The neo-psychedelic critics (Reynolds; Gilbert; Stubbs, 1989) draw on Kristeva's,
Cixous' and Barthes' post-structuralist accounts of *jouissance*: ' "bliss" and
"noise" are the same thing – a rupture/disruption in the signifying system that
holds (a) culture together' (Reynolds, 1990, p. 13). What is lost here is the distinction between utopian and dystopian versions of *jouissance*, between the hippy

culture and the Factory scene. Accordingly the tendency in criticism has been to treat the Velvets as increasingly part of the psychedelic revolution. This requires two (problematic) moves – the marginalisation of the Velvets' connection to punk rock (Reynolds finds punk's emphasis on amateurism, primitivism and irony over-literal and inhibited, arguing instead for a (slight) return of progressive pretension, ambition and vulgarity) and the eliding of hippies from psychedelia (Reynolds, 1990, pp. 37–8). Thus the Velvets become the true originators of the psychedelic tradition: 'A line can be drawn from the hypnotic drone of the Velvet Underground to the disorienting swirl of My Bloody Valentine' (DeRogatis, 1996, p. xi). This elision of hippiedom is ideologically significant, as it allows the authors to present psychedelia without reference to the specific material circumstances of its production, as well as in some ways reifying it as a 'youth' culture by sundering it from its historical roots with the older generation (which could work against its perceived radicalism).

Reynolds, Gilbert and DeRogatis all offer an aesthetic of psychedelia as 'mind-expanding', gender-problematising music that transcends the particular location of psychedelia only in the 1960s. This in turn is allied to the split between active and passive masculinities. Gilbert argues that 'it's a consideration of how the Velvets might fit into this [Reynolds and Press's] scheme that will enable us ... to rewrite it' (1999, p. 41). The Velvet Underground 'treated the moment of over-amplification as a moment at which the musician's individual control is *problematised* ... by the materiality *and* collectivity of sound' (Gilbert, 1999, p. 42). This sound problematises authorship (1999, p. 42). It decentres rock phallocentricism, by promoting *jouissance*, which breaks down rational binaries like gender – the Velvets can thus be regarded as 'androgynous' and 'queer rock' (Gilbert, 1999, p. 43; Humm, 1995, p. 135). Reynolds argues that British indie band My Bloody Valentine extend this tradition: 'reconciling the two great pleasures in rock ... the masculine pleasure of the oppressive, spine-crushing arse quake and the feminine bliss of the border-dissolving, spine-melting oceanic wash' (1990, p. 121). This 'oceanic' music is marked by its exotic (non-Western) sound: a continuous droning quality, lack of harmonic development, decentralisation of vocals and repetition, and, of course, drugs:

> Psychedelic music ... aspires to ... the rushing roar of the Original sound, the primal OM. You can trace a thread through ... gamelan, didgeridoo music, raga ... the Velvet Underground, the Byrds ... simple patterns, repeated, can generate both complexity and immensity ... drone music blurs the gaps between the notes to hint at the supramusical roar of the cosmos breathing ... Through (ac)quiescence the listener lives in the present. (Reynolds and Press, 1995, pp. 181–2)

However, while one can discern the analogy between the type of music (repetitive, additive, rhythmic and textural rather than harmonic, process rather than goal-oriented) and the purported 'decentring' affect, I don't think any music produces its affects divorced of social context, and equally there is no reason why such affects should be tied to any particular musical form. Barthes (1990, pp. 293–94, 299–300), whose formulation of *jouissance* informs the discussion, heard it in all kinds of music.

As I stated in Chapter 1, such an approach tends towards a simplified idea of the feminine as multiple and fragmented. One way in which such an aesthetic is expressed in (indie) rock criticism is by an insistence on 'pure sound' or white noise over voice and lyrics – the triumph of polysemy over authorial intention. For example, New Zealand rock critic Matthew Hyland (1990), rather like Simon Reynolds, celebrates the death of meaning: 'early Sonic Youth, Bailter Space et al. … exploit the qualities unique to music: the ability of sounds to affect the listener in a directly sensual and emotional way … the music itself is inauthentic, truthless, not only because as pure sound it has no meaning … but because it is dedicated to the production of surreal, unfamiliar sensations.' A quality of anonymity and mystery is seen to be preferable to structure, the good song, or the humanity of the artist. Abstract, impersonal 'pure noise' replaces a purist 'fixation with meaning' (Reynolds, 1990, p. 12). Ignorance is 'bliss'. However, prominent vocals and lyrics, Hyland's bugbear, do not necessarily restrict meaning: rather they are another site where the listener may construct different meanings and interpretations, adding to, rather than restricting, the free play of possibilities. Hyland simply replaces the authority of the voice with the 'pure' sound of electric guitars, arguing that in noise we have the freedom to construe what we like and this is somehow better than being 'tied down' by the hegemony of the voice.

These writers assume an affective fallacy, an over-deterministic relationship between the type of sound and the affect it produces: 'making it look as though socially, historically constructed delineations are somehow inherent in the musical notes and processes themselves' (Green, 1997, pp. 128–9). That is, it's basically Adorno in reverse. No doubt psychedelic music can produce such an affect of *jouissance*, but why could a listener not get the same out of the Beatles, the Supremes, Duke Ellington or Mozart? Gilbert (and Reynolds and Press) are trying to have it both ways, implying *jouissance* can somehow connote. But *jouissance* is by definition a freedom from connotation; it is outside language. It also seems restrictive to limit it to one type of music; hence making any one artist/genre a special case on the basis of musical style alone seems insupportable.

Reynolds and Press also simplify in their 'organic' and essentialist reading of psychedelia, which ignores the praxis of many of the artists discussed. An excellent example is Pink Floyd, whom Reynolds and Press (1995, pp. 170–75) discuss as types of the 'psychedelic mummy's boy' (and not just the Syd Barrett era). But this overlooks the technological mediation of the music, and the way that it buys into a rather different type of masculinity: the band's well-documented studio perfectionism and the hugely technological spectacle of their live shows. Pink Floyd then, as well as being psychedelic, also construct themselves as technological authoritarians, masters of a huge array of equipment. To hear their music purely as an expression of 'male passivity' overlooks aspects of technological mediation and performance. Psychedelia's use of technology problematises its association with male passivity. The Beatles' psychedelic period was inseparable from their growing mastery and manipulation of studio technology, assisted by George Martin and the other Abbey Road sound engineers. Tracks like 'Strawberry Fields Forever' were the product of hours of overdubbing, varying tape speeds to achieve unusual timbres, and phasing, limiting and backwards recording. Although the Beatles shared the evocation of childhood and passivity that Reynolds describes as typical of psychedelia, this was achieved through technological mastery. Eno (another primary indie influence) is open to the same charge – his stated idealisation of passivity is at odds with his highly technological mode of production. 'Eno's object was to eliminate himself from his work ... to cleanse his art of the idea of the individual' (Frith and Horne, 1987, p. 118). Control is relinquished at the level of musicianship, only to be reasserted at the higher level of production. I will discuss Eno at more length in Chapter 5.

Conclusions

'One of the best ideas pop music ever had was not to have too many ideas' (Smith, 1995, p. 78). The prevalent ideology in the popular music world is that intellect is anathema, but this acts to disguise the ongoing importance of high art or avant-garde discourses in the production and reception of popular culture and music. Attitudes of anti-intellectual disrespect towards high culture are usually disguised forms of intellectualism (Ross, 1989, p. 6). Such intellectualism, insofar as it produces power, through distinctions of class for example, has some relation to hegemonic masculinities.

High culture is complicit with patriarchal capitalism, and masculinised high cultural paradigms are reproduced in popular music – through subcultural capital and Warhol's aestheticisation of mass culture. These approaches take mass rather than high culture as their object, but their mode of perception, I have argued, is very similar, producing disembodied, alienated subjects who worship art not as an enhancement of, but as a replacement for life – obsessional, narcissistic and withdrawn, controlling indirectly through the gaze. They represent very well the alienation of the bourgeois subject in modern society – refining himself out of existence.

In essence I argued that rock culture (especially art rock) plays out a similar set of problems as in high culture's attempts to cope with the onset of modernity. The notion of ego death, apparently a challenge to hegemonic masculinity, whether achieved through ascetic withdrawal, camp masquerade or psychedelic 'derangement', affirms patriarchal discourse by asserting a fragmented, multiple, essentialised feminine opposite to a unified, separate masculine self. Ego death was central to rock's implicit critique of the straight establishment, and upsetting of gender binaries. However, rock culture (and commentaries on it) simply reverse the poles of the binary system of mass cultural critique, and identify either with primitive id or with the passive consumer of Adorno's critique, while ironically retaining its most salient feature – the superiority of art to life.

Because of the dualistic terms of the discourse, no satisfactory synthesis of the opposing terms is possible within the terms of that system. Critics who hail the Velvets' problematisation of the subject elide the negative implications of their and Warhol's aesthetic, and overlook the way in which a consideration of masculinities in relation to this scheme demands that we see active and passive masculinities as two possibilities of the same masculine subject – rather than idealising feminine passivity and fragmentation at the expense of a masculine illusory wholeness. In the next chapter, I will focus on defining indie guitar rock as a genre, before going on to consider gender politics in more detail in relation to that model.

Notes

1. The term 'monomaniacal' seems especially appropriate given Spector's 'back to mono' credo and his obsessiveness about control of others (Thompson, 2004, pp. 17, 53).
2. For an indie example, see Lawrence of Felt (Cavanagh, 2000, pp. 219–24, 237–40).
3. And a bit of a joke as well, as the 'banana' cover of their first album demonstrates.

Chapter 3

What does it mean to be alternative? Indie guitar rock as a genre

Indie (independent) guitar rock is a post-punk subgenre of independent or alternative rock, featuring mainly white, male groups playing mainly electric guitars, bass and drums 'that sound a bit like The Byrds, The Velvet Underground' to primarily white, male audiences, recording mainly for independent labels, being disseminated at least initially through alternative media networks such as college radio stations and fanzines, and displaying a countercultural ethos of resistance to the market (Larkin 1995, p. 196). In the 1980s, indie guitar rock occurred all over the First World, from the USA to the UK to Australia and New Zealand, marked increasingly by a comparative stylistic homogeneity partly attributable to the recurrence of similar influences, mainly punk and 1960s white pop/rock, but also to the dissemination and globalisation of the alternative/avant-garde aesthetics of popular culture discussed in Chapter 2 (Shuker, 1998, p. 104).

Adding 'guitar' to 'indie' excludes genres like industrial and electronic music, and highlights the fact that most studies of indie seem to be predominantly of guitar bands. The prevalence of guitars is a preliminary indication of indie's canonical nature – it immediately suggests affiliation to rock tradition. But the presence of guitars also complicates attempts to understand the genre in terms of an alternative ethos, which may explain why it is not highlighted in other studies.[1] I have henceforth referred to the genre as 'indie' but, as indicated, I use this term in a selective manner.

Many studies of indie present it as authentically autonomous and unique, produced in isolated, marginal, local scenes, uncaptured by ideology, free of commercial and other pressures, but also of high culture elitism (Kruse, 2003, p. 1). Critiques and/or accounts of indie (and canonical groups like The Velvet Underground), written by fans or advocates, make absolute claims – that the music is avant-garde, postmodern, subversive or radical (Arnold, 1995, pp. 4–11; Azerrad, 2001, pp. 3–11; Felder, 1993; Gilbert, 1999; Harrington, 2002, pp. 373–93; Reynolds, 1990, pp. 11–13). In their concern to position (some) indie music as valuable and innovative, they overlook or simplify indie's historical, social and cultural context, and risk essentialising it as resistant to the dominant culture, or as a postmodern, ahistoric form of 'play' (Zuberi, 2001, p. 4). David Hesmondhalgh has gone some way to redressing the balance by showing the complex relations of production between UK indie labels and the industry, and addressing the question of how indies balance financial viability with street credibility, making a living without 'selling out'. However, he only discusses UK indie, and I intend to take a more international perspective (Hesmondhalgh, 1999; Negus, 1992, pp. 15–17).

Jason Toynbee argues, following Bourdieu, that a genre is a localised grouping within a larger culture, a section of a field (in rock music) defined in time, space and through the practices of a particular taste community (Bourdieu, 1984, pp. 101–2; Toynbee, 2000a, pp. 36–42). Neither principally an imposed regime nor the product of talented individuals, it is more like a way of doing things: 'the new is generated through the selection, combination and revoicing of what is already there' (Toynbee, 2000b). Such an approach may avoid treating genre as either exclusively authored and intentional or purely structural and impersonal.

However, genres (or generic texts) also function as representations, and representation is a site of power and struggle as well as a source of identity, naturalising certain points of view at the expense of others (Burton, 1999, pp. 85–91). Hence I would turn Toynbee's statement about 'what is already there' into a question – genre can never be divorced from questions of distinction, social capital and power. In Foucault's terms (1978, pp. 68–9), it is not a question just of what representations are present but of how these representations function in a system of power.

Genres are not just made out of 'what is already there' but are also shaped by 'what is not'. Identity is made up of relationships, not inner essences – it is constructed through 'significant difference' (Neale, 1980, pp. 48–50). Indie, by virtue of its very name, had a strong investment in difference, concerned with 'what not to do', and this was central to ideological conflicts within the nascent genre between indie 'pop' and 'rock', and with the maintenance of generic purity (Buckley, 2002, pp. 78–9). However, certain models of music practice became hegemonic within indie – the alternative ethos that rock media had been debating and formulating: Bangs' punk rock aesthetic (assault, minimalism and amateurism), Ellen Willis's 'rock and roll art', Eno's minimalism, Warhol's Pop Art, which in turn drew on bourgeois values of negation and refinement (as I argue in Chapters 2 and 5). Debates about punk and indie in the UK music press demonstrate how indie as a genre was preshaped and influenced by media discourses which set boundaries for what alternative rock could be. Indeed, the dominant form of indie rock became almost precisely what the critics had prophesied – white noise made by amateur white boy 'losers' (Bangs), aestheticised pop trash (Warhol), purified of pleasure (Ellen Willis) and delivered with offhand, studied detachment (Eno). But not everyone was happy with this set of meanings.

In Chapter 2 I argued that rock, and indeed most oppositional or avant-garde aesthetics, tend to draw on folk and art discourses to legitimate their difference mainly in terms of either a distinctive folk authenticity of marginal localism or a camp discourse of ironic elitism (it has to be ironic or else it becomes indistinguishable from high culture elitism). Both in different ways elevate the 'low' to aesthetic status. As such we might expect that alternative rock music tends to call on some combination of these discourses. An example of the folk approach would be the idea of indie as local.

Local scenes and global genres

'Recurrent in narratives of indie pop/rock is the conscious geographical and ideo-logical positioning of the "peripheral" local sites and practices of indie music pro-duction and consumption in opposition to the "centers" of mainstream music production' (Kruse, 2003, p. 1). This mythology has been prominent in accounts of NZ indie: 'the Dunedin Sound was generated through a cultural geography of living on the margin, producing "a mythology of a group of musicians working in cold isolation, playing music purely for the pleasure of it"' (Shuker, 1998, pp. 103–4, quoting McLeay, 1994, p. 39). The obvious problem is that it tends to exaggerate local originality.

Local scenes are often seen as preceding, anticipating or redefining musical genres, providing new grassroots input and innovation into existing mass-medi-ated categories; perhaps creating new genres. However, given the ubiquity of mass media, any claim to the originality of local music making needs to be taken with a grain of salt. New Zealand, for example, has historically high levels of imported content in its media, and while there was little coverage of alternative rock in mainstream media, the local (Auckland-based) monthly free rock magazines *Rip It Up* and the *NME* (though several months late) were both available. UK alterna-tive and post-punk music was available (if distributed by major labels) – for example, The Jam, The Cure, Joy Division, the Korova bands and Two-Tone.

Moreover, Will Straw states that indie scenes involved 'the eclectic revival and transformation of older musical forms' (1997b, p. 496), and that 'points of musical reference are likely to remain stable from one (indie) community to another' (for example punk rock, The Velvet Underground) (1991, p. 378). Musical and stylis-tic continuities between diverse indie scenes tend to complicate any idea of local originality. There were significant groups of people listening to the same records in different places. So, for example, Robert Forster (The Go-Betweens) could travel from Brisbane to Glasgow in 1981 and discover 'Edwyn [Collins, of Orange Juice] … down on his hands and knees listening to the first John Fogerty solo album. He turned to me and said, "Do you think that second guitar is a Stratocaster or a Rickenbacker?" I just looked at him and went, "We've found 'em!"' (Nichols, 2003, pp. 88–9). Accounts of indie as local and independent are going to play down such unlikely alliances. They are also going to ignore the way in which sonic orthodoxies emerged, shaped partly by 'tastemakers' and partly by the glo-balisation of certain models of music practice.

Holly Kruse (2003, pp. 137–38) suggests that Straw underplays differences between scenes, for example between Southern Californian hardcore, LA psychedelic pop and Georgian jangle. One might further argue that these scenes were in themselves split: for example, the Minutemen's music is not all 'archetypal hardcore', despite Toynbee's protestations (2000a, p. 105; Minutemen, 1984). From a broader perspective, however, there are also significant common factors – small groups of white men playing guitars, influenced by punk and 1960s white pop/rock, within a broader discourse and practice of (degrees of) independence from mainstream musical values. Additionally, as indie became a 'global' genre and a more defined market, this necessarily entailed some standardisation and codification of its 'difference'.

Indie and the mainstream

The positioning of indie as local (as opposed to global) was also continuous with the sense that indie music was now carrying the flag for innovative pop/rock: 'Rock had reached the crossroads where popularity and creativity would separate' (Harrington, 2002, p. 322). Hence punk/indie was seen as a kind of rebirth of rock as a minority rather than a mainstream culture: 'we were entering the age in which anyone doing anything creative in the name of rock'n'roll existed within … the underground, because mainstream rock had become just another wing of the entertainment industry … Punk … now meant any music which challenged the restrictions of the mainstream culture' (Harrington, 2002, p. 333). This approach buys into a Frankfurt School high/low dichotomy that relies on the vapidity and banality of the mainstream as default mode for understanding the uniqueness and difference of punk/indie music: 'punk meant … entering a whole new and more satisfying community of outcasts' (Arnold, 1995, p. 4).

'Virtually every band did their best and most influential work during their indie years' (Azerrad, 2001, p. 5). Indie practised a kind of aesthetic purism in which commercial influence was taboo: '[US indie] SST was like a *Good Housekeeping* seal of approval, guaranteeing that the music was … completely outside the mainstream' (Arnold, 1995, p. 58). This ethos was particularly marked in some US scenes, especially those based around hardcore (US punk), which in turn became a paradigm of authenticity for aspiring US indie bands (see Chapter 4). In New Zealand it was represented by 'punk puritan' Chris Knox and continues to flavour accounts of local music (Churton, 2000; Robertson, 1991). In the USA, fanzines like *Conflict, Forced Exposure* and *Maximum Rock'n'Roll* advocated, as their titles imply, a 'take no prisoners' attitude, championing music that was the most extreme, uncompromising and generally obnoxious: 'goddamned blood-curdling, screaming rock'n'roll like a fucking car crash' (Cosloy, 2005).[2] Any band looking or sounding or becoming remotely commercial was rapidly denounced.[3]

Many (especially US) accounts of indie scenes and bands have little place for the many indie bands and scenes that were more pop or commercially oriented, such as those based around Hoboken, NJ or LA's Paisley Underground (Arnold, 1995, pp. 83–4, 113–16; 'Punk Rock City, U.S.A.', 1993). David Buckley (2000, p. 53) suggests that, in the USA especially, the recent success of 'power pop' 1960s influenced guitar groups like The Knack had given 'pop' a bad name. Plus, the size and economic organisation of US popular culture meant that US indie acts were unlikely to get the kind of exposure available to UK bands (hence touring the UK and Europe were important ways for US acts – for example, Sonic Youth, Sub-Pop – to become better known, not just there but also at home.

However, in the beginning, not all indie was so dismissive of 'pop'. Of course, what was meant by 'pop' was complex: for some it meant an idealisation of 1960s pop naivety – a style; for others it meant an actual desire to be commercially successful. As Geoff Travis explained, 'There were two different sets of musicians … one set … definitely had an agenda. They wanted a career in pop music and their aspiration was to be on a major. Being on an independent … was just mucking about' (Cavanagh, 2000, p. 38). Sneaky Feelings definitely fell into this camp (at least in our minds) – like The Jesus and Mary Chain 'we wanted to be pop stars … we didn't want to be part of that indie scene' (Jim Reid, quoted in Cavanagh, 2000, p. 175). But Reid's initially surprising comment (The Jesus and Mary Chain – a pop band?) suggests a measure of naivety about the commercial realities of the charts (Cavanagh, 2000, pp. 185–6). For, whatever the group's intentions, there was clearly a disparity between intention and result. Indie 'pop' bands were often a lot more indie than they cared to admit, and this was also true for Sneaky Feelings: 'To like the Sneakys you had to appreciate the songs first and foremost, and had to be prepared to forego all the other aspects that are usually the hallmark of the successful rock and roll package' (Graeme Downes of the Verlaines, quoted in Horton, 2002). Out-of-tune singing and guitars, onstage scruffiness and disorganisation, lack of cool and an accent on content ('the good song') over presentation – we were 'indie', whether or not it was what we wanted to be.

Indie pop

Indie 'pop' as a term and musical style generally enjoyed more currency in the UK than in the USA. This can be explained partially by the higher status of indie media in the UK. *New Musical Express* and *Melody Maker* were far more accessible than the macho style of US 'zines, and reflected a less polarised worldview. In contrast to the USA, the indie scene in the UK enjoyed *national* media coverage, as well as through Radio One's John Peel and the indie charts, first published in *Record Business* in January 1980 (Lazell, 1997). Consequently, some measure of popular success was seen as achievable and even desirable by many UK indie musicians.

The use of 'pop' also suggests the UK rejection of US folk 'authenticity' (see Chapter 1). In the UK 'pop' has always been favoured as a general term to describe popular music, but in the USA 'rock' is favoured (Goodwin, 1992, p. 36; Keightley, 2001, p. 127; Thomas, 1990, p. 88). UK rock critics were accordingly much less committed to punk *rock* as a measure of stylistic authenticity. For example, Simon Reynolds (who wrote for *Melody Maker*) was dismissive of punk's influence on indie, which he saw as 'a gamut of taboos … about what was sonically permissible' (1990, p. 12), suggesting that punk rock scenes could play a policing role in indie.

Alan Horne's Postcard label provides a case study of the nascent 'pop' approach. Horne used the idea of pop as a way of distancing himself from the dourness and earnestness of contemporary alternative 'rock' music, such as Joy Division and the Cure: 'to us these groups were lower than dogshit' (Horne, quoted in Nichols, 2003, p. 90). He used the word 'pop' in a camp, Warholian manner – emphasising its ephemerality and artificiality. However, somewhat paradoxically, he found these ideal pop qualities mainly in the past, and particularly in 1960s pop/rock. In a manner that we will later see is actually rather widespread (see Chapter 5), he acted as a musical mentor to the Postcard bands, educating them in 'magical hipness', producing 'classic rubbish', actively shaping the tastes of the bands on his label (Nichols, 2003, p. 87). Like Alan McGee (Creation) '[h]is thinking showed a siege mentality. If he was powerless to challenge for the charts, he could at least imply that the chart groups were playing an inferior version of pop; that the only reason they'd achieved success was because they were not good enough to fail' (Cavanagh, 2000, p. 103). In turn, the Postcard ethos seems to have triggered aspects of the UK indie scene (analysed by Reynolds, 1989), although not in a way that Horne endorsed (Cavanagh, 2000, p. 53). The Go-Betweens (Australian, but also on Postcard for a time) were 'very, very pop … because we did no heavy metal, which 99.9 percent of bands in Brisbane were doing' (Robert Forster, quoted in Nichols, 2003, pp. 33–4). Forster didn't want to play with musicians who 'just wanted to do "Black Magic Woman", "Honky Tonk Woman" [*sic*] – all songs that had "woman" in the title … I wanted to sing about *girls*' (p. 37). This in itself highlights a basic irony in indie's appropriation of 1960s 'naivety', because in feminist parlance 'woman' is preferable to 'girl'. It also suggests that more androgynous styles of representation were not necessarily less sexist. Middle-class white men flirted with pop androgyny partly as a way of defining themselves against heavy metal machismo.

Simon Reynolds describes the early UK indie pop scene as a reaction to the commercialised 'yuppie' hedonist consumerism of Thatcherite Britain, defining itself against the mainstream association of the New Right agenda with the hedonistic commercialism and artifice of dance music, New Romantics and New Pop (Reynolds, 1989, pp. 246–7). Instead there was nostalgia for the innocence of childhood, and by extension the 1960s: 'The Sixties are like pop's childhood, when the idea of youth was still young' (Reynolds, 1989, p. 248; 1990, p. 23).[4]

Such an overtly nostalgic and regressive genre was hard for commentators to take seriously, however: 'Indie stylists are the spiritual successors to the student fans who consumed progressive rock in the early and mid-1970s ... they are not usually from art schools. In their account of authenticity, the indie charts are the only indicators of pop quality' (Frith and Horne, 1987, p. 177). What Frith and Horne do not acknowledge, however, is that the UK art-school concern with androgyny, irony and visual style that they celebrate as central to UK rock music had by the 1980s become too commercially successful to be representative of emergent, 'marginal' social groups.

Indie pop was gradually replaced by indie rock as the dominant form. Accordingly, critics had to change their line. In *Blissed Out* (1990, p. 37), Reynolds redefines indie pop as 'regressive' rock: 'the attenuated remnant of punk ... shorn of its spirit ... reduced through shortsighted, dogged adherence ... antihippy hippies'. Indie lacked irony, and that made it rock, whatever its pop pretensions. Instead Reynolds champions a new psychedelic progressivism: Butthole Surfers, Sonic Youth, My Bloody Valentine, Spacemen 3 and the Pixies (1990, pp. 37–44, 63–7, 115–25, 145, 147–50). Reynolds here anticipates or comments on what was indeed occurring in indie – a heavier, more rock, more US approach was taking precedence over visions of indie as 1960s pop purity. Cavanagh (2000, pp. 186–8) notes that US bands blew much of the UK indie pop scene away with their superior playing ability. But Reynolds doesn't want to admit as much. Instead, he redefines indie pop as a stunted remnant of punk rock dogmatism which allows him to see the new indie rock movement as utopian pop. Rock and pop reverse positions:

> around the turn of '87, it became clear that a miraculous turnaround had taken place. Everything that was most suffocatingly stable and stabilizing, drearily coherent, and anxiously worthy about 'rock' discourse had taken hold of pop (Band Aid was the culmination of this maturation) and all the glorious incoherence and Dionysiac gratuitousness that Nik Cohn had first defined in pop, had somehow resurfaced in rock. (Reynolds, 1990, p. 11)

By this neat inversion, Reynolds avoids having to identify exclusively with rock 'authenticity' because that is now the preserve of pop.

In the positioning of indie, US and UK commentators used a similar strategy – the splitting off of mainstream and alternative – but envisioned the split in opposite ways. The USA went for the traditional split of mainstream pop and authentic indie rock but, for UK commentators like Reynolds, rock was the mainstream, and indie rock was split between regressive pure pop (which was really rock) and the authentic neo-psychedelia which promised the 'glorious incoherence' of pop (Reynolds, 1990, p. 11). NZ indie tended towards the US authenticity approach, but exceptions could be and were made – for example, Martin Phillipps (The Chills), whose perceived 'pop genius' put him at least temporarily above criticism on these grounds (Brown, 1984b, p. 22; Colbert, 1985).

Splitting and purity

Reynolds (1990, pp. 12–13) deconstructs the indie myth of 'punk purity', but then contradicts himself by reifying *jouissance* as a 'pure' response to the indie music he advocates. 'This myth of purity … is today as defining a pop myth as any other. In England it defined punk from the beginning' (Marcus, 1999, p. 25). For all genres or subcultures, the impure is an important operating principle for practice: 'Struggles over musical propriety are themselves political struggles over whose music … whose rules of order shall prevail' (Susan McClary, quoted in Keil and Feld, 1994, p. 257). In Chapter 2, we saw how purity was central to both folk and high art discourses. Anthropologist Mary Douglas has written: 'ideas about separating, purifying, demarcating and punishing transgressions have as their main function to impose system on an inherently untidy experience. It is only by exaggerating the difference between within and without, above and below, male and female, with and against, that a semblance of order is created' (1970, p. 15). Purity and taboo are a way of creating unity in experience, or in a genre, although Douglas overlooks the degree to which this system is based on the suppression of 'otherness'. I've already suggested how rock/pop provided one means of differentiating indie, while also suggesting that this required some rather complex moves within different scenes. But indie initially defined itself not only by its opposition to commercial contemporary pop, but also by its opposition to 'rockism', the traditional association of rock music with machismo, spectacle, virtuosity, excess and self-indulgence – in other words, forms of 'vulgarity' (Bourdieu, 1984, p. 486; see also Reynolds, 1990, p. 23; Shuker, 1998, p. 104). So indie musicians had to somehow differentiate themselves from the adverse connotations of both a rock and a pop mainstream (although the 'rock' stance gradually became fashionable again, as categories of 'bad taste' were normalised and aestheticised (Cavanagh, 2000, pp. 297–8)).

David Buckley, in his excellent biography of R.E.M. (2002, p. 70), suggests that the band's stylistic choices were severely limited by the plethora of taboo (mainstream) practices they felt compelled to avoid. Mitch Easter, who produced the band's first two albums, remarks: 'In those days, you really had to watch who [what music] you mentioned or you got people really upset' (Buckley, 2002, pp. 70–71). Michael Stipe explained: 'We work by a process of negation. We know everything we don't wanna do and what's left are our options' (Buckley, 2002, p. 78). Indie came to describe a rather restricted set of musical practices. 'As with so many oppositional genres … indie was contradictory: its counter-hegemonic aims could only be maintained … by erecting exclusionary barriers around the culture' (Hesmondhalgh, 1999, p. 38).

If outside influence was a threat to autonomy, then one way around this problem was simply to deny it – the DIY ethos of 'just doing it' which I described in the Dunedin scene, and which was also a feature of hardcore. The admission of influence was used as a means of marginalising some groups, including my own, because it could be seen as proof of impurity. Certain styles were seen as natural or self-evident; others were highlighted as deviant. Perhaps the most obvious marker of deviance was 'black' musical influences.

For 1980s and indeed 1990s indie, the taboo mainstream was often defined as black (McDonnell, 1995). This continued the marginalisation of black influences in art rock and most punk, discussed in Chapter 2. Indie rejected dance music's emphasis on the body, which seemed complicit with the 'work hard play hard' New Right ethos. This attitude was also continuous with punk's hatred of disco. Rap was viewed with suspicion, while black 'soul' was seen as commodification of passion and hankering for old-fashioned authenticity (Reynolds, 1990, pp. 79–85, 152–60). Perhaps the most notorious UK example of contemporary indie attitudes to black music was the controversy surrounding the Smiths' 'Panic' (1987) with its line 'Hang the DJ', which some condemned as racist or an attack on dance music (Rogan, 1992, pp. 252–3). While the song is ambiguous, some of Morrissey's statements about black music are less defensible: 'Reggae to me is the most racist music in the world. It's an absolute glorification of black supremacy' (Wrenn, 1988, p. 25; see also Cavanagh, 2000, p. 225; Reynolds, 1990, pp. 19–20).

This stance is confirmed in relation to the USA by Will Straw, who claims that 'African-American musical forms … [stand] implicitly for a relationship to technological innovation and stylistic change against which [alternative culture] has come to define itself' (Straw, 1997b, p. 497; see also Reynolds, 1990, p. 23; Shuker, 1998, p. 104). This ethnic angle also crops up in NZ indie (as discussed below). In terms of indie's complex positioning in relation to pop/rock, blackness was attributed both to contemporary pop/dance music and the rockist blues influences of macho 1970s rock. This relationship is discussed further under the genre categories below. Rejection of 'black' musical styles was another means of asserting indie 'purity'.

Genre description

Jason Toynbee points out that 'increasing the amount of detail in order to specify [genre] only makes the definition more difficult. For as the number of required traits increases so the number of texts which conform … will decline' (2000a, p. 105). Moreover, any description, so far as it is used to prove a point, will tend to construct generic attributes in a particular way. A classic aesthetic approach (such as high modernism), which assumes aesthetic values as autonomous and uniquely expressive, would regard the extent to which a text could be constructed as generic as proof of its lack of aesthetic value, for example soap operas and reality TV, or in music, disco and teenybopper pop. Adorno's classification of popular music as standardised and repetitive uses generic similarity and social function to qualify aesthetic value (1990, pp. 302–9). So when Azerrad claims that 'the key principle of American indie rock wasn't a circumscribed musical style; it was the punk ethos' (2001, p. 6), this is actually very similar to Adorno's argument: it claims 'uniqueness'. In contrast, my approach could be seen as a reductionist attempt to show that indie is really just a musical genre like any other, with no claim to special consideration – a 'demystification' of its aura. However, I have at all points tried to avoid making this chapter into a list, by tying musical and stylistic features to a broader socio-cultural context, and by noting and trying to explain the many contradictions within indie, although by the late 1980s, I argue there was a dominant style, which basically set up grunge and Nirvana in the early 1990s.

Although I've suggested that no descriptive account of a genre is entirely satisfactory, it still seems like a worthwhile exercise, if only to supply some concrete examples to argue about. So I have employed Franco Fabbri's genre definitions: formal and technical aspects; semiotic aspects; behaviour (performance); social and ideological aspects; and commercial and juridical aspects (Fabbri, 1982, p. 52; Frith, 1996, pp. 91–4). I do not mean to imply that these definitions are rules, though equally some may function in some contexts as such (Negus, 1999, pp. 24–30). In line with my argument about 'significant difference', splitting and purity, I've also tried to include a sense of what is being rejected or excluded. It seems apt to deal with commercial and juridical aspects first, given that indie is the first genre to be named after its mode of production (Hesmondhalgh, 1999, p. 35).

Production (commercial and juridical aspects)

The rise of independent labels, connected to local scenes, became a central feature of the post-punk 'alternative' musical landscape (Shuker, 1998, p. 170). Of course, independent labels had been central to the rise of rock and roll – the difference was that these new labels claimed they did not aim for mainstream success but rather created an alternative space for non-mainstream musical practice, that 'at the heart of the politics of cultural production was the issue of how music came to its audiences' (Hesmondhalgh, 1999, p. 37). This was especially the case in the USA, where 'jamming econo' (working independently and cheaply) presented a critique of capitalist excess, as did the reiterated insistence that real indies could not, under any circumstances, deal with majors (a line that UK and NZ scenes did not follow, partly due to the different conditions they were working under) (Azerrad, 2001, p. 5).

Some indie labels started as bands releasing themselves and their friends; sometimes it was a local record shop owner and his clientele. Such small-scale operations were rarely run for profit, at least initially. Distribution was the biggest problem indies faced, requiring a lot of money, time or contacts (Negus, 1999, pp. 57–8). Over time scenes linked up, whether through touring bands, specialist record shops, student/college radio, fanzines, mail order or word of mouth. According to Azerrad (2001, pp. 14, 120), in the USA early networking was done through hardcore: Dischord Records, set up by Ian MacKaye (Minor Threat) in Washington DC, and SST, set up by Greg Ginn (Black Flag) in LA. Azerrad (2001, pp. 5, 14) claims that in the face of local opposition to their music and lifestyle, hardcore groups like Black Flag were forced to tour to survive. In the process, they pioneered an alternative network of scenes, 'zines, venues, labels and bands, which aimed to avoid mainstream involvement. This provides another point of difference from earlier indie labels, and could be seen as counteracting 'the processes of concentration and oligopolization which had been characteristic of the recording industry' (Hesmondhalgh, 1999, p. 37). These networks became global.

US college radio, which initially played mainly UK post-punk, started to play hardcore, and in its wake also other music that was not necessarily as hardline (Arnold, 1995, pp. 26–38). In New Zealand, student radio was also extremely important. Most NZ university stations were owned by the relevant student association, so at this point profit was not an issue and the stations were relatively free-format (most were privatised and restructured in the early 1990s, however).

Indie guitar rock occurred from 1980 (approximately) in US scenes like Athens, Georgia (R.E.M., Pylon), Minneapolis (Hüsker Dü, The Replacements) and LA (which contained several scenes), and also through groups like Sonic Youth (New York) and Dinosaur Jr. (Amherst, Mass.). Again, geographical proximity did not necessarily mean interconnection – LA was marked by a range of relatively autonomous scenes from hardcore (Black Flag, Minutemen) to middle-class neo-psychedelia (the paisley underground – Dream Syndicate, Rain Parade, Green on Red, The Bangles), while The Replacements and Hüsker Dü in Minneapolis were more rivals than friends (Arnold, 1995, pp. 56–7, 83–5; DeRogatis, 1996, pp. 173–8). The LA indie SST signed many of the bands mentioned; Twin/Tone in Minneapolis had The Replacements and IRS (LA) had R.E.M.

The UK scene was also based around post-punk indies, such as Factory, Mute, Cherry Red, Beggar's Banquet, Postcard and Creation. Rough Trade, originally a London record shop run by Geoff Travis, emerged as one of the most important because of its role in distributing smaller labels, such as Creation, Cherry Red and Postcard, as well as its own in-house label. It also expanded abortively into the US market (Kruse, 2003 p. 54). Early UK indie was often marked by a strong ideological agenda, usually feminist or Marxist (Gang of Four, The Raincoats, The Slits, Au Pairs). There was also diversity in musical style, with punk, funk, electronica and reggae. Thanks (I think) to the influence of the US scene, guitar pop/rock became increasingly central. Indie guitar acts in the early 1980s UK included Orange Juice, The Smiths, Felt and The Go-Betweens (Australians, really). Later bands included The Jesus and Mary Chain, My Bloody Valentine, Teenage Fan Club, The Wedding Present, That Petrol Emotion and, later, Britpop groups such as Oasis (who stylistically epitomise indie guitar rock but fall outside the scope of my study). Most of the music was associated, more or less, with local 'scenes', although London was still the main focus of activity. The final point about the UK was that there was more traffic between majors and indies than in the USA – for example the setting up of boutique labels like Blanco y Negro by majors (WEA), who signed The Jesus and Mary Chain (Cavanagh, 2000, pp. 96–7, 137).

There were few independents in New Zealand until 1980, when there was a sudden rush, paralleling the rise of independent labels overseas (Cammick, 1998, p. 14). Flying Nun formed in Christchurch in 1981. Unlike the short-lived Auckland indies, Propeller and Ripper, which aimed for mainstream popularity and success, Flying Nun was more informal and less ambitious, but its more obvious opposition to the mainstream capitalised on the growth of a discrete alternative audience – young, urban consumers who became identifiable in the aftermath of punk, tending to be associated with student radio stations. When despite its homemade sound, The Clean's first EP *Boodle Boodle Boodle* (Flying Nun) spent several months in the singles charts in 1981–82, eventually earning a gold record (5000 sales), the industry had to take some notice. But the album charts, the most profitable part of the business, remained firmly in the grip of the majors (Mitchell, 1996, p. 217). However, independents have allowed many artists to release several albums, which was previously a rarity in New Zealand (Cammick, 1998, p. 14). Flying Nun therefore participated in, and arguably encouraged, a period of considerable commercial and cultural growth in the local music industry.

Flying Nun's early commercial arrangements were extremely informal. Commercial pressures as such were not initially a major factor in music production, except insofar as lack of money sometimes held up the production of records for up to a year (Bannister, 1999, p. 73). Sneaky Feelings never signed a recording contract. We funded our own recordings and only later started asking the label to help out. In return, Flying Nun paid the mastering, pressing, production and distribution costs. This arrangement was pretty standard (Bannister, 1999, p. 82). Most records covered their costs; in such a tiny market, 2000 was accounted a good sale (the per capita equivalent of about 180000 in the USA, or 50000 in the UK). There are strong similarities to the financial environments of indie labels elsewhere (Azerrad, 2001, pp. 41–3, 283; Cavanagh, 2000, pp. 38–40; Hesmondhalgh, 1999, pp. 35–7; Kruse, 2003, pp. 34, 51).

Flying Nun was initially rather limited in its networking, given the lack of similarly inclined local indies. However, it did increasingly network globally with other indie scenes, licensing The Chills' album *Kaleidoscope World* (1986) in the UK with Creation, which led to US licensing for some NZ bands with Homestead (Arnold, 1995, p. 119; Cavanagh, 2000, p. 214).[5] Flying Nun UK/Europe, established in London in the mid-1980s, was distributed through Rough Trade UK and Normal (FDR). In New Zealand, it entered into manufacturing and distribution deals with WEA and later Mushroom, which eventually bought a controlling interest in the label.

Indie production supposedly rejected major company practice, seen as profit-based, formalised, politically and aesthetically oblivious, corporate, professional, soulless and impersonal. It proposed an alternative system that would operate 'under the radar' (Joe Carducci, quoted in Azerrad, 2001, p. 3). Roy Colbert (1985) reminisces about: 'records transported ... by a band's rattling Bedford, carried processionally through city streets by a procession of untrained hands to be deposited on a record shop counter with apologies for losing the invoice'. However, Hesmondhalgh (1999, pp. 40–1) usefully points out how indie labels managed to reconcile such romantic visions with paying the bills, because in practice, very few labels were ever totally independent. Most depended on majors through distribution; most were bought out sooner or later. Very few fitted Azerrad's hardline US definition of no 'major' involvement (2001, p. 5).

Moreover, the relationship between genre and mode of production has often been essentialised: 'indie proclaimed itself superior to other genres ... because it was based on new relationships between creativity and commerce' (Hesmondhalgh, 1999, p. 35). It is very easy to slip into a folk/romantic fallacy of indie as a 'pure' form of 'local' production. Steve Neale observes that 'genres ... exist within the context of a set of economic relations and practices', though he adds that 'genres are not the product of economic factors as such. The conditions provided by the capitalist economy account neither for the existence of the particular genres that have hitherto been produced, nor for the existence of the conventions that constitute them' (1980, pp. 51–2). That is, we should be suspicious of any account that makes a causal linkage between mode of production and genre conventions, for example the idea that indie sounds cheap and raw only because of the economic circumstances of the bands. More important is the ideological justification of such amateurism in the light of an overall indie aesthetic. I look at this issue in more detail in Chapter 5, where I argue that many indie labels were very much controlled by the taste of their owners for a certain ideal of amateur youth music, rather than by the performers themselves.

Formal and technical aspects – aural characteristics, instrumentation, rhythmic and melodic rules, studio sound, balance of mix elements

Most indie guitar bands followed what Carducci terms the 'small band' format – drums, bass, guitar and vocals (Christgau, 1991). Gendron attributes this line-up to the influence of Bangs' punk ethos: 'rock'n'roll is at its best when "stripped down" to its "bare essentials" ... In its purest form, the minimalism meant the use only of guitars and drums, simple riffs, a maximum of three chords, and the avoidance of long guitar solos' (Gendron, 2002, p. 234). The 'simplicity' of this line-up also approximates the authenticity of live performance (Buckley, 2002, p. 70; Gendron, 2002, p. 234; Jones and Featherley, 2002, p. 34). Guitar is usually 'rhythm' (accompaniment) rather than lead. Keyboards are sometimes used (usually piano, organ or synthesiser), although hardline indie ideologues would question their inclusion (Christgau, 1991). Modern electronic instruments, sequencers, and samplers are generally infra dig (with the occasional exception of drum machines and loops, which were too useful in lo-fi recording to be totally unacceptable). There is often a preference for old technology (valve amps over transistors, analogue over digital) (Buckley, 2002, p. 81; Knox, 1989).

The punk discourse of authenticity sets indie against the sugariness or polish of mainstream sounds – a modernist dichotomy. Permissible mediation is limited to electric guitars 'following the root chords pretty religiously' – form follows function (Knox, 1991). Tonally and timbre-wise this results in an overall sameness of tone, dominated by the midtones of (usually electric, sometimes distorted) guitars. Toynbee suggests that the 'guitar sound does not so much define the genre as become the object of its aesthetic practice', providing a context of repetition in which individual practitioners may innovate to some degree – mainly by writing songs, which, given the engulfing sameness of the genre's sound, provide 'a tool for producing small variations along a bed of iterated texture … it is from the vantage of different listenings in the different songs that we can hear the full, engulfing sameness of the … sound' (2000a, p. 107). Toynbee's example is actually hardcore, but guitar sound is equally central to indie.

Sometimes this minimalism is attributed to technical/economic limitations – many early Flying Nun recordings were made on Chris Knox's four-track tape recorder, but in general this approach, even where expedient, has tended to be promoted to a credo (Bannister, 1999, p. 54; Buckley, 2002, p. 80; Mitchell, 1996, p. 218). Home-style lo-fi recordings such as Echo and the Bunnymen's 'Pictures on my Wall' (Korova, 1979) are early indie 'classics'. Financial considerations did limit studio time, especially for new bands.[6] Hüsker Dü's Grant Hart claims that most of their early album tracks were done first-take (Azerrad, 2001, p. 169). A hurried schedule would mean little time for overdubs, but this all added to the 'authenticity' of the work. The Replacements' albums like *Hootenanny* take the live 'warts and all' approach to almost comic extremes. Hardcore bands 'jammed econo' – musical minimalism was just one facet of an overall lifestyle of indie austerity (Azerrad, 2001, pp. 73–5). Clearly there is a close association here between the folk authenticity of the music, and the minimal technological intervention or resources involved in playing and recording it – a DIY ethos (Azerrad, 2001, p. 6; Bannister, 1999, p. 102; Kruse, 2003, pp. 10–12). However, one exception to the minimal approach was volume – guitars, especially, tended to be mixed loud, often obscuring the vocal, and this again could replicate the effect of 'liveness'.

In terms of aural characteristics, the music tended to be slightly 'top heavy', favouring higher frequencies. Over time, harsh treble frequencies became increasingly dominant – rendering even a relatively accessible song like Dinosaur Jr.'s 'Freak Scene' (1989) quite hard to listen to. This was partly a matter of technical limitations – cheap guitars and amps often have a tinny sound, as do cheap studios, and early recordings cut for independent labels were often mastered bass-light (because bass can make the needle jump during cutting) (Bannister, 1999, p. 58; Buckley, 2002, p. 58). The lack of bass may also affect the prominence of rhythmic elements – again this feature became generic, rather than a result of technical limitations. It also relates to the prominence of guitars, marked by a 'drony' or 'jangly' quality which results from the use of 'pedals' – repeated patterns of treble guitar notes sustained through chord changes, and mixed prominently, competing with vocals. In contrast to mainstream practice, authenticity was increasingly established through the highlighting rather than the elimination of 'noise' – a 'cheap', tinny, unproduced sound, lacking in the conventional 'hooks' of a strong vocal, a compelling rhythm or funky bottom end. Although set against the supposed monotony of commercial music, it is in fact, rather monotonous itself.

For bands that only had one guitarist, drone/jangle was a way in which musical novices could fill out the sound, establishing sonic presence, continuity or musical flow. The obvious influences were 1960s groups like The Velvet Underground (for example 'Heroin', 1967) – a massive drone effect 'like a jet engine' created partly by guitar feedback and partly by John Cale's viola style, influenced by classical avant-garde minimalist La Monte Young (Heylin, 1993, pp. 6–8)[7]. This drone approach is particularly notable in Sonic Youth, Hüsker Dü (USA), My Bloody Valentine, The Jesus and Mary Chain (UK) and Bailter Space, Snapper and The Clean (NZ). Jangle can be understood as a subspecies of drone: trebly, relatively clean (undistorted) guitar sound played in (often) a chordal style: either strummed or arpeggiated (sounding each string in a chord separately) but generally repeating notes (pedal) over the top of a chord sequence. Pedals are normally open strings that also resonate overtones (like the sympathetic strings on a sitar) – in the Dunedin Sound, for example, bands would often play chord shapes on the lower strings only, allowing the higher open strings to sound throughout.[8] This style was strongly identified with 1960s guitar bands, especially the Byrds (Bannister, 1999, pp. 71–2; Buckley, 2002, pp. 74–7; Reynolds, 1990, pp. 37–8). However, the effect changed depending on how the notes were played – Sneaky Feelings strummed and arpeggiated, which produced a more 'jangly' effect than the punk down-stroke approach. Jangle characterised the sound of acts like R.E.M. and The Smiths, typically played on a Rickenbacker 12-string, like Roger McGuinn of The Byrds (and before him George Harrison) (Buckley, 2002, pp. 80–1). Although jangle and drone imply electricity, they also have folk music resonances and, as in folk, open tunings were widely used: for example, by the Verlaines, The Smiths and My Bloody Valentine. 'One of the keys to [Kevin] Shields' guitar sound was the tuning of two neighbouring strings to almost the same pitch' (Cavanagh, 2000, p. 34), combined with the use of the tremolo arm and a reverse reverberation effect creating the distinctive 'glide guitar' sound ('Off Your Face', 1990) (Azerrad, 2001, pp. 243–4). Open tunings also relate to 1960s avant-garde minimalism, for example Sonic Youth (Heylin, 1993, p. 8; Unofficial Sonic Youth Guitar Tunings List, 2004).

'Jangle' implies a more pop, mainstream approach – as such it is strongly associated with indie pure pop. Jangle bands tended to 'cross over'; the style was increasingly seen as not truly alternative (Azerrad, 2001, p. 5; Reynolds, 1990, pp. 37–8).

The drone was felt to be a more authentically rock approach, and became increasingly dominant. The main stylistic innovation in this area was the Pixies' idea of dramatically contrasting choruses of loud drone guitar with a more skeletal approach in the verse – a device which became common in grunge (Nirvana). The prominence of guitars also dissociates indie from contemporary mainstream rock and pop, based more on synthesisers, sequencers, digital effects and rap 'breakbeats'. At the same time, indie guitarists are not usually virtuosos, favouring a simpler, punk-based approach (however, lacking the shock value of punk). That said, many indie bands feature quite complex guitar parts (That Petrol Emotion, 1986) and accomplished players (Bob Mould, Johnny Marr).

Harmonically, the songs tend to be simple and repetitive, with a few repeated chord changes (tonic-subdominant, like the Velvets, being a particular favourite).[9] US punk/indie band The Feelies feature 'layered rhythm guitars that frantically strum simple two- and three-chord progressions' (DeRogatis, 1996, p. 150). The Bats are an NZ example, and in the UK, The Wedding Present (1987). Over time, some indie bands tended towards an 'ideal' of no chord changes, echoing New York avant-garde minimalism, for example Snapper, Spacemen 3 and some Sonic Youth. This works with the drone approach, as sustained pedals or repeated notes clash with a complex harmonic scheme. More complex harmonies were used, but even here the affect tends to be integrated into an overall drone approach, either by the use of pedals (Verlaines, Sneaky Feelings, R.E.M.) or by the use of a relatively monotonal vocalist, like Morrissey of The Smiths. Song structures tend to echo punk or 1960s pop/rock. Some bands used middle eights (Sneaky Feelings, for example), but this was not particularly common (and became less so with time). On the other hand, rock devices, such as blues riffs, were relatively uncommon initially, but became gradually more prominent – Primal Scream serves as an example of a punk/indie band that evolved towards a more rock'n'roll sound (Cavanagh, 2000, pp. 374–5, 381). (See Chapter 5 for indie use of technology and the 'wall of noise'.)

Melody, vocal and instrumental, tends towards basic diatonicism, with frequent repetition and use of 'primitive' melodic devices – chord triads, monotones, ascending and descending scales, and pentatonic scales.[10] The melodies of singers like Morrissey and Stipe often repeat a limited number of diatonic tones; however, sometimes this leads to suspensions, where notes are not supported by the chord structure, giving a feeling of disembodiment, suspension or irresolution.[11] Morrissey's singing is also somewhat rhythmically unhinged, which adds to the affect of disconnection. An interesting characteristic of indie is the use of two separate lead singers in a song – for example The Go-Betweens and Hüsker Dü. The Beatles are the obvious prototype. Sometimes more complex and ambitious melodies are used, though the effect may be undercut by the limitations of the player or singer, not quite reaching the note or going out of time (Verlaines, The Go-Betweens). Sometimes vocal/melodic elements are obscured by the loudness of the guitars (Hüsker Dü, for example).

Blues scales and tonality are infrequent. The overall effect tends to be primitive, but white not black, a slightly 'keening' or Celtic sound – for example, Morrissey, Stipe and, in New Zealand, The Bats – sometimes reinforced by the use of vocal harmonisation in 'primitive' octaves, parallel fourths and fifths (Buckley, 2002, pp. 87–8; Eggleton, 1994, p. 44). Flying Nun music was characterised as 'un-Afro' (Stead, 1990–91, p. 85). Lead guitarists like David Kilgour of The Clean and, later, David Long of The Mutton Birds, were influenced by the twangy, low-note, country-influenced style of Duane Eddy – the Great Unwashed recorded a song called 'Duane Eddy' on their debut EP (1985) – or by the similar 'surf' style of Dick Dale, which can be seen as 'pure' in its lack of blues tonality. Overtly black references in music were generally frowned upon (Bannister, 1999, pp. 57, 106). Contemporary pop, blues, soul, boogie, R&B, disco, jazz, rap and reggae did not feature much in NZ indie or within indie guitar rock globally.

In rhythmic terms, these groups tend to favour 4/4 in straight eights – the most common rock time signature. Flying Nun tends towards the monadic beat of punk rock and its antecedents; however, there was some metric experimentation: 6/8 and 12/8, suggesting 1960s folk archivalism, and swing time were not uncommon, and even 5/4, 6/4 and 11/4 also feature occasionally, suggesting a certain intellectualism.[12] Hardcore and its descendants favour a punk approach to rhythm (Minor Threat, however, raise the tempo to the point where the drummer has to play 2/4 to keep up). Some groups employ the Velvet Underground approach of accelerating and decelerating tempo.[13] This refers to a classical rather than a popular music tradition, and thereby to white rather than African-American tradition.[14] Even where punk monadism is not the norm, rhythmic repertoire tends towards a few basic rock beats, for example R.E.M.'s use of the *baion* (derived from The Beatles and The Byrds) or The Replacements' characteristic 1970s hard rock beat (hi-hat in crotchets rather than quavers). In general, rhythm is de-emphasised: drums are often mixed low compared with guitars, giving a sound that throbs rather than moves. Rhythmic elements are also in some ways 'primitive', by which I mean lacking in swing or syncopation, and not particularly danceable (early Velvet Underground is a big influence here). Again this tends to indicate indie's suspicion of black dance music.

But not all indie groups/scenes were dismissive of black music. In Scotland, Postcard Records 'were interested in the fifties, the sixties, disco, Chic, Motown, Stax and we wanted to get a black thing into music' (Nichols, 2003, p. 90; see also Cavanagh, 2000, pp. 23–4, 28). This had some effect on the musical style of groups like Orange Juice, most obviously in their 'chicken scratch' guitar style. The band even covered Al Green's 'L.O.V.E.' on their first album, albeit incompetently (Orange Juice, 1981). Their second album *Rip It Up* (1982) deployed black influences, especially Motown, to better effect – indeed the group also had a black drummer by this time. But indie purists tend to dismiss their later work, probably because it was done for a major label (Nichols, 2003, p. 129). UK group The Housemartins also played with soul styles ('Build', 'Caravan of Love'). In the

USA, Camper Van Beethoven were notable for their use of ska within an indie rock framework, and the Minutemen (1984) used funk rhythms. In New Zealand, Sneaky Feelings' 'There's a Chance' (1982) and 'Coming True' (1987) attempted a Philadelphia soul sound. All these groups took elements of earlier black pop (however, they did not attempt blues or rap – too many negative macho connotations?) Finally, few of these groups became central to indie style, which moved towards harder and louder styles.

Semiotic aspects – musical expressivity, lyrics, intertextuality, degrees of intimacy and distance

Generally the music eschews individual expression in favour of a group approach. Improvisation is generally rare – guitar solos (where present) tend to be integrated into the overall form of the song; simple and naive (The Go-Betweens, The Chills); repetitive and drony, thus underplaying the individually expressive (and therefore 'rockist') element (The Clean, Hüsker Dü, Sonic Youth); or messy and anarchic (Bob Stinson of The Replacements, Sonic Youth). It wasn't until the late 1980s and groups like Dinosaur Jr. that the extended 'virtuosic' solo became acceptable again. There are no drum or bass solos, again deriving from the 'less is more' credo and a democratic, team approach. Expressivity tends to be located more in the sound.

Flying Nun bands favoured a lot of reverberation in performance and on record, not just on the vocals but on the instruments too (especially guitars), as if the group were playing in a large hall. This was not uncommon indie practice.[15] Its effect is to de-emphasise individual elements (as with the drone). Reverberation fills out the minimal instrumentation of groups like The Clean: 'The spring reverb unit, especially used on guitar, is as much a feature of Dunedin music as slap echo was of Sun Studios in Memphis' (Bannister, 1999, p. 72). Reverberation also has the effect of covering up mistakes, an important consideration for relatively amateur musicians. It was also used extensively by UK indie acts (The Smiths, The Jesus and Mary Chain, My Bloody Valentine, Spaceman 3) and US groups (R.E.M. and Hüsker Dü).

Jangle and drone plus reverberation create a contemporary equivalent of Spector's 'Wall of Sound' – a massive, ringing, cavernous noise and a device used by many indie groups: Flying Nun, from Sneaky Feelings' *Send You* to Straitjacket Fits and the JPS Experience. One reviewer described The Jesus and Mary Chain as the sound of 'a giant bee in a ventilation shaft' (Cavanagh, 2000, p. 118). Historic references for this approach include 1960s psychedelic and garage rock (for example The Byrds' 'Eight Miles High', 1966b) and Phil Spector's Wall of Sound. As we have seen, this tendency towards white noise was interpreted by many critics as implying freedom from learned technique and the rational controlling ego (Reynolds and Press, Gilbert) – hence their increasing tendency to disparage as 'old fashioned' or 'regressive' groups that took a more conventional song-based approach. Rachel Felder claims that the drone of indie music replicates the sound of radio interference, of 'unwanted noise': 'a supercharged combination of an oldies station and frazzled static' (1993, p. 128). This 'hypermediacy' obtained through 'noise' can be interpreted as postmodern fragmentation, but clearly also served more tangible functions for audiences and musicians wishing to highlight their difference.

Singing

Vocals tend to be indistinct, because they are not prominent in the mix, a feature that may derive from punk, although some have argued it is a central feature of rock (Gracyk, 1996, pp. 106–7; Laing, 1986, pp. 53–4). Even when the vocal is 'mixed up' it doesn't use a lot of expressive devices like sudden changes in tone, rhythmical subtleties – the type of devices associated with vocal virtuosity and African-American music. There is a tendency towards a matter-of-fact, deadpan or monotone (Jim Reid of The Jesus and Mary Chain is an excellent example). Some Flying Nun singers (and instrumentalists) eschewed the use of vibrato, as a false 'sweetening' of the note, which can give an effect of naivety. Of course, some singers (myself included) were incapable of holding a tune. But again this limitation was sometimes seen as a virtue because it implied honesty and authenticity, as for example, in early Go-Betweens records (1982).

On the other hand, in UK indie, Morrissey and Edwyn Collins (Orange Juice) go to the opposite extreme with a campy exaggeration of vibrato, which gives a quasi-operatic, semi-comic effect. In The Go-Betweens, both modes of vocalisation are present, often in the same song – Grant McLennan's dour sincerity and Robert Forster's histrionic campness.[16] The main point is the avoidance of orthodox models of 'good' singing, and the general lack (or ironisation) of expression. US indie vocals, however, tend to be in more conventional rock modes – a rawer, angrier sound (Hüsker Dü, The Replacements). They also tend to be more technically accomplished.[17] However, as stated above, vocals are typically low in the mix. This decentres them – even when angry and defiant in tone, the affect is generally one of impotence. This can be interpreted in different ways – the most important being Reynolds's and Gilbert's concept of a wordless *jouissance* – implying that voice somehow restricts possible readings (Gilbert, 1999, p. 43; Reynolds, 1990, p. 13).

Lyrics in this genre eschew or parody the romantic devices and subject matter commonly identified with pop music (Buckley, 2002, pp. 121–2). The word 'love' is usually avoided, or only used ironically. Lyrics are often pessimistic but more often obscure (Mitchell, 1996, pp. 218–19).[18] The Go-Betweens, R.E.M., The Smiths and the Verlaines tend towards a poetic vagueness, often using literary devices such as third-person description.[19] Literary or cultural allusions abound in the UK and New Zealand, as in The Smiths' 'Shakespeare's Sister' (1987a) (a feminist essay by Virginia Woolf) and 'Cemetry Gates' (1986).[20] US indie tends to be less overtly literary and intellectual. Relationship (you and me, me and her) songs are reasonably common but are usually presented in a non-romantic, sometimes accusatory mode.

Isolation is a typical subject position: 'Nobody's touched me in such a long time' wails Robert Forster on 'Ask' (The Go-Betweens, 1983). 'Sometimes I think I feel too much and I don't want to feel at all' ('Thumbs Off', The Clean, 1981, 1999).[21] This may become solipsistic ('The Living End', 'My Little Underground', 'In My Hole', The Jesus and Mary Chain, 1985). Accordingly, relations with others (love or relationship songs) are often represented as an unequal struggle between a weak (male) singer and a powerful (and often androgynous) other, for example Morrissey or The Jesus and Mary Chain's 'Taste of Cindy'.[22] One consequence of this is a sense of helpless guilt, resulting in a number of indie songs that are apologies: 'Apology Accepted' (The Go-Betweens, 1986); 'I Apologise', 'Sorry Somehow' (Hüsker Dü, 1985, 1986); 'So. Central Rain (I'm Sorry)' (R.E.M., 1984), 'All Apologies' (Nirvana, 1993). UK indie band The Wedding Present (1987) made a career out of romantic humiliation, writing song after song about losing your girlfriend, and then watching her run around with another guy.

On the other hand, there is also a preoccupation with (childlike) regression and fantasy (Reynolds, 1989, p. 247). The opening lines of The Chills' 'Kaleidoscope World' run: 'If we were floating in a space capsule/You'd look at me and perhaps you'll/Smile at me, loving our kaleidoscope world.' Floating in a pod, far from the world, being contemplated with love – a picture of infant bliss. Naturally it is an eternal vision: 'We'll never die/In our kaleidoscope world' (The Chills, 1986). The idea of floating in space or the sea clearly evokes earlier psychedelic voyagers across oceans or space: Tommy: the deaf, dumb and blind boy who lives in 'a strange vibration land' (The Who, 1968), Bowie's 'Space Oddity' (1970). In other words, the theme of isolation returns in fantasy. The 'psychedelic mummy's boy' thesis of Reynolds and Press is relevant, as well as Jim DeRogatis's history of psychedelic rock (1996, p. xi). (A more ironic rendering of the child-man trope is Jonathan Richman's faux naif punk). Such lyrics speak of happiness and bliss, but usually only in terms of a nostalgic and solitary fantasy.

Irony is not infrequent (DeCurtis, 1999, p. 32).[23] This relates most obviously to the valorisation of 'failure' as part of punk's legacy to indie, and the inversion of straight values characteristic of subcultures (Bangs, 1987, p. 273; Carson, 1996, pp. 108–17). The most recurrent technique is self-deprecation: 'I'm not strong' (for example, The Go-Betweens' 'About Strength', 1982).[24] But increasingly there are also harsher ironies – the US scene was especially preoccupied with violence and sick humour, for example in the way in which Steve Albini (Big Black) deals with images of violence and abjection, and takes the point of view of bigots, psychopaths, racists and rapists (Azerrad, 2001, pp. 324–6, 331). While this is presented as ironic, it clearly is open to other interpretations. The mode of utterance is not dissimilar to US 'zines, for which Albini wrote a good deal (Azerrad, 2001,

p. 323). On the other hand, Morrissey also has his moments of violence and bigotry (Reynolds, 1990, pp. 19, 27; Wrenn, 1988, p. 25). The lyrical concerns of indie can be viewed as an inversion of pop values: anti-romantic, pessimistic, ironic, intellectual and often serious (not dissimilar to high culture values). Again, this inversion became more pronounced as the 1980s progressed and lyrical subject matter became more self-consciously extreme (Big Black, Sonic Youth). Again, this seems to be basically down to the US influence.

Intertextuality

Both Buckley and Straw suggest indie was highly reflexive in its consciousness of rock and pop culture tradition (Buckley, 2002, pp. 4–5; Straw, 1997b, p. 496). Indie had a strong investment in 1960s popular culture – Flying Nun, for example, took its name from a 'trashy' US TV sitcom starring Sally Field, while Creation took theirs from an obscure British group. The Smiths' Morrissey was obsessed by post-war British culture, especially film (Zuberi, 2001, p. 20). This retrogressive tendency is also reflected in what Hesmondhalgh (1999, p. 46) terms the 'connoisseur' or archivalist aspect of indie – the idea that it was largely the product of young men listening to old records in their bedrooms (Straw, 1991, pp. 377–8). Flying Nun was the first record label or musical style in New Zealand to be based on this sort of 'canonism', connecting to similar practices within independent record labels like Creation in the UK. The authority of indie musicians and fans is strongly associated with their investment in certain kinds of culture, and their judgment of it as superior to mainstream taste. Moreover, as we already saw in the discussion on lyrics, many indie bands also referenced high culture in their work, sometimes ironically (The Smiths), sometimes not (Verlaines). There is a sense, then, in which indie anticipated the continuous recycling of past musical styles which has become increasingly common in modern (especially white) popular music.

Intertextuality includes both influence and quotation. There are instances of direct self-conscious quotation, sometimes ironic – for example, Dunedin's The Stones, who defaced the cover of the Rolling Stones' *Exile on Main Street* in a facetious gesture towards 1970s rockism, thereby getting the jump on Pussy Galore by four years ('Dunedin Double', 1982). The Replacements pulled a similar trick on *Let it Be* (1984), presumably sending up the taste of label owner and manager Peter Jesperson (Azerrad, 2001, p. 200). On *Hootenanny* (another ironic take on 1960s Americana), the song 'Mr Whirly' (about having the 'bed spins') incorporates snatches of the introduction of 'Strawberry Fields Forever' (played on a loud distorted guitar) while the body of the song alternates between Chubby Checker's 'The Twist' and The Beatles 'Oh! Darling' (1969). The band also wrote a song to Big Star founder: 'Alex Chilton' (1987).[25] Generally, references were mainly to white 1960s music, with the exception of Postcard (for example, Orange Juice's 'I Can't Help Myself', 1982) who gave black music a more equal billing (as did my band, and we took plenty of flak for it, too)

(Bannister, 1999, p. 55). The Smiths habitually refer to different musical genres and sometimes even particular songs. These references to rock tradition may have counterbalanced Morrissey's perceived effeminacy for some male rock fans (see Chapter 4).

The other literal form of quotation is cover versions (performing songs by other artists). One might not expect this to be common, given the punk ethos of originality, but this is complicated by archivalism. The most covered artists and genres in the Dunedin scene were The Velvet Underground, punk and 1960s material (Churton, 2000, p. 241).[26] The scene most resistant to covers was hardcore, because of its emphasis on autonomy and originality. However the Washington DC Dischord bands had a well-known affinity for The Monkees' 'Stepping Stone', a 1967 hit with 'garage' rock undertones (Azerrad, 2001, p. 131). Hardcore may have heard covers as a concession to commercial pressures. Some indie guitar bands had 'alter-egos' who performed cover versions.[27] Much of R.E.M.'s early reputation was based around their repertoire of mainly 1960s covers. Hüsker Dü's versions of 1960s 'classics' may have acted as a way of distancing themselves from the hardcore scene.[28] (Dinosaur Jr. later paid homage to the 1970s, covering 'Show Me the Way' by Peter Frampton, while Seattle grunge clearly owes a big debt to 1970s metal) (Buckley, 2002, p. 48; Gray, 1993, pp. 277–85)). Clearly, covers functioned in a number of ways – they could be a popular move (as in the case of the recorded versions); they could act as tributes to influences, invoking a common tradition and audience solidarity and recognition. However, they were also used as a way of frustrating audience expectations, as we shall see in the case of The Replacements.

The Replacements used covers in live performance both as sloppy tributes – *The Shit Hits the Fans* (a 1985 live release which includes covers of Black Sabbath, Thin Lizzy, the Stones and Tom Petty) – and as a weapon: 'In New York they played a show at CBGB packed with music industry types interested in signing the band. They … played nothing but shambling covers for the assembled execs. After destroying the Rolling Stones' "Start Me Up", Westerberg leaned into the mike and said, "Do we get a record contract now?"' (Azerrad, 2001, p. 227). Covers in this case become a way of confirming the band's total indifference to the industry.

Indie use of covers suggests a fairly strong debt to the past. Musically we might say that the harmonic and melodic basis of much indie music is pretty traditional – indeed 'the good song' was sometimes represented within indie as a paradigm of authenticity, as in the indie 'pure pop' model, which drew in turn on the idea of the three-minute pop classic (Hyland, 1990; Reynolds, 1989, p. 252, 1990, p. 42). But, increasingly, focus shifted to the way in which bands would then 'pervert, pound, personalise these [traditional] elements' (or, perhaps simply obliterate them with incompetence) (Felder, 1993, pp. 6–7). 'Fucked-up feedback is piled on to the top of what would otherwise be classically structured, three-minute, stick-in-your-head pop tunes' writes Rachel Felder of The Jesus and Mary Chain (1993, p. 117).

She continues: 'The Mary Chain's targets are clear; groups like the Shangri-Las and the Beach Boys' (p. 123). However, songs like 'Kill Surf City' are clearly also homages, albeit ramshackle, a case perhaps of each band killing the thing they love. I would describe indie's attitude in terms of Jameson's concept of postmodern pastiche: 'blank parody' without any political bite: 'Pastiche is, like parody, the imitation of a peculiar or unique, idiosyncratic style, the wearing of a linguistic mask, speech in a dead language. But it is a neutral practice of such mimicry, without any of parody's ulterior motives, amputated of the satiric impulse, devoid of laughter' (Jameson, 1983, p. 117; Gendron, 2002, pp. 288–90). This rather studied indifference seems a useful way of characterising indie's relation to the past, relating to Warhol's flatness of affect – his numbness in the face of modernity (Chapter 2). Clearly, too obvious a highlighting of influence could connote dependence and unoriginality: 'every time there's a new music scene everybody thinks they are forging entirely new territory. Part of that of course was the need to destroy the past' (Mitch Easter, R.E.M.'s producer, quoted in Buckley, 2002, p. 70). The complexity of influence in indie is a theme I develop in Chapters 4 and 5.

Behavioural aspects – performance, packaging

Although indie groups were influenced by punk musically, in performance they generally avoided the transgressive, offensive aspect of punk and favoured a post-punk, non-performance 'shoe-gazing' ordinariness, dressing in street clothes and eschewing expressive 'rock' gestures: a group approach, in which no single member is the 'star' – 'dressing down, a minimum display of musical prowess, and a deliberate muting of charisma' (Hesmondhalgh, 1999, p. 38).[29] The Clean once performed behind a sheet of transparent industrial plastic, reducing their onstage presence to amorphous blobs (Shepherd, 1998): 'in Dunedin, standing still was the acceptable mode of performance' (Bannister, 1999, p. 20). Where a group member was highlighted, as in Morrissey of the Smiths or Michael Stipe of R.E.M., this display was problematised by the use of irony and sexual ambiguity – Morrissey's 'celibacy', for example. De-emphasising vocals or 'bad' singing could be interpreted similarly – vocal ability highlights the body of the performer and foregrounds him as an object of display and as distinct from the homosocial band milieu (Green, 1997, pp. 27–30).

This account of seeing The Clean live in June 1980 at the Captain Cook Tavern in Dunedin demonstrates some of the above points:

> At some stage guitar cases and a very old set of black, beat-up drums materialised on stage. Then band members began to materialise, out of the audience. They wore woolly scarves (inside). One of them ... plucked tentatively at a white Ibanez, tortuously comparing notes with a squat boy with glasses, holding a bass as one might hold a weed-eating device. They were out of tune. Gradually they became more out of tune. The drummer hit things in a testing way.

Then quite unexpectedly they started playing. The band were still but tense, as if they were standing in a stiff wind, apart from the drummer, who waved his head around like he was in a trance. He played with his hands uncrossed and had his rack tom set so it was almost horizontal. To play it he leaned forward and dipped his stick in, as if testing a casserole. He hit the bass drum on every beat; it was a rhythmic drone. The sound was grating – it chafed, it gouged, it left a wound. The guitarist wore a violent paisley shirt that looked like it was made out of curtain material. It was buttoned right up the neck. Any sudden movement could cause him to choke. His head and feet seemed rooted, though when he sung, he swung his hips gently, like a creeper in a breeze.

After about a minute the guitarist stopped playing. After a moment the rest of them stopped too. He was talking to the bass player – showing him something on the guitar. He was teaching him the chords. (Bannister, 1999, pp. 22–3)

Flying Nun groups were often extremely amateur and, over time, this could take on the status of an ideology of 'ordinariness' – the refusal of 'showbiz' conventions such as 'the show must go on'. The Clean, at this point, couldn't really play at all. However, within a year, The Clean had become a formidable live act, and in practice bands that could actually play made a much bigger impact than those who couldn't, as R.E.M. proved in 1983 when they toured the UK (Cavanagh, 2000, pp. 186–8). In the success- and image-oriented 1980s, clearly 'shambling amateurism' acted as a refusal of mainstream values – indie groups generally tried to avoid looking like they were having fun, unless their idea of fun was not fun for the audience (The Replacements). The idealisation of incompetence served an important ideological function within all indie scenes, and relates to punk amateurism. The Jesus and Mary Chain's early reputation seems to have been largely based around their incompetence – which band manager Alan McGee (Creation) exploited as a means of provoking the audience and gaining media notoriety (Cavanagh, 2000, pp. 107–8, 142–5, 149–53, 159–65).

Other presentational aspects include band and record names, record and poster artwork and videos. Many band names are curt, deadpan or ironic monosyllables that seem designed to resist any obvious interpretation, perhaps emulating the 'blankness' of some punk names, like Wire – The Clean, The Stones. Others are simply obscure, for example Hüsker Dü,[30] or not very 'rock and roll' – Orange Juice. Some signify ordinariness, anonymity or superfluity – The Smiths, R.E.M., The Replacements and The Go-Betweens. When asked to explain their choice of name, R.E.M.'s Michael Stipe suggested, 'we just like the dots' (Buckley, 2002, p. 40). Some contain high cultural references – The Go-Betweens, the Verlaines, the Jean-Paul Sartre Experience, emphasising the middle-class backgrounds of many indie groups. Later in the 1980s, band names became more 'expressive' like the Headless Chickens and Straitjacket Fits, My Bloody Valentine and the Butthole Surfers, tending to suggest violence or horror, following the transgressive punk tradition – Bad Brains, Suicidal Tendencies, the Sex Pistols. Again, the intention to refuse mainstream values is clear through an obvious failure to 'sell' the product by conventional appeal.

Record artwork tends not to feature a photograph of the band, especially on the front, as this is identified with 'pop' (as with bands like The Go-Betweens, Orange

Juice and Sneaky Feelings) (Buckley, 2002, p. 86). On the other hand, some 1970s prog rock groups had similarly used obscure cover art – though usually more professionally done. Flying Nun artwork tends to be 'primitive' and often messy, again perhaps because of technical limitations or a punk ideal of amateurism. The Clean (1981) and the *Dunedin Double* (1982) exemplify a childlike, 'hand-drawn' look. R.E.M. (1984) used the work of 'naive' Georgian artist The Reverend Howard Finster, contrasting with the use of digital and computer-generated imagery in more mainstream media.

Artwork, if not amateur, was often obscure and arty, for example The Jesus and Mary Chain's *Psychocandy* (1985). Intertextual references were common (for example, The Smiths' use of archival images from film). Increasingly indie bands like Dinosaur Jr. favoured a dark, messy, sludgy, sordid look, which tends to also be reflected in their album and song titles, for example 'Bug', 'Tarpit', 'Puke and Cry' (1989, 1991). Early SST hardcore was heavily associated with the artwork of Raymond Pettibon, harsh black and white cartoons, often of violence against women, for example the 1983 SST compilation *The Blasting Concept* (indie guitar rockers tended to distance themselves from such explicitly misogynistic images, favouring a more generalised anomie) (Azerrad, 2001, p. 187). Finally, there was the extreme approach of the Butthole Surfers and Big Black who tended towards explicit images of horror and carnage. Some indie groups took it upon themselves to offend not just ordinary people, but also PC (politically correct), right-on New Left types (Azerrad, 2001, p. 321). Such practices suggested disillusionment not only with right-wing but with all political rhetoric, anticipating a slacker-type 'whatever' apathy.

Many indie bands disliked videos – for them, MTV was a betrayal of the basic principles of rock and roll, not only because it was clearly industry-driven, but also because videos required a 'fake' performance (lip-synching was especially abhorred) and emphasised personal appearance, as opposed to sound. Moreover, MTV was unlikely to play independent productions, and there were few alternative broadcasters. The Replacements, Hüsker Dü and The Go-Betweens all avoided videos for as long as possible; others lacked resources. When videos were made, they would often be comparatively simple, rough clips of the band playing, perhaps with a few arty montages thrown in (*Very Short Films*, Flying Nun, 2004). This enforced the idea of liveness.

Social and ideological aspects – the social image of the musician and audience

Early UK indie was often political, ranging from left-wing agit-rock (Gang of Four, The Pop Group, PIL, early Human League, Billy Bragg) to women's and/or feminist groups (The Slits, The Raincoats, Au Pairs), to ethnic issues, especially in ska (The Specials, The Beat, Two-Tone) (Thompson, 2000, pp. 1–77). There were strong cross-associations with groups like Rock against Racism and CND (Hesmondhalgh, 1999, p. 37). Relative stylistic diversity was underpinned by strong, broadly left-wing ideological and political convictions about what was and was not PC. Indie guitar rock was not particularly in sympathy with this (Cavanagh, 2000, pp. 41–2, 48–51, 91). Its emphasis was on aesthetic rather than political change; musical/cultural preferences were the main area in which it advocated overt resistance to dominant values: 'Aesthetically my life was so unpleasing … Ugly, ugly, ugliness, that was all I knew' (Arnold, 1995, p. 8). It might be possible to say that PC-ness was rearticulated at the level of stylistic choice (Horne's Postcard label, for example; Arnold, 1995, p. 11; Cavanagh, 2000, pp. 23–9). Given the contemporary importance of identity politics for some white middle-class youth, stylistic minimalism may connect to conventions concerning sexist or racist behaviour. One way for indie to stay 'politically correct' was to avoid overt 'rock' gestures: ' "Rock'n'roll" had become unsightly, and sensitive, arty, young men like Michael Stipe of R.E.M. wanted nothing to do with it' (Nichols, 2003, p. 26). So, in indie guitar rock, political correctness was reinterpreted as aesthetic correctness (Hesmondhalgh, 1999, p. 36). This was paralleled by a long slow movement away from the vaguely anarchist and collectivist principles of early indie towards and eventually back to a more 'rock'n'roll' approach (Creation is a good example; see Cavanagh, 2000, pp. 199, 212).

Indies such as Rough Trade (UK) or SST (USA) aimed to provide an alternative, rather than explicitly attacking the establishment (Azerrad, 2001, p. 21; Cavanagh, 2000, pp. 36–42). The main idea was to make music available and, as such, indie was basically capitalism, albeit practised at a localised level, on a more modest scale than the 'majors' and with a degree of philanthropy. Political rhetoric centred on basically aesthetic and personal politics – not selling out (profiteering) and personal political issues like feminism, racism, vegetarianism and, in the USA, 'straight edge' abstinence (Azerrad, 2001, pp. 135–7; Cavanagh, 2000, p. 91). The obvious model was the hippy counterculture, and indeed 'ex-hippies' were instrumental to the founding of many indie labels – for example, Travis, Ginn and Knox – but without its 'naive' idealism (in theory). However, the US indies were sometimes more businesslike, if only because they operated in a harsher environment. But overall, early indie was music- rather than money-centred – Flying Nun artists, for example, were reasonably free to produce what they wanted without interference from financial interests. 'Because the bands were the important thing, Roger [Shepherd] would say "okay, I'll help you do this"' (Chris Knox, quoted in *Heavenly Pop Hits*; Cavanagh, 2000, pp. 50–1).

Indie culture, unlike punk, had a strong tendency to avoid direct confrontation with society: 'Independent rock and roll does not present itself as a challenge … to the dominant culture although it may function as such. It apparently exists outside of its relation to the dominant culture; it does not want the world. It seeks to escape, to define a space which neither impinges upon nor is impinged upon by the hegemony: "we want our world"' (Grossberg, 1997, pp. 486–7). Punk activism was largely replaced by a more passive, mediated approach, an argument Reynolds advances with reference to UK indie band The Smiths: 'the rebellion of The Stones, Who, Pistols, Jam was based in some kind of activism … but The Smiths' rebellion was always more like resistance through withdrawal' (1990, p. 19). Instead musicians and critics advocated an alternative canon based mainly on punk and white 1960s guitar music, but also on trash and cult TV, film, comic books and other forms of popular culture (Bannister, 1999, pp. 105–7; Brown, 1983c; Knox, 1986).[31] 'Fill your head with alcohol, comic books and drugs' as Martin Phillipps sang on 'This is the Way' (The Chills, 1986). Indie, then, anticipates the disengagement of 'slacker culture' (Rushkoff, 1994, pp. 5–7; *Slacker*, 1991). This resignation of agency has been critiqued as implying an acceptance of the dominant social order (Poniewozik, 2001):

> But as much as we 80s vets would like to remember ourselves as having created and enunciated an alternative during Reaganism, we have to consider how much our resistance meant shutting ourselves off in a kind of privileged privacy while the forces we were supposedly resisting, too, were advancing a politics of privacy – the private sector, deregulation, free markets, etc. To appreciate this we, and Arnold [whose book is being reviewed here], might take another look at the three shy, private boy stars [Stipe, Mould, Westerberg] listed above (whose bands make up the core of Arnold's book) and realize that they're all boys, and that at least two of them are, to varying degrees, closet cases. And that's precisely what gets elided in an account like this – that in the fantasy about meeting in this private, utopic space, we become blind to the fact that certain people are still getting more access than others. And that a certain identity is still privileged, and, surprise, it's not middle-class girls. For all its identification with idealistically leftist communities, the implicit message of the 80s scene was that only straight [*sic*] white boys make music. (Stadler, 1995)[32]

A further point here is the fairly strong correlation between indie and educational institutions, especially universities, important as venues, as meeting places for future bands and for their radio stations and newspapers. Thornton observes that (in the 1980s) 'college students now make up the bulk of the audience for live popular music and the live circuit is heavily dominated by a few subgenres, like alternative rock and indie music … the largest share of middle-sized gigs … are hosted by university student unions' (1995, p. 48). What this tends to suggest is that indie is 'a white middle-class bohemianism … separated from … delinquent lifestyles' (Reynolds, 1989, pp. 254–5). It is not usually confrontational. It generally de-emphasised dress, withdrew from the 'the street' and engaged with popular culture in private through practices like archivalism (Frith, 1992, p. 181). Indie practitioners could claim some male authenticity in indie's 'local' and 'grassroots' modes of production and distribution, but this locality was not particularly reflected in a corresponding diversity of influences and sound. Hence indie's relation to rock 'authenticity', in conventional masculine terms, was complex, because indie masculinities were implicitly critical of the dominant mode, but this criticism was signalled through retreat and withdrawal rather than active engagement.

White males dominate indie personnel (Cohen, 1997). A number of Flying Nun bands have had female members, mostly playing keyboards, an instrument with more female connotations than the guitar (through the history of the piano as a domestic and therefore female instrument) (Walser, 1993, p. 133). The Chills used keyboards, played by Martin Phillipps' sister, Rachel, and also a female drummer in 1987 (Caroline Easther). Both left due to the pressures of touring (Davey and Puschmann, 1996, pp. 25, 29).[33] These tendencies are repeated throughout indie scenes: 'the indie scene was less welcoming to women than the punk scene before … I never heard of any female lead guitarists' (Arnold, 1995, pp. 164–5; see also Kruse, 2003, pp. 138–44). Some of the shoegazer bands had women members, notably My Bloody Valentine and Slowdive, though the extent of MBV's female members' involvement in recording is a matter of some debate (Cavanagh, 2000, pp. 414–16). However, woman managers of indie groups are more common: Straitjacket Fits (Debbi Gibbs), Jean-Paul Sartre Experience (Domanik Nola) and My Bloody Valentine, managed by Kevin Shields' sister, Ann Marie (Cavanagh, 2000, p. 425). A number of record companies were also headed by women, for example Lisa Fancher (Frontier), and there were/are significant female writers (Gina Arnold). But overall, indie guitar scenes were blokey and exclusive of women (Cohen, 1997, p. 29). My experience of the Flying Nun social scene and audience suggests that this was also true in New Zealand indie – the wistful Romanticism of some Flying Nun performers had to be balanced against the necessity of 'rocking out' to keep the primarily male pub audience happy.

This relative conservatism about gender was continued in indie attitudes to ethnicity. For example, while there was little overt racism in Flying Nun, the marginalisation of non-white music was widespread. Flying Nun 'founding fathers' Chris Knox and Dunedin record shop owner Roy Colbert were both evasive about other ethnicities in music, Knox handing over his *NZ Listener* record column to a guest to review dub, funk and reggae, Colbert ghetto-ising black music in a separate bin from rock music, which occupied pride of place, next to the entrance (Bannister, 1999, p. 21; Knox, 1985b). Colbert's liner notes for Flying Nun act Bill Direen's CD reissue of *Split Seconds* (1995) also contain some racist jibes, ostensibly anti-Australian, but focusing on Aboriginals. Auckland bands influenced by the brief 'white funk' craze of the early 1980s often received a hostile reception, especially in the South Island, home of Flying Nun (Churton, 2000, p. 251).

In 1983, journalist Russell Brown of NZ music paper *Rip It Up* and Chris Knox discussed a 'lineage … the Velvets, John Cale, The Saints, Wire, The Stooges, The Birthday Party and authors like William Burroughs … who have tried to describe the White Man's Condition … it is soul music in the sense of the *white man's soul*' (my italics). Knox responded by describing Dunedin band the Stones as 'plugged into the white man's heartbeat' (Brown, 1983a). This highlights an increasing tendency within indie culture to reproduce a canon of mainly white musicians and bands, as can also be seen in indie discographies and overviews (Strong, 1999; Thompson, 2000). Reynolds describes UK indie music as 'whiter than white "pure pop"' influenced by the *'pure* voices of Syd Barrett, Roger McGuinn, Arthur Lee' (1990, p. 23; 1989, p. 247).[34] This implied a similar canon to other indie scenes: 'strictly albino roots like The Velvet Underground, Television, The Byrds, psychedelia, folk, country' (Reynolds, 1989, p. 246; see also Cavanagh, 2000, p. 228).

However, this was also the era of Rock Against Racism, so there was a conflict between being anti-racist and not liking contemporary black music. But one possible way of resolving this conflict was to pronounce white imitation of black styles as unacceptable appropriation. In indie, this sometimes resulted in a wholesale renunciation of black moves and styles by white musicians, saying in effect, they had no right to pretend (or desire) to be black any more. 'I can't help it that I'm not Schoolly D' (Peter Buck of R.E.M. quoted in Arnold, 1995, p. 87). I have worked with white NZ musicians who refuse to perform black styles of music live (although they don't necessarily mind playing them for 'fun'). Since appropriation of black style is central in the history of pop music, this was a radical renunciation. At the same time, feminism was also telling young middle-class men that 'sexual' moves were no longer acceptable onstage or off. This discourse often combined with the renunciation of blackness, thus redoubling the ban.

US scenes made a similar equation – black music equalled commercialism, therefore it was no good: 'the radio blared out cheesy disco songs unendingly' (Arnold, 1995, p. 8). Henry Rollins spotted 'Derrick Bostrom of tourmates the Meat Puppets carrying a copy of the Jacksons' *Triumph* album. "I always knew you were one of *them*," Rollins sneered' (Azerrad, 2001, p. 47). Both Black Flag and Minor Threat wrote songs ('White Minority' and 'Guilty of Being White') that have been interpreted as racist, although both claim it was a reaction to being beaten up by black kids at school (Washington in the 1970s was, in Parliament's phrase, 'Chocolate City') (Azerrad, 2001, pp. 25, 141)). Later indie groups such as Sebadoh termed indie rock 'a new generation of electric white boy blues' in a similar manner to Knox ('Gimme Indie Rock', 1991). Some of the fanzine writing of the times was blatantly racist, for example Gerard Cosloy in *Conflict*: 'Only thing in this world that's worse than listening to some spliffed-out moron who ain't washed his hair in three years singing "I love Jah" is watching white college students throw frisbees around to the strains of the above Rasta fool' (quoted in Arnold, 1995, p. 120). Steve Albini claimed in *Forced Exposure*, 'I don't give two splats of an old Negro junkie's vomit', later claiming such statements were ironic 'overkill' (Azerrad, 2001, pp. 321–3) (see the discussion of Albini in Chapter 6).

UK indie scenes were overall the most likely to 'play' with ethnicity. Many UK indie acts and performers crossed over into dance music: New Order, Norman Cook of The Housemartins (aka Fatboy Slim), Primal Scream and the Happy Mondays; even The Jesus and Mary Chain experimented with hiphop beats (*Automatic*; *Honey's Dead*) (Cavanagh, 2000, pp. 350–54). Why the difference? One possibility is the importance of minstrelsy in the UK context (Frith, 1988, pp. 45–63). The distance, both geographical and cultural, between the UK and the USA means that minstrelsy can be maintained as a space for British white middle-class cultural play. Arguably in the USA and New Zealand, race is more overtly highlighted as a means of social stratification, as opposed to the UK concern with class. Finally, some of the points I make in Chapter 4 about media in the UK may also be relevant – just as dedicated national media engendered a certain potential for mainstream crossover, and a consequent reflexivity in gender representation in UK indie, so it also perhaps affected the way UK musicians and scenes approached ethnicity.

To sum up indie attitudes to ethnicity, there seems to be a double sense of blackness as somehow exceptional – on the one hand, because it is too commercial, commodified and feminised (basically the mass culture critique) but on the other, because it is too violent, threatening and masculine (the feminist critique). Both are constructed around a rejection or objectification of blackness as body, instinct or id. I argued that purity is a significant criterion for indie guitar rock and that ethnicity, broadly speaking, functions as a type of 'impurity' which the genre defines itself against. The problem with indie, as I see it, is that it rejected 'blackness' (or its construction thereof), when it should have rejected its accompanying ideological baggage – of blackness as a 'pure' folk culture (see Chapter 2). Instead it ran with the idea of purity, with the black parts removed. In other words, indie shot the messenger, when it should have burned the message.

Conclusions

I have shown in this chapter that there are broad similarities in production, text and reception across the board in 1980s indie music. I have also tried to show how indie's oppositionality was part of its identity – how it was in some ways negatively defined, by avoiding certain styles and connotations. This relates to the complex pressures on the emergent genre – a desire to reject the 'mainstream', identified as black-styled dance music (pop) on the one hand, but also a feminist/ punk informed critique of 'rockist' machismo (Hesmondhalgh, 1999, p. 38; Reynolds, 1990, p. 23). Indie guitar rock was a tightly bounded space/genre: on the one hand, one couldn't be too 'pop' or 'dance'; on the other hand, 'rock' was also at least initially loaded with negative connotations. The result was a music that was gesturally restricted: not obviously black or danceable or too macho and 'rock and roll' – few blues scales or phrases, little syncopation, relatively uniform in tone and texture, performed loudly but understatedly and without much individual expression. Guitars strum continuously to create an effect of drone or jangle, with a consequent masking of the vocal, which (along with the harmonies) derive from punk or 1960s pop. Lyrics (often inaudible) tend to be introspective, pessimistic, passive, sometimes ironic or apologetic. The image of the musician is often as anti-star – 'ordinary', modest. Recordings often sound cheap, with amateurish, childlike or obscure cover art. There is a tendency towards an aesthetic of mini-malism – 'less is more'. Some of the limits were in some cases pregiven: cheap guitars, primitive recordings and relatively amateur musicianship (especially singing), but equally there was a tendency to regard such 'limitations' as intrinsic to the genre, making a virtue of what was not always a necessity. This idea of pro-ducing an autonomous music whose freedom is constrained by the necessity of avoiding references to taboo genres is in some ways similar to Adorno's concep-tion of modern art music as a negation of society that achieves truth through denial of meaning and convention (Adorno, 1973, pp. 19–20, 34; Subotnik, 1976, p. 260). Adorno also says that this music will seem repetitive and barbarous to uneducated ears, alienated and void of emotional expression (1973, pp. 41–3, 49). These same qualities recur, I think, in most strains of 'alternative' music.

In terms of gender, clearly the struggle over pop and rock values, and the triumph of the latter, is significant. Rock's taken-for-granted oppositionality to straight society made it too powerful a symbol of difference to be ignored. Hence there was a slight return over time of rock machismo, not so much in performance personae, but rather in the way in which sound and themes became increasingly associated with violence and extremity – the increasing prominence of the fuzzbox, 'white noise', minimalist approach, marked most obviously in the USA by 'pigfucker' bands, in the UK by the 'shoegazers' and in New Zealand by 'noise' bands like SPUD, Bailter Space and Solid Gold Hell (Arnold, 1995, pp. 118–19; Azerrad, 2001, p. 366; Cavanagh, 2000, p. 315). If early indie's biggest bands were 'jangle pop' groups like R.E.M. and The Smiths, then their relative success made them and similar groups no longer 'indie' – in order to go on being different, the style had to go on remaining different from the mainstream. As the 1980s progressed, Flying Nun bands tended towards a slower, more hypnotic feel, increased use of the 'wall of guitars', more distortion, more aggression and a generally 'darker', gloomier, more 'rock' sound, contemporaneous with the increasing influence of groups like The Jesus and Mary Chain and Sonic Youth. The Jean-Paul Sartre Experience typify this progression, initially experimenting with pop and soul styles before set-tling into the classic indie mould (1987, 1990). Their career and musical develop-ment closely parallels stablemates Straitjacket Fits, with whom they often shared bills. Both developed a grandiose sound, with distorted guitars, much echo, obscure but threatening lyrics, anthemic choruses and generally slow tempos. Abstraction and grand gestures replaced immediacy and locality. This was also reflected in naming practices, which tended towards the acronyms characteristic of global cor-porations – indie itself was becoming a globalised phenomenon at this time. The Jean-Paul Sartre Experience later shortened their name to an acronym – JPS Experience – as did Flying Nun artists Not Really Anything (NRA) and SPUD. Some labels' corporate-type acronyms – SST, IRS – may have had similar connota-tions. The association of artists with faceless corporations and technology can also be read as indie masculinities linking with discourses of globalisation, technologi-cal mediation and abstraction of authority that are characteristic of modernity. Thus masculinities in this music are associated with the impersonality of modern life and the power invested in technology and corporations, a connection I will explore further at the end of Chapter 5. One has to consider to what degree the production of this extreme difference reproduces hegemonic gender values, in the same way that I would argue that the high culture avant-garde reproduces the reification of art and thereby reinforces dominant power structures.

Given indie's personnel, influences and characteristic tendency towards gestural restriction and aesthetic codification, I think there is a case to be made for reading indie in terms of homosociality, as constructing a mediated cultural space which depends on othering and objectifying a third party – the feminised mainstream. The tendency towards reading indie scenes as autonomous, independent and self-policing constructs them, in some significant way, as masculine. On the other hand, it would seem that in indie, masculinity is not performed in the same manner as in earlier rock traditions – it is not so directly performative or aggressive and homosociality, if it is important, is being articulated in other ways. So in the next chapter, I take a closer look at the possibilities and limitations of the homosocial model for understanding indie.

Notes

1. Alternatively it could be argued that guitars are being used in a new way in indie – as Steve Waksman (1999, pp. 3–13) points out, the guitar's centrality to discourses of rock makes it a key site for investigating ever-shifting articulations of power in relation to technology in popular music.
2. See also Thurston Moore's account (1992) of a Sonic Youth tour, originally printed in *Forced Exposure*.
3. Although these magazines had small audiences, the writers' and editors' influence was not limited to print: for example Cosloy, editor of *Conflict*, also ran Homestead Records, managed Deep Wound (precursors of Dinosaur Jr.) and is now co-owner of Matador Records, a leading US indie.
4. One can see this approach in other contemporary UK indies, for example the popular Cherry Red *Pillows and Prayers* compilation (1982), with its many 'Girl from Ipanema' retreads.
5. Flying Nun was also distributed (nominally) in the UK through the Cartel, an indie distribution network allied to Rough Trade.
6. The Clean recorded their first single, 'Tally Ho' for NZ$50; Nirvana their first album *Bleach* for US$603. The Minutemen recorded a double album *Double Nickels on the Dime* for US$1100 (Azerrad, 2001, p. 82).
7. Perhaps the pioneering punk guitar drone was Keith Levene on Public Image's eponymous first single. Drone features prominently in Spacemen 3 (UK), Hüsker Dü and the Jesus and Mary Chain, and reaches its apotheosis in Sonic Youth and My Bloody Valentine (Heylin, 1993, p. 7). Sonic Youth members played drone-based pieces with Glenn Branca, part of the same NY avant-garde scene as Young (Azerrad, 2001, p. 232).
8. 'Anything Could Happen' (The Clean, 1981); 'Flex' (Jean-Paul Sartre Experience, 1986), 'Dialling a Prayer' (Straitjacket Fits, 1987), 'PIT Song' and 'Husband House' (Sneaky Feelings, 1984, 1985).

9. 'Waiting for the Man', 'Heroin', 'Femme Fatale', 'There She Goes Again' (all 1967), 'Some Kinda Love' (1969), 'Sweet Jane' (1970), 'The Ocean' (1974). Such chord progressions also recur in Flying Nun: for example, 'Kaleidoscope World' (The Chills, 1986); 'Joed Out', 'CD Jimmy Jazz' (Verlaines, 1988); 'Quickstep' (The Clean, 1999).
10. 'Pink Frost' (The Chills, 1986) is like the *Z Cars* theme or 'Michael Row Your Boat'; 'Getting Older' (The Clean, 1983); 'Seven Chinese Brothers', 'Good Advices' (R.E.M., 1984, 1985).
11. 'Bigmouth Strikes Again' (The Smiths, 1987a); 'Harborcoat' (R.E.M., 1984).
12. Swing: The Chills, 'Kaleidoscope World' (1986, Bannister, 1999, p. 28); 6/8: Sneaky Feelings, 'Throwing Stones' (1984); Jean-Paul Sartre Experience, 'Flex' (1986); 5/4: Sneaky Feelings, 'Letter to You' (1987); 6/4; Verlaines, 'Burlesque' (1988); 10/4: The Go-Betweens, 'Cattle and Cane' (1983). The Clean's 'Tally Ho' (1981) is similar in approach to 'I'm Waiting for the Man' (The Velvet Underground, 1967).
13. 'Heroin' (The Velvet Underground, 1967); 'Quickstep' (The Clean, 1999); 'Pyromania' (Verlaines, 1988).
14. The Modern Lovers' punk/monadic approach influenced The Clean's rhythm section, with the bass and often kick drum playing 'four on the floor' – a continuous bass rhythm without breaks or syncopation, but with the snare falling on the third measure as usual (for example 'Roadrunner' (The Modern Lovers, 1976), also used by early R.E.M. (Buckley, 2002, p. 54).
15. 'As a producer, McGee knew only one trick: reverb' (Cavanagh, 2000, p. 275). In the 1960s, most reverb effects were generated mechanically with resonating plates or springs. Indie bands often favoured this over digital reverb.
16. Especially on their early LPs *Send Me a Lullaby* (1982) and *Before Hollywood* (1983).
17. For example, Michael Stipe. Hüsker Dü's 'New Day Rising' (1985), is, by indie standards, a vocal tour de force.
18. 'Looks like we're in this together, and it's a comforting thing / But it's not' ('Flex', Jean-Paul Sartre Experience, 1986); 'In the doledrums on the dole' ('Doledrums', The Chills, 1986).
19. 'Cattle and Cane' (The Go-Betweens, 1983); 'Camera', (R.E.M., 1984); 'Pyromania', 'Baud to Tears', (Verlaines, 1984); 'This Night Has Opened My Eyes', 'Girl Afraid' (The Smiths, 1987a).
20. The Verlaines' 'Baud to Tears' (Baudelaire), 'CD Jimmy Jazz and Me' (Claude Debussy, James Joyce), 'Death and the Maiden' (Verlaine and Rimbaud) (1988); 'The House that Jack Kerouac Built' (The Go-Betweens, 1987).
21. 'The Boy with the Perpetual Nervousness' (The Feelies, 1980) is an obvious influence on The Clean's 'Billy Two' (1981): 'Billy didn't have a lot to say; he never spoke at all'; 'Within Your Reach' (The Replacements, 1984); 'Freak Scene' (Dinosaur Jr., 1989).
22. In The Chills' 'Pink Frost' (1986), 'she' is not characterised except in terms of the possibility of her death, which is associated with the narrator's guilt: 'How can I live when you see what I've done? ... What will I do if she dies?'
23. Examples range from the sophisticated literary ironies and wit of Morrissey, to musical jokes like Dunedin band the Stones singing 'three blind mice' ('Gunner Ho', 1983), an absurdist approach that derives from punk.
24. See also Hüsker Dü, '59 Times the Pain' (1985); The Wedding Present, 'My Favourite Dress' (1987); The Smiths, 'Still Ill, 'Accept Yourself', 'You've Got Everything Now (1984b).

25. Ex-Straitjacket Fits member Andrew Brough formed Bike (from a Pink Floyd song by Syd Barrett, 1967). The Clean refer to Bob Dylan's 'Sad-eyed Lady of the Lowlands' (1966) on 'Sad-eyed Lady' (1981, 1998). Other Dylan references include The Go-Betweens' 'six white horses who turned electric' on 'That Way' (1983), referring to 'Absolutely Sweet Marie' (1966), and the Verlaines, 'Burlesque' (1984): 'built a fire on main street and shot it full of holes' refers to 'Stuck Inside of Mobile' (Dylan, 1966). Other references to 1960s icons include 'You said you liked the Rolling Stones, but the Beatles were better' ('Hold onto the Rail', The Clean, 1998; see also The House of Love's 'Beatles and the Stones', 1993).

26. Live covers included 'Femme Fatale' (The Velvet Underground, 1967), 'Career Opportunities' (The Clash, 1977) and 'You Can't Put Your Arms Around a Memory' (Johnny Thunders) by the Verlaines; 'Love Minus Zero (No Limit)' (Bob Dylan, 1965) and the James Bond theme by The Clean; 'Matthew and Son' (Cat Stevens) by The Chills; 'Different Drum' (the Stone Poneys, who featured Linda Ronstadt on lead vocals, 1974) by The Bats; 'Hang on Sloopy' (The McCoys, Nuggets) and 'Hey Joe' (Jimi Hendrix, 1968) by Sneaky Feelings; 'So Long Marianne' (Leonard Cohen, 1968) by Straitjacket Fits. Only the last has been released (Straitjacket Fits, 1988). Notably, all songs covered are sung by men in both versions, with the exception of 'Different Drum', sung by guitarist Kaye Woodward.

27. The Feelies and Dr Robert and The Velvets in Foggy Notion, R.E.M. and Hindu Love Gods (DeRogatis, 1996, pp. 151–3).

28. Hüsker Dü's covers included The Byrds' 'Eight Miles High' (1984), The Beatles' 'Ticket to Ride' (1986), Donovan's 'Sunshine Superman' (1983) and the Mary Tyler Moore theme, 'Love is All Around' (1985).

29. However, this does not mean that the bands were internally democratic – many centred around a main performer/songwriter – J Mascis (Dinosaur Jr.), Paul Westerberg (The Replacements), Martin Phillipps (The Chills), Graeme Downes (Verlaines), Kurt Cobain (Nirvana).

30. Hüsker Dü means 'do you remember?' in Norwegian, and apparently refers to a 1960s board game 'where the child can outwit the adult' (Azerrad, 2001, p. 161).

31. Flying Nun groups also identified themselves to some extent with 'junk culture'.

32. Mould is, of course, gay (not that you'd know it from listening to his music).

33. Christine Voice played keyboards in Snapper, but they didn't tour much. Only The Bats have had a full-time female guitarist throughout their career (Kaye Woodward). Sneaky Feelings had a female bass player until 1984 (Kat Tyrie). Look Blue Go Purple were the only well-known all-women group on Flying Nun. Women have managed a number of indie groups, however (Bannister 1999, p. 162; Cavanagh, 2000, p. 443).

34. Lee, of LA band Love, was not white, however.

Chapter 4

The singer or the song?
Homosociality, genre and gender

It is a critical orthodoxy that rock music and the discourses surrounding it are homosocial and homophobic (Arnold, 1995, pp. 163–5; Cohen, 1997, p. 34; Davies, 2001; Gaar, 1992, xii–xiii; Shuker, 1994, pp. 101–2). Musicians and audiences often regard femininity as dangerous and disruptive to the integrity or authenticity of music. This includes but is not exclusive to women appearing onstage – it is also articulated through the ways the musical and stylistic boundaries of the genre are defined and patrolled, and the need to maintain a distinction between the music and the ways it is received and used in the media or by audiences (Bayton, 1990). However, this tendency to reiterate the ways in which femininity is problematic in rock can lead towards a reification of rock as monolithic masculinity. Mary-Anne Clawson writes: 'Until recently, attention to gender issues [in rock music] has largely meant attention to the experience of woman musicians … However, such studies do not sufficiently problematise the "normality" of masculine musicianship, and thus fail to understand rock as a gendered activity' (Clawson, 1999, p. 99; see also Coates, 1997). Such studies may elide the ways in which masculinities and femininities are continuously under reconstruction in the maintenance of gender hegemony. 'For history to become organic to theory, social structure must be seen as constantly *constituted* rather than constantly reproduced … Groups that hold power do try to reproduce the structure … but it is always an open question whether … they will succeed' (Connell, 1987, p. 44). To assume the 'normality' or inevitability of rock as masculine/homosocial presents as a universal truth what is in fact an ongoing operation.

In this chapter I want to look more closely at male homosociality in rock, and especially indie. My contention is that homosociality is not, on its own, a sufficient model for understanding masculine hegemony in rock. The homosocial discourse, which depends on an idea of men as independent, autonomous and in control, is always in conflict with the idea of rock as a performance in which the male body itself becomes an object for the delectation (potentially homosexual) of others: 'the idea that men are masculine … because they possess the symbol of male power, the phallus, only works if it can guarantee that the phallus is not an object of male homosexual desire' (Easthope, 1986, p. 121). Such representations of masculinity include live performance, but also media.

It is the presence of an audience that 'feminises', and it is the continual job of masculinity is to make sure that it remains in control of representations and is able to readjust them to confirm masculine values. As such, this argument implicitly suggests that the indie ideals of autonomy and independence, defined through a limited musical style, as adumbrated in Chapter 3, are inherently masculinist, because they are based on the idea that it is possible to split off good (homosocial) from bad (feminine) musical practice. What I want to show is how these splits, characteristic of homosocial indie discourse, are continuously being maintained, but also that they are self-destructive – they are a key element in why so many male indie groups break up.

A related problem for rock masculinities in mass media is the idea of influence. By this I mean the idea that participation in mass media represents a potential compromise or sell-out – the music becomes influenced by outside forces; its artistic autonomy and purity are no longer guaranteed. This also includes the ways in which rock scenes were (are) represented as local, patrilineal and thus autonomous from the feminisation of mass media, and from influence by other music. The idea of influence is a threat to (masculine) originality and autonomy. Finally, I want to look at how this ongoing conflict is played out within bands – that is, how the presence of an audience, or women, highlights problems with homosocial bonds between men – specifically, the latent homosexuality and other suppressed emotions within male–male bonding, which, again, may cause problems within bands (Cohen, 2001).

Homosociality is a male-defined social hierarchy based around one's susceptibility to accusations of homosexuality. It engenders a split between male friendship and homosexuality: one is properly masculine, the other effeminate and taboo. Male homosocial and homosexuality exist on a continuum 'whose visibility, for men in our society, is radically disrupted' (Sedgwick, 1985, pp. 1–2). The maintenance of male identity is achieved through the continuous rejection of feminine possibilities (Easthope, 1986, p. 6). Sedgwick argues that such categorisations have meaning far beyond the 'special interest groups' with which they are normally identified: 'categories of gender ... can have a structuring force for nodes of thought, for axes of cultural discrimination, whose thematic subject isn't explicitly gendered at all' (1990, p. 34). Writing in the context of a 'newly virulent homophobia of the 1980s' (p. 38), the same time that indie rock was starting up, she states that: 'many of the major nodes of thought and knowledge in twentieth century western culture ... are structured ... by a chronic ... crisis of homo/heterosexual definition, indicatively male' (p. 1). The implication here is that homosociality is not just understood in explicit statements about 'faggots' but is more generally applicable to an implicitly gendered worldview that argues for the superiority of cultural work that is masculinised. In culture, this split is most often managed through Frankfurt School dichotomies between popular and high culture. This process was fairly explicit in US and NZ scenes, where punk/hardcore was the main paradigm of masculine authenticity, policed through personal interactions and media discourses (Arnold, 1995, p. 10; Azerrad, 2001, pp. 150, 314–15). In the UK the situation was a little more complex with regard to the gender model used, but the splits were still policed with ferocity. The greater prominence of media coverage in the UK scene provides a clue as to differences in the representation of masculinity. I will examine each scene in turn.

Southern California hardcore

The US hardcore scene presents us with an extreme example of homosociality. At the same time, most commentaries present it as a paradigm of authenticity for aspiring indie rockers (Arnold, 1995, p. 68; Azerrad, 2001, p. 14; Harrington, 2002, pp. 373–4). This authenticity was produced through its 'uncompromising' and extreme stances in areas such as production (setting up of indie networks, record labels, live circuits, 'econo' approach), musical and performance style (similar to punk), influence on other underground media (for example fanzines, artwork) and finally through 'straight edge' (total abstinence from drugs, alcohol and sometimes sex, mainly a feature of East Coast hardcore) (Azerrad, 2001, pp. 135–7). Homosociality and authenticity, therefore, are closely linked.

Black Flag was formed in 1978 by Greg Ginn of Hermosa Beach, California, a tall, quiet, geeky kid who eschewed surfing in favour of poetry and ham radio and found inspiration in punk rock and the Grateful Dead (Azerrad, 2001, pp. 15–16). According to Azerrad, Black Flag pioneered the indie ethic through the incessant touring that was instrumental to the setting up of an alternative venue circuit, through SST, the label the band founded, which became arguably the most influential US indie of the 1980s (and thereby the most influential label, period), and through their aggressive live shows, recordings, artworks and the fanzines they inspired. '[T]he band's selfless work ethic was a model for the decade ahead … [they were] among the first bands to suggest that if you didn't like the system, you should create one of your own' (Azerrad, 2001, p. 14). Of course, such a view depends on ignoring other early 1980s US scenes, such as LA's 'Paisley Underground' and Athens, Georgia, because they are seen as too commercial, middle class or feminine.

The US indie scene, and especially that around SST, was envisioned as embattled and difficult to sustain: 'a ground war strategy in an age of strategic nuclear forces' (Joe Carducci, quoted in Azerrad, 2001, p. 3). It lacked national media coverage and, unlike in the UK and New Zealand, going 'on the dole' was not an option for musicians: US indie bands were operating in a much more aggressive, individualistic and competitive society. Amateurism, in this sense, was not an option, and many hardcore bands seemed to have lived pretty much hand to mouth, hence the Minutemen's emphasis on 'jamming econo' – basically doing things as cheaply and efficiently as possible (Azerrad, 2001; pp. 41, 73–5). Total DIY self-reliance (releasing and manufacturing your own records, setting up your own tours, bussing and setting up your own equipment) was seen as a virtue. This was partly because music was not seen as a 'manly' lifestyle. Most indie musicians were 'serious nerds', routinely bullied by local jocks (police harassment of hard-core was also common) (Azerrad, 2001, pp. 64, 31). For example, D. Boon and Mike Watt of the Minutemen (from San Pedro, California) were amazed when surfer jock George Hurley joined their band. As Watt explained, 'for Georgie, a *popular* guy, to like punk was incredible. Everybody knew me and D. Boon were weirdos – when punk came, of course *those* assholes would be into it. But Georgie, he took blows for that' (Azerrad, 2001, p. 66).

Hence 'jamming econo' was also a performance of masculinity 'at work' that might gain musicians kudos from their masculine peer group in a way that music alone could not, for example setting up and breaking down equipment at live shows. According to Watt, 'That was a respect thing … You wanted to look like you knew what you were doing. Because guys were always giving you shit like you were assholes' (Azerrad, 2001, p. 74). But pressure towards masculine con-formity also came from within the music scene, especially given the band's affili-ation with SST. This manifested at a personal level (as when they toured with Black Flag) but also at the level of audience expectation – some saw the band's musical eclecticism as an unacceptable deviation from the hard, fast, heavy hard-core style (Azerrad, 2001, p. 76).

Clearly the aura of violence that surrounded hardcore did not encourage female participation (Azerrad, 2001, pp. 150–51). Greg Ginn's brother Raymond Pettibon's artwork for SST (on Black Flag records, for example) was consistently anti-women. Many hardcore and indie fanzines were openly misogynistic (Arnold, 1995, pp. 55, 164). Hardcore was also homophobic: one Pettibon Black Flag flyer depicted a cop with a gun jammed in his mouth, with the caption 'Make me come, faggot!' (Azerrad, 2001, p. 21). Obviously homosociality was also articulated at the level of style – the louder, faster, harder ethos of hardcore was expressed in terms of a lan-guage of aggression and extremity. But misogyny was and is a prominent feature of US society and culture, not just of hardcore (Arnold, 1995, p. 9). Hardcore misogyny has to be seen in its social context, for example in relation to other uses of the term, such as pornography. A theorisation of gender highlights the contradic-tions inherent in hardcore's extreme stance in terms of continuities with the domi-nant culture – in the US case, specifically the Rambo-isation of popular culture, and its reproduction of neo-liberalist ideologies of individual freedom and auton-omy: 'dependency is weakness' (Rollins, quoted in Collins, 2000). Self-control and para-military organisation were central to Black Flag – Ginn had 'a monster work ethic' (Azerrad, 2001, p. 31) – the band routinely practised several hours a day, most days of the week, drilled by Ginn. As Rollins ironically notes: 'There was never any anarchy in our lifestyle' (Azerrad, 2001, p. 38). On tour, Ginn 'took the business down to a level that was beneath the level lightweights could handle: they couldn't handle sleeping in the van, they couldn't handle not knowing where they were going to stay … on the road the band got $5 a day' (Carducci, quoted in Azerrad, 2001, p. 40). Ginn remarks: 'I think people would consider it rough but that's all relative – there's things I would consider rough, like war' (2001, p. 42).

Hardcore authenticity was a highly gendered discourse that attempted to produce a music/lifestyle that was not only perceived as autonomous and independent from the dominant culture, but also minimised all influence – musical, emotional, social – tending towards a ideal (and hence unachievable) purity or singularity. It is this attempted autonomy from influence that I believe is hardcore's most distinctively masculine characteristic. Of course, hardcore had its own set of influences – namely punk rock. But it was less than open about acknowledging them: 'There was a quantum difference between early punk and hardcore – it was something like the difference between bebop and hard bop in jazz, or the leap from Chuck Berry … to Jimi Hendrix' (Azerrad, 2001, p. 130; see also Harrington, 2002, pp. 373–4). This judgment is, to put it mildly, an exaggeration, on the basis of the recorded evidence. Minor Threat ('the Beatles of hardcore' (Arnold, 1995, p. 68)) certainly sped up the music, but the effect (on record, at any rate) is slightly comical (Minor Threat, 1989). Black Flag weren't musically innovative at all: their early material (on which their reputation seems to be based) sounds rather like generic UK punk (Black Flag, 1979, 1980, 1981). In this light, Ginn's statement that his main connection with punk was 'as a place where anyone could go who didn't fit in the conventional rock mode' seems somewhat disingenuous (Azerrad, 2001, p. 16). Black Flag may have been of huge institutional importance, have done the touring groundwork and been instrumental in setting up networks. But on record, they're no great shakes.

Acknowledging diversity of influence in hardcore parlance came close to selling out – both Black Flag and Minor Threat broke up over issues of commercialism (Azerrad, 2001, pp. 58–9, 154–5). This dynamic between masculine hardcore purity and autonomy on the one hand, and a 'softer', more commercial approach on the other, was also played out in bands like The Replacements, whose early records (for example *Hootenanny*, *Let it Be*) oscillate between quasi-hardcore such as 'Run It' and 'Gary's Got a Boner' and more sensitive, introspective material such as 'Unsatisfied' and 'Within Your Reach'. The latter song was included on *Hootenanny* despite the objections of other band members that it wasn't 'rock'n'roll' enough (Azerrad, 2001, p. 210). Grant Hart (Hüsker Dü) explained: 'I found the hardcore thing very limiting … it was just … "let's jump into a more stringent set of rules than what we're supposed to be rebelling against." I've never enjoyed that macho, "Here are the rules, here's how you conform" stuff' (Klein, 2002, p. 132). Although hardcore was hugely influential, many musicians found it simply too limiting or too masculine to emulate. Lou Barlow commented: 'I loved hardcore, but I felt like I wasn't powerful enough and didn't have enough of an edge to really make it' (Azerrad, 2001, p. 350). This meant moving away from the 'purity' of hardcore towards diversity (relatively speaking).[1]

Straight edge

The clearest articulation of the association of hardcore purity and autonomy was through the philosophy of straight edge. To put this in a historical context, some punk/indie scenes used 'straightness' (that is, not being on drugs) as a way of articulating their difference from hippy excess. Jerry Harrison (later of Talking Heads) played in Richman's band The Modern Lovers: 'We were all anti-drugs … we'd go onstage and start our sets with this number called "I'm Straight", which would immediately cause the audience to start throwing things – rotten fruit, bottles, cans, anything – at us' (Gans, 1985, p. 44). Likewise, for Alan Horne (Postcard), 'the thinking we had … was based on a lot of punk and Jonathan Richman ideas, we had an antidrug stance' (quoted in Nichols, 2003, p. 90).

This stance was developed furthest in the Washington DC scene based around Minor Threat. Band leader Ian MacKaye pioneered the 'straight edge' stance, apparently partly inspired by the fact that 1970s hard rocker Ted Nugent didn't do drugs (Azerrad, 2001, p. 121). By 1981 they had released their first record, an untitled EP, on their own label, Dischord. MacKaye then wrote 'a forty-six second outburst' called 'Straight Edge' which advocated abstention from casual sex, drugs and alcohol (Azerrad, 2001, p. 136). This was to some extent making a virtue out of necessity, since most DC punks were underage and could not enter licensed venues (hence 'Minor' Threat). However, for MacKaye, it was about taking control of one's life: 'Try to find out a little more entertainment from your own resources. As opposed to … buying it' (Azerrad, 2001, p. 137). But it also caused some to accuse the band of puritanism (p. 139). The question of how much MacKaye's stance was also the band's was contentious – leading to a dispute over the lyrics of 'Out of Step' which declared 'don't drink; don't smoke; don't fuck'. Band member Jeff Nelson insisted on inserting the word 'I' before each imperative, thereby distancing himself from the statements; however, on the Minor Threat compilation *Complete Discography* lyric sheet, most of the 'I's have disappeared (p. 140). Other bands took the straight edge stance as a 'set of rules', although MacKaye claimed that he never intended it to become an orthodoxy – he just wanted kids to think for themselves (p. 140). This paradox, of deviation becoming dogma, is clearly a recurrent problem in alternative scenes, and seems to connect to the way in which many aspects of hardcore seem to reproduce patriarchal values.

Keightley (2001, p. 124) suggests that the 1960s concept of rock as youth music is continued in alternative rock's reification of naivety, purity and amateurism. Taken to an extreme, as in 'straight edge', this discourse became a rejection of all forms of rock 'excess' apart from the music itself, and violence. This in turn might be seen as one way in which indie rearticulated rock authenticity away from 'black roots', by rejecting bodily indulgence and replacing it with physical discipline and punishment.

In the same way, albeit in a less extreme fashion, the punk/DIY ethos of NZ indie produced an ideology of Dunedin music as autonomous – a music generated by boredom, isolation and the desire to 'just do it' (McLeay, 1994, p. 39; Robertson, 1991, p. 9; Shuker, 1998, pp. 103–4). Accordingly, influence was often invoked in evaluation of bands like Sneaky Feelings. This is not quite as simple as saying that our influences were more obvious than others, because 'obviousness' is itself ideologically loaded. Rather it means that there was a canon of acceptable influences that were taken as self-evident and were not much discussed. Influences that came from outside the square were more likely to attract comment. In the case of the Dunedin Sound, the influence of punk, The Velvet Underground, garage rock and early Pink Floyd (in the case of The Chills) was 'self-evident'. More mainstream influences were likely to be commented on, however: 'Sneaky Feelings have always admitted and even coveted the 1960s tag and the big studio has allowed them to fulfil ringing guitar fantasies. At times you could swear you were listening to the Byrds. The effectiveness is undeniable but … I hope for their sakes the next album doesn't sound the same. Get the picture?' (Brown, 1984a). 'One of the Dunedin Band's [sic] influences are more than just on their sleeves with this song … Wind this one up and WALLOW in it' (Colbert, 1985). Denial of influence was a way of reproducing the autonomy of the local scene through rejection of a 'feminised' nostalgia.

Chris Knox has had a huge influence on local rock discourses in New Zealand (partly because the limited media coverage of the scene meant that a few people had a lot of influence). As leader of Dunedin's 'original' punk band, The Enemy, one of the 'founding fathers' of Flying Nun, effectively running the Auckland end of the operation for several years, and as a casual journalist and commentator, he was in an influential position, able to shape the ideology of a label, sometimes by bullying the bands involved (Bannister, 1999, p. 102):

> I did get reasonably well known for sort of drunkenly and stonedly going up to bands and saying 'aw for chrissakes you gotta stop playing that song, that song and that song, and you gotta get rid of that bloody bass player.' I'd like to think I was the Jiminy Cricket, sort of conscience on the back of the Pinocchio that was Flying Nun. I tried to keep things pure. (Chris Knox, quoted in *Heavenly Pop Hits*, 2002)

Sneaky Feelings was definitely the most 'pop' band on Flying Nun, and therefore the most ideologically suspect to Knox, who frequently badgered us about our musical direction and once remarked to me that one of our records was 'wimpy crap' (*Heavenly Pop Hits*, 2002; Bannister, 1999, pp. 67–8, 84, 100, 160–61). Effectively, he and other 'gatekeepers' to the local music scene were performing a kind of homosocial 'policing', checking that bands stayed true to the true spirit of punk.[2] Knox and his cohorts also produced a patrilineage: 'There is a lineage in Dunedin rock, a sacred torch – with an aromatic smell – that is passed down from "father to son", belying the parricidal reputation of some of its practitioners. The line starts with Chris Knox and the Enemy, who begat the Clean, who begat the Chills' (Bannister, 1999, p. 27). In local scenes, this sense of patrilineage acts to minimise outside influence, by implying that the essential creative spirit is transmitted exclusively from 'father to son'. We also see this in US hardcore:

> It would be easy to christen *Our Band Could Be Your Life* as an 'indie-rock Bible':
> The egocentric Greg Ginn and his narcissistic protégé Henry Rollins would probably
> love to be painted as God and Jesus Christ, respectively; Ian Mackaye [*sic*] would be
> Moses, bearing the tablets of stone declaring what ethics should be embodied (his
> 'straight-edge' followers of today are to some degree just as ludicrous as fundamen-
> talist Christians); and the Butthole Surfers would be the infidels that rule Sodom,
> eventually playing Judas by signing with Capitol Records and suing their former
> indie allies Touch & Go Records. (Finn, Cohen, 2001)

Such approaches are similar to rock canonism more generally: 'Without Hank Williams and Arthur Crudup, there would be no Elvis Presley; without Little Richard and James Brown, no Prince; without Chuck Berry, Buddy Holly and Lonnie Donegan, no Beatles' (Dafydd and Crampton, 1996, p. 4). But one might expect alternative rock to be a little more reflexive in its relation to rock tradition.

UK indie and homosociality

In UK indie scenes, punk did not have quite the same undisputed precedence that it enjoyed in the USA and New Zealand, and indie scenes were arguably less openly macho. Influences were more self-consciously displayed, and rockism militated to some degree against hardcore displays of misogyny. Labels like Cherry Red and Rough Trade promoted a generally gentler, more PC approach than in the USA and New Zealand (Cavanagh, 2000, p. 91; Nichols, 2003, p. 119). UK indie was also more androgynous in its performance styles (the glam rock tradition) (Cavanagh, 2000, pp. 24–5, 190; Frith and Horne, 1987, p. 178; Reynolds, 1989). The lack of overt homosociality in the UK scenes as compared with the USA and New Zealand may be partly attributable to the national culture – gender is subordinate to social class in the UK context. However, boundaries were still patrolled; for example, Postcard Records' Alan Horne was especially critical of the contemporary UK alternative scene. Postcard's elitism more obviously related to distinctions of social class than gender, for example in the way they despised 'dope-smoking hippies'. At the same time, women were notably absent (Cavanagh, 2000, pp. 34–7; Nichols, 2003, p. 90).

Another major factor was that UK scenes were not as isolated as those in the USA and New Zealand – oppositions between mainstream and alternative, while ideologically significant, were not as absolute. The relative abundance of national media coverage made recognition or even crossing over into the pop charts a real possibility – hence the idea of a local, pure, autonomous scene evolving out of the media spotlight, untrammelled by attachments to influence, didn't really make sense (unless, of course it came from outside the UK, as with grunge, discussed in

Chapter 1). Conversely, the lack of favourable or mainstream media coverage of hardcore helped preserve its sense of its exclusivity and purity. This is to suggest, then, a reverse correlation between homosociality and media coverage, or that masculinity is problematised by the insertion of an audience.

This was not a new problem: Simon Frith and Howard Horne suggest that since the early 1970s 'what [male] rock stars were up against was the sexualisation of consumption – *they* were the objects of desire ... the only way to maintain some sense of control was to take charge of this process, to serve oneself up as fantasy ... to disrupt the behaviour assumptions of natural sexuality' (Frith and Horne, 1987, p. 154). The problem with this approach was that 'once pop stars began exploring the semiology of glamour, then women could employ their superior experience and expertise' (Frith and Horne, 1987, p. 155). Bowie may have led the way, but it was Madonna who cashed in. If 'by the 1980s even "raunchiness" was clearly a pose' (Frith and Horne, 1987, p. 154), then how could a real sense of authentic masculinity be affirmed? 'Stars are involved in making themselves into commodities; they are both labour and the thing that labour produces' (Dyer, 1986, p. 5). The commodification and feminisation of the star was deeply troubling for many male rock performers, as it was for the whole indie ideology of independence. The idea of the star as commodity is anathema to the traditional masculine split between the artist and his art. Did indie react against masculine commodification by creating an anti-style subculture? What this tends to suggest is that traditional male homosociality is problematised by media. The increasing commodification of the male body runs against traditional gender roles. But it's also clearly part of rock's cultural legacy. To understand this problem (for masculinities), I will introduce two further concepts – that of 'the gaze' and that of homosociality as a system of kinship.

Kinship and the male gaze

Gayle Rubin and Eve Kosofsky Sedgwick offer a feminist reinterpretation of Levi-Strauss's theorisation of kinship as a triangular (Oedipal) structure by which male–male bonding is valorised as long as it is mediated through a third party, archetypally a woman (Rubin, 1975 pp. 169–82; Sedgwick, 1985). Sedgwick argues that 'our intellectual tradition schematises erotic relations' in terms of this triangular structure: 'two males are rivals for a female' (1985, p. 21). Conventionally we think of rivalry (between men) and love (for women) as mutually exclusive, but according to Sedgwick, 'the bonds of "rivalry" and "love" ... are equally powerful and in many senses equivalent' (1985, p. 21). That is, the socially acceptable goal of a woman acts to disavow the potentially erotic relationship between the men – they sublimate their desire for each other, and project it onto the woman instead. The woman becomes an object of exchange – the '"conduit of a relationship" in which the true *partner* is a man' (1985, p. 26; see also Levi-Strauss, 1969,

p. 115). This mediation through a third party avoids the possibility that the men might desire each other and directs desire down more socially 'useful' channels. Freud argued that 'the successful repression of homosexual desire in men … formed the basis for male bonding upon which human culture [and, he might have added, male dominance] is built' (Segal, 1990, p. 159). Male–male desire can be sublimated and mediated through social structures: 'Desexualised, sublimated love for other men becomes available to form the male bond, enabling men to work together for each other' (Easthope, 1986, p. 15).

The third party in this male–male relation does not have to be a woman, it could be a common goal, such as playing music: 'there is a special relation between male homosocial (including homosexual) desire and the structures of maintaining and transmitting patriarchal power' (Sedgwick, 1985, p. 25). Many forms of masculine association are goal-directed – work, sport, a common activity (for example a rock band). As such we could say they are primarily instrumental, and that the subjectivity of the members tends to be subjugated to the common goal. Indeed process-oriented subjective 'caring and sharing' is usually described as 'woman's work' and could be seen as actually impeding the achievement of a goal. Those displaying too much subjectivity or otherness may be stigmatised by the rest of the group for their latent homosexuality.

The second point is that kinship is based around the male gaze – men look at and objectify women. In this way they confirm their own power, and also police other men, constantly nullifying the possibility that they could become the subject of each other's erotic gaze. The maintenance of homosocial solidarity is dependent on control of the gaze. 'Woman … stands in patriarchal culture as a signifier for the male other, bound by a symbolic order in which man can live out his fantasies … through linguistic command by imposing them on the silent image of woman … as bearer, not maker of meaning' (Mulvey, 1989, p. 15).

However, the presence of an audience throws the homosocial model into disarray, because the men become objects. I have already suggested how the gaze is central to the sexual politics of musical performance (Green, 1997, pp. 22–6; Mulvey, 1989, p. 20). The extreme example is the singer, whose body is highlighted to a greater extent than other performers; more generally, the emergence of a natural 'frontman' or 'star' highlights that person in a way that can cause problems within the group. This gives them some power and consequently often causes resentment. The star's bond with the audience can be seen as a betrayal of his male solidarity with the group: 'In the politics of a band, a singer without an instrument is essentially unarmed and outnumbered, and must turn his back to the players at the precise moment their resentments are made concrete by the live audiences' (Carducci, 1992, p. 127). Carducci's remark is clearly relevant to Black Flag (given Carducci's close relationship to SST and the band).

Male singers are often criticised, especially by more 'hardcore' or alternative elements who may feel the singer's visibility and accessibility, in short his position as a 'star', equate too closely to selling out. Carducci argues that the singer (implicitly Rollins) is compromised by his position: 'when the sex groupies and the mind groupies line up after gigs in front of the singer it tends to turn off the players who may have written the music and in any case played it' (1992, p. 127). The singer occupies a more sexualised position than the other musicians. According to Carducci, this threatens the homosocial solidarity of the group onstage: 'when musicians let their payoffs slip from musical ones to those supplied by the audience they are in trouble' (1992, p. 127). Clearly Carducci is referring here to groupies, and in his view sex and music are incompatible, an equation that goes back to classical music (see Chapter 2). The body of the singer, because it may be sexually desirable, is incompatible with the 'pure' response to music that most Western theories of aesthetics demand, including punk. 'Everyone knew that singers were prats and showoffs, like Mick Jagger and Bob Geldof. Singers had to jump around and put on a show' (Bannister, 1999, p. 20). In indie music, the very performativity of the singer was at odds with the authentic 'ordinariness' of the band. Extroverted performance combined with a vulnerability to the gaze immediately suggested 'sell-out'.

For example, Rollins's increasing visibility during his tenure with Black Flag as singer, media representative and in his own solo career as a performance poet, clearly raised a few eyebrows at SST. It was felt that being in the band wasn't enough for him and that he also wanted to be a 'star' (Azerrad, 2001, p. 48). The band's confrontational stance meant that Rollins was also the centre of negative attention – he was typically the one who bore the brunt of the audience's ire. None of the other band members either attracted or dispensed such violence. 'I think Henry, his ego, in a way, brought some of that stuff across,' says Ginn. 'At some times he had a condescending attitude towards the audience, and people pick up on that' (Azerrad, 2001, p. 46). The dynamic between guitarist, leader, songwriter Greg Ginn and Rollins was fundamental to the band. Ginn, 'the strong, silent' type provided the musical framework, but Rollins provided the performative aspect: Many of the band's songs can be read in terms of this intra-band relationship: '"I conceal my feelings so I won't have to explain/What I can't explain anyway,"' Rollins hollers on "Can't Decide". Ginn's lyrics certainly applied to their aloof author, but it was Rollins who was acting them out' (Azerrad, 2001, p. 47). Ginn's strong silent persona and status as chief taskmaster suggest a classic homosociality – Rollins's 'acting out' caused him to be seen as potentially compromised.

Equally the 'star' in turn may become conscious that his role is emasculating – he has become, for the audience, an object of desire. As the audience's primary point of identification, he may find that his very life has become other people's property. A lot of men are uncomfortable with this kind of attention – certainly it gets you more sex, but it also risks losing the respect of your masculine peer group. Male singers like Morrissey and Michael Stipe are continually forced to remind the audience that their 'real' self is not available for public scrutiny: 'I'm not about to split myself open, gut myself on stage and spill myself all over people' (Stipe, quoted in Gray, 1993, p. 61; see also Buckley, 2002, p. 27). Morrissey has strenuously resisted attempts to reveal the 'real' Morrissey, and remarked of unauthorised biographer Johnny Rogan: 'I hope [he] ends his days soon in an M3 pile-up' (Rogan, 1992, p. 1).

In Sneaky Feelings, David Pine was the most socially attuned, outgoing and charismatic member of the group. His relatively conservative (boys' school) background meant he was well versed in the performance of hegemonic Kiwi bloke masculinity (James and Saville-Smith, 1994; Philips, 1987). This was both an advantage (it facilitated dealings with third parties) and a disadvantage (real 'blokes' are not expressive). Sneaky Feelings' reputation was made on our first album *Send You* (1984), a record written and sung mostly by David. Songs like 'Throwing Stones', 'Won't Change' and 'PIT Song' had an emotional and almost confessional directness, which, combined with touches of Dylanesque spite, proved quite popular. Effectively it made David into a bit of a local star, but he did not feel comfortable in this role. Especially I think he regretted being so candid – it made him vulnerable, as if his inner feelings were now public property. Subsequently he moved towards modes of lyric writing that were more indirect or dramatic ('Trouble with Kay', 1987).

There is a parallel here with Grant McLennan of The Go-Betweens, who also found that being an indie pop star put his personal life under the microscope in a way that he didn't enjoy. Accordingly he denounced attempts to interpret his writing personally, claiming that his musical output was merely a craftsmanlike approach to 'classic' songwriting (Nichols, 2003, p. 160). However, many of his songs ('Cattle and Cane', 'Dusty in Here', 1983) certainly invite an autobiographical reading, leading band biographer David Nichols to observe: 'few writers try so fervently to cover their tracks at the same time as they produce such transparently personal material' (2003, p. 162). Why? Nichols surmises that 'the image he projected ... laid him open to ridicule from the particularly masculine men whose company he often sought' (p. 160). In the same way David must have felt, even more keenly than the rest of us, shame and embarrassment when we were derided as wimpy 'pop' wannabes, that our music 'lacked drive', energy or radicalism (Bannister, 1999, p. 188; Churton, 2000, p. 228).

Moreover, the public aspect of band performance often intersects with internal band relations in quite complex ways. Theories of kinship posit that same-sex desire between men is sublimated into pursuit of a common goal or common desire. But this repression is rarely complete – desire and identification, distinct in Freud, are usually both present in human relationships, and arguably especially so in fan/star relationships, whose fantasy content means that that the usual binaries do not have to be respected (Zanes, 2002, pp. 299–301). The band is not a purely instrumental unit; they are also each other's audience – they gaze at each other, they recognise 'star' quality – and this questions the absolute disjunction between band and audience, music and sex, masculinity and femininity that recurs in rock discourse (S. Cohen, 2001, pp. 230–31).

The typical means by which rock discourse copes with this contradiction is by splitting the objective and subjective so that the former is entirely the property of the band and the latter is entirely the audience, or world. Hence the recurrent elegiac mode of the rock bio, which typically mourns the loss of original purity as the band is increasingly invaded and destroyed by feminised outside forces (women, drugs, commerce). But these outside forces are usually latent within the band itself – the presence of the gaze of the media simply exacerbates them, as it highlights the subjective interactions which are disavowed in the homosocial model.

Many rock groups form around a 'partnership' of young men, 'joining forces' usually with a common goal in view – playing music, becoming 'stars' (Clawson, 1999, pp. 106–8). But it is also an emotional relationship, or friendship, often with an intensity that gives it some homosexual undertones, for example Lou Barlow and J Mascis in Dinosaur Jr. (Azerrad, 2001, p. 349), Grant McLennan and Robert Forster in The Go-Betweens (Nichols, 2003, pp. 39–40) and myself and David in Sneaky Feelings (Bannister, 1999, p. 11). Arguably any intense relationship between two men that involves them withdrawing from the public domain and spending time together in private is likely to be interpreted in this way. Sooner or later, one of them gets a 'serious' girlfriend and this often causes (or perhaps more accurately highlights) emotional tensions that were present (but usually not acknowledged) between the men. The homosocial tradition of male solidarity in rock dictates that emotional relationships are the province of women – who are usually seen as the troublemakers, threatening to split the bonds between men (Yoko and Linda and The Beatles, Anita Pallenberg and the Stones). Women musicians are apt to be treated in the same way, especially if they enter into a sexual relationship with one of the other band members.

Women in indie bands

As I've already said, most indic guitar bands were male, so women, where present, were always in a minority (for example Sneaky Feelings, The Go-Betweens, Sonic Youth, the Pixies and the Verlaines). Moreover, they usually played bass or drums, not guitar. This often meant that they were not perceived as being central to the group in the way that guitarists usually are (for example in terms of songwriting). However, often these women's stories and perspectives highlight a 'normative' homosociality that is otherwise hidden, taken for granted or occasionally romanticised. In the Pixies, the marginalisation of Kim Deal's songwriting by Frank Black led to the band splitting ('History of the Pixies', 2004; Peters, 2002–2005). Jane Dodd left the Verlaines because she got fed up with being told what to play. Gina Roessler was forced to leave Black Flag partly as a result of the band objecting to her wearing feminine clothing in performance (Azerrad, 2001, p. 56).

Many indie women musicians had a background in feminism or activism and were inspired by punk rock: Kathryn Tyrie (Sneaky Feelings) used to say that she really wanted to be a terrorist, but compromised on a rock band. Lindy Morrison was looking for an all-woman band, but she found The Go-Betweens' somewhat indeterminate sexuality an acceptable compromise: 'Robert ... didn't know if he was Arthur or Martha' (Nichols, 2003, p. 97). She in turn 'was not the kind of "woman drummer" the two ... had in mind when they would try to pick up women at dances with the winning line: "Uh ... you don't play *drums*, do you ...?" She was not likely to fall in with their flights of fancy involving Warhol-style clubs with girls in fishnet stockings on trapezes, nor to have the respect they did for a more traditional sexist like Bob Dylan' (p. 96). In other words, there were obvious tensions in most mixed-sex indie groups between men and women, because of differences around questions like canonism, musical style and perception of gender roles. Also as isolated women, female musicians did not have recourse to the type of group solidarity available to men, and this would tend to make them, for want of a better word, 'stroppy' (S. Cohen, 2001, p. 239).

Sneaky Feelings were formed around an alliance between two groups – myself and David, and Martin, Max and Kathryn (who were initially looking for other women members, and were perhaps hoping to form a more political punk group). About a year later, Kathryn and I started a sexual relationship, which for me was partly compensation for the fact that David had a girlfriend and hence had less time for me. David and Kathryn did not particularly like each other, and probably my relationship with her exacerbated this dislike. The Go-Betweens experienced a similar dynamic, with Forster and drummer Lindy Morrison's relationship 'disrupting' Forster and McLennan's relationship. Morrison: 'He (McLennan) actually said in front of me ... "it was all so easy when it was just the two of us, Robert, and now it's so hard that there's three" ... I was of so little value to him that he would say things like that in front of me' (Nichols, 2003, p. 100).

According to Nichols (2003, pp. 79–82), Morrison became sexually involved with Robert Forster about a year after she joined. Morrison stayed in The Go-Betweens to the end (despite breaking up with Forster) – however, when the group reunited in the late 1990s, Morrison was not included, which caused her great distress (Nichols, 2003, p. 252). Kathryn was kicked out of Sneaky Feelings in early 1984, mainly because after our relationship ended she became increasingly unreliable (Bannister, 1999, p. 88). We got some criticism for this from the feminist community – on one occasion a female student radio DJ quizzed me on-air on the subject. Martin, who was also present, contributed a flip comment to the effect that Kat and I had an 'Ike and Tina'-type relationship. I was furious – I may have neglected Kathryn, but I never hit her – but the broader point is that Martin, who was probably trying to 'mythologise' our relationship, inadvertently revealed the inherent sexism of the rock context.

To reflect on the episode in a slightly more theoretical fashion, Kathryn (intentionally I think) broke a homosocial code of playing in bands – she let her feelings affect her performance and intra-band interactions. If she felt bad, her playing and general attitude expressed that. For David and me, personal feelings were something that had to be put aside in the performance context (or anywhere else). Psychoanalytically speaking, our feelings were sublimated into the production of a band performance – a collective enterprise that was 'bigger than both of us'. I don't think my relationship with David ever quite recovered, but this was not really to do with Kathryn – indeed arguably one of the reasons I went out with her was that she was committed to me in a way that David was not. She made me more aware of the differences within the group.

Sneaky Feelings were not an emotionally attuned band. For example, our manager carried on a homosexual relationship with another group member for two years without Martin or I realising it. We got on well on a musical level – but there was a lot of personal stuff that bubbled under, which eventually broke up the band. One of the ways it came out was in the form of songs we wrote about each other: I wrote 'Not to Take Sides' (1984) about the increasing alienation I felt in my relationship with David. David in turn wrote a rather bitter song about me – 'Now' (1987) – which masqueraded as a lover's farewell (again, that gender ambiguity). It seems rather odd, this displacement of emotions into songs, this communication by proxy, but I don't think it is atypical. For example, it's not difficult to read Lou Barlow and J Mascis's relationship in the songs they wrote, especially after Barlow left the band and formed Sebadoh, for example 'Asshole' (Azerrad, 2001, p. 373).[3]

Dinosaur Jr. – you're living all over me

US indie rockers Dinosaur Jr. provide an interesting case study in terms of the intra-band relationships (or lack of the same) between 'frontman' J Mascis and the rest of the band. Mascis has often been represented as a classic indie 'anti-star': an 'idiot savant', whose musical ability is complemented by an almost total lack of social skills, as a 'slacker' poster-boy – culturally knowledgeable, socially oblivious and emblematic of the 'GenX' sensibility (Azerrad, 2001, pp. 366, 370). Mascis's 'weird' behaviour always worked as a way of getting himself noticed, even at the University of Massachusetts (Amherst) school cafeteria: 'J would walk over to the table carrying this mountainous plate of food and proceed to sit there and not even really eat it – he'd just begin to organize it in different patterns and shapes,' says (Gerard) Cosloy, '… it was hard not to be impressed. You just sort of knew you were dealing with a visionary' (quoted in Azerrad, 2001, p. 350). This perception of Mascis as a countercultural anti-hero is confirmed by bandmate Lou Barlow's first impressions: 'He'd cut pieces of hair out of his head – there were bald spots in his hair. He had dandruff and he had sleepy stuff in his eyes. Everything "sucked" which was, like, amazing. I was like "Oh my God, he's *too cool*"' (Azerrad, 2001, p. 348).

But Mascis could not handle Barlow's idolatry, and Barlow in turn became convinced that Mascis's distancing was related to homophobia (Azerrad, 2001, pp. 363–4). 'Barlow felt bandmates should be close friends but Mascis was utterly uninterested in that kind of intimacy.' Barlow commented: 'I realized there was no way I'd know what was going on in his head … He's a really, really, really uptight person, but he comes off the whole time as being really mellow' (p. 359). Hence Barlow began Sebadoh so he could write songs without having to involve Mascis.

Rather than assert themselves, the other members of Dinosaur became more and more passive. Barlow became a 'silent partner' – he played J's songs, but did not contribute, becoming 'super passive-aggressive'. 'We both did that a lot,' says [drummer] Murph, 'but that causes tension' (Azerrad, 2001, p. 360). However, Mascis's insularity was getting to him as well: 'if he saw somebody socially having fun … he would probably try to put a damper on it … that was the major part of it, J being such a control freak and just not letting up' (p. 360). This control extended to Mascis writing the others' parts, which naturally caused resentment. Barlow recalled: 'I just totally took this martyr role … OK you don't like me, well, I'll just try to be as inconspicuous as possible' (p. 364). This soon extended to also doing more of the work – breaking down the equipment after shows, driving the van and so on. Barlow's perspective is confirmed by Mascis, who contrasts Barlow's early biddability with his later assertiveness: 'He didn't really talk until he got his girlfriend … and somehow that jump-started his ego, and he went from "I am Lou, I am nothing" to "I am the greatest." He … just flipped the scales' (p. 371).

Mascis's perspective on the band's internal problems inadvertently reveals the extent of his own disengagement. Repeatedly he casts himself in the role of observer rather than participant, describing other members' tantrums and personal quirks. 'I can see Lou getting beat up at high school a lot' (p. 348); 'Murph and Lou would fight a lot … which was hilarious' (p. 362). This tendency culminates in a sleepwalking episode while the band are on tour in Holland in 1988: 'I just remember Murph sleepwalking, getting up like some primitive animal … going at Lou like he was going to kill him … I was thinking "Either Murph's going to wake up or he's going to kill Lou". And I was waiting to see what happened' (pp. 369–70). Mascis's role in these little dramas is as a 'sadistic voyeur' whose displaced emotions are acted out by the people around him (like Warhol). In turn, Mascis's own narcissism would have been fortified by his own increasing presence and power in the media as the 'star'.

Tensions came to a head at a show in Naugatuck, Connecticut in 1988, when a newly assertive Barlow started 'messing' with the songs. Mascis recalled: 'And I'm playing and I'm like, "I think Murph's going to beat up Lou" and it goes on a bit more and I'm thinking, "Yup this is going to be bad, Murph's going to beat up Lou".' Rather than acknowledge that he's angry, he projects his feelings on to other people. However, in this case it doesn't work. 'Finally I think, "Huh, I guess

Murph's not going to beat up Lou. I guess I'll have to do it"' (p. 371). Mascis attempted to hit Barlow with his guitar, and then walked offstage yelling 'I can't take it!' 'Barlow called after him, "Can't take *what*, J? Asshole!" and raised his fists in triumph … "I felt like he'd proved to me that he actually had feelings"' (p. 372). Not surprisingly, Barlow and Dinosaur parted ways soon after (in a typically messy fashion; see Azerrad, 2001, p. 372). Barlow subsequently enjoyed some success with Sebadoh. Dinosaur Jr. ended up as basically a Mascis plus sidemen project.

Mascis's musical and artistic ability and reputation, combined with his habitual mode of passive disengagement, his 'negative charisma', wreaked havoc on intra-band relationships. Interestingly, this maladjustment cannot be attributed (directly) to drugs, because Mascis was at the time 'straight edge'. What interests me is the development of a sadistic/masochistic relationship between Mascis and the rest of the band (and how this relationship was mediated by socio-cultural context as well as by psychology).

Although Dinosaur Jr. represents a rather extreme case of dysfunctional band relationships, clearly indie was full of maladjusted boy wonders who attracted and then alienated scores of budding hopeful sidemen musicians. Martin Phillipps of The Chills comes to mind, especially in the light of the number of line-ups the band has been through. Rogan's account of The Smiths makes some similar points about dysfunctional and unequal band relationships (which in this case ended up in court). Sneaky Feelings had a milder version of the same thing. There was a lot of passive aggression – rather than discussing problems, we would simply act out, David by not writing songs, by prioritising work above music (which Martin also did) and more generally through our level of disorganisation, which hit epic pro-portions once we lost our manager. But of course all this was exacerbated by our lack of success, and the feeling that we did not fit in to the indie scene, either in New Zealand or in Europe when we toured there.

Some masculine coping strategies – R.E.M. and The Smiths

If the singer or star runs the risk of becoming feminised (or to put it another way, makes the group accessible to a larger audience, as in the case of R.E.M. and The Smiths), then how do the group keep their masculine integrity? One strategy for the singer is to have a partner in the group who supplies the masculine elements that the singer could be seen as lacking. The classic example here is the Rolling Stones' Mick Jagger and Keith Richards. Together they are the 'Glimmer Twins', a male homosocial partnership, leading the group, doing the songwriting and pro-viding a masculine iconography of rock and roll magic and excess. Richards pro-vides a traditional 'proletarian' rough and ready masculinity, technical and musical ability, and a reputation for excessive substance abuse, grounding Jagger's camp-ness and bourgeois aspirations (as was illustrated recently in Richards's reaction to Jagger's knighthood). The point here is not that Richards is really proletarian or

Jagger bourgeois but that that the two enact and naturalise class and gender difference under the aegis of their common masculinity. Such a lead singer/lead guitarist dynamic has become standard rock music ideology, albeit inflected slightly differently in each case: Robert Plant and Jimmy Page of Led Zeppelin; Roger Daltrey and Pete Townshend of The Who; David Bowie and Mick Ronson; Johnny Rotten and Steve Jones of the Sex Pistols; Bono and the Edge of U2.

This tradition continues into indie guitar rock: both R.E.M. and The Smiths feature a similar dynamic of powersharing between lead singer and lead guitarist, Morrissey and Johnny Marr, Michael Stipe and Peter Buck. The guitarist provides the 'rock and roll' element – technical skill, rhythmical drive and the ability to 'party' – while the singer provides intellect and a distinctive performing style (Buckley, 2002, pp. 24–7; Rogan, 1992). The guitar is inseparable from what we understand as masculinity in rock; the singer provides feminine glamour. Musical arrangement grounds the singer in a legitimating, recognisable rock tradition. Marr's speciality is the emulation of (often) British rock classics – hence 'Panic' (1987a) remodels T-Rex's 'Metal Guru'(1972); 'Shoplifters of the World Unite' (1987a) recreates the quasi-classical multi-guitar solos of Bryan May of Queen; 'Handsome Devil' and 'What Difference' (1984b) nod towards 1970s rockers Thin Lizzy; and 'How Soon is Now' (1985) borrows elements of Led Zeppelin's 'When the Levee Breaks' (1971) (which in turn refers back to Bo Diddley's 'Who Do You Love?'). These references (mostly to hard rock) act to distance the band from any accusations of foppery. Morrissey's musical tastes are in contrast mainly feminine (1960s UK girl singers). Peter Buck and Michael Stipe act out a similar dynamic. Stipe remains studiously ignorant of rock tradition, while Buck is knowledgeable (Buckley, 2002, pp. 25–6). Buck's guitar style refers mainly to The Byrds and their various progeny (Big Star, Television) – lots of jangly 12-string (or flanged) riffs and arpeggios, with the occasional country picking interlude – while Stipe parades 'art' influences such as Surrealism (Gray, 1993, p. 107).

Again sexuality is to the fore in relation to the singer; the difference being that the overt sexuality of Plant, Jagger and Bowie (androgynous certainly, but definitely sexual) has been to some extent supplanted by androgyny or asexuality. Morrissey and Stipe both idolised Patti Smith, notable for her relatively androgynous appearance (for example the cover of *Horses*, 1975) (Bret, 1994, pp. 11–12; Buckley, 2002, p. 25). Both have allowed and perhaps encouraged speculation about their sexual preferences. Morrissey's 'celibacy' creates an ambivalence heightened by the way his lyrics float between gender positions (Bret, 1994, p. 85). Stipe repeatedly refused to 'confirm or deny' and his lyrics give few clues either way (Buckley, 2002, pp. 121–2). He finally came out in 2001.[4] Why the ambiguity? Well, a little controversy never hurt sales, but the main reason is the post-punk reaction to 1970s rockism – the association of authentic rock and roll with machismo, and the influence of feminism (which both singers have acknowledged).

Both bands in performance generally presented a relatively low-key, dressed down approach, low on confrontation (apart from the singer), an ethos that also comes through in the anonymity of the band's names. In parallel ways, Morrissey and Stipe problematise their own onstage presence. Subject positions and lyrics are important here – Stipe's (early) lyrics are usually virtually indecipherable – if the voice speaking words is conventionally regarded as indicating a subject and hence the possibility of meaning through words, then Stipe's disembodied moans and howls suggest the opposite – that he is 'not there' (an impression further reinforced by the obscurity of the song titles, for example 'Wolves, Lower' (1982), an impressionism that encourages the listener to read their own meanings into the words. Again, when Stipe's lyrics became more comprehensible, some suggested that the band was 'selling out'. Both Stipe and Morrissey problematise their own presence and masculinity. It could be argued that this represents a reassessment of gender 'roles', but this would be to ignore their relationship with the rest of the band, and particularly the 'guitar heroes'. These figures act to normalise the aestheticism and tendentiousness of the lead singers by grounding them in 'rock and roll'.

It seems possible that one reason why R.E.M. and The Smiths are both relatively successful is that they display a version of this classic rock masculine partnership, a singer who is the star and acts as point of audience identification and a guitarist who confirms the rock authenticity of the group. If nothing else, this may broaden the appeal of the band in gender terms. Gina Arnold says of R.E.M.: 'There was nothing violent or passionate or frightening in their seduction, we weren't enslaved by the seedy romance of drugs or rhythm or bowled over by ideals or proselytized ... their niceness stood in bright relief against the scary world of angst and pain that the rest of rock n'roll [*sic*] celebrated' (1995, pp. 78–9). Likewise, Morrissey had more appeal to female listeners than any demagogue of punk authenticity.

Conclusions

'The closer we come to an exemplary masculinity, the more shot through with contradictions it is' (Segal, 1990, p. 123). The contradiction I have addressed in this chapter is that of the representation of masculinity in a patriarchal discourse, and how that conflicts with the 'male gaze'. A strategy of masculine hegemonic groups is to encourage the assumption that they have direct access to the truth without mediation – (documentary) objectivity (Easthope, 1986, p. 82). Power in such a discourse is constructed not through representations of hegemonic groups, but through control of representation – but rock, by highlighting male representation, performance and display onstage, problematises the traditional mind/body dichotomy that allowed masculine power to be articulated as an 'invisible' force. In Chapter 1, I discussed how representations of masculinity in masculinities studies are constructed as other to the subjectivity of the researcher. The homosocial model, if too simply applied, can similarly give rise to readings that simplify and reify masculine domination as 'machismo'. However, if we recognise the close interconnection of homosociality with homosexuality, the picture starts to get more interesting. I used 'kinship' to highlight the emotional and sometimes homoerotic investment that men have in each other (but rarely acknowledge), and showed how the presence of women within bands tends to reveal these hidden, non-instrumental relationships.

I suggested that masculinity in indie scenes is often closely tied to the representation of such scenes as autonomous, original and pure (relating back to Chapter 3). Media coverage (the insertion of an audience) is seen as threatening this 'pure' masculinity – it exposes the scene to a 'gaze' which constructs men as objects, and questions their control. The singer or 'star' highlights the tensions between the homosocial band model and the band as an object of media representation. At the same time, this stardom highlights latent homoeroticism within the band. Successful rock groups often construct a public representation of masculine partnership, in which the star's potentially femininity or commercialism is offset by the 'seriousness' and earnestness of his partner, usually a guitarist/songwriter.

In Chapter 2 I wrote about how, in classical music, association with technology acts to normalise and hide masculinity in performance. Clearly this is also important in rock music, for example in the way that it is the singer, not the guitarist, who is 'feminised' by the gaze of the audience. More broadly, use of technology in the Frankfurt School model of masculinity is essential to maintaining control. But at the same time, too obvious a technological virtuosity, too obvious a display of knowledge and/or technique could be problematic in a rock aesthetic that is supposedly inclusive, community-based and built on opposing dominant discourses of power and control.

So how is this apparent paradox to be renegotiated?

Notes

1.   As the US indie scene developed, bands started getting interested in other musical influences: for Hüsker Dü, it was 1960s pop/psychedelia; for Dinosaur Jr. 1970s FM rock; for The Replacements 1970s stadium rock and white R&B; for the Minutemen Creedence Clearwater Revival and UK indie band the Pop Group. Unlike hardcore, later indie bands were more likely to pay tribute to past music by recording covers, indicating a wider awareness of popular music as a field of possibilities rather than just taking an anti-establishment stance, for example Hüsker Dü's 'Eight Miles High', 'Sunshine Superman', 'Ticket To Ride'; Dinosaur Jr.'s 'Show Me the Way'; The Replacements's 'Black Diamond' (Kiss); the Minutemen's 'Don't Look Now' (Creedence Clearwater Revival). Lists of Dunedin Sound covers are given in note 26 below.
2.   Knox also attacked Flying Nun's 'pop genius' Martin Phillipps, in a song called 'Self-Deluded Dream Boy (in a Mess)' (Tall Dwarfs, 1994).
3.   The Chills' 'Dream by Dream' (*The Lost EP*, 1985) is another example.
4.   See, for example, 'Michael Stipe: I'm Gay', http://news.bbc.co.uk/1/hi/entertainment/showbiz/132994.stm, 14 May 2001.

Chapter 5

'Someone controls electric guitar': indie and technologies

'I can only understand really amateur performers ... because whatever they do never really comes off, so therefore it can't be phony.'

(Warhol, 1975, p. 82)

Rock and particularly punk and post-punk music have an ambivalent attitude to technology, because of the perceived conflict between technology as commodification/instrumentalisation and authentic personal musical expression on the one hand, and between technologies of musical reproduction and 'live' performance on the other (Thornton, 1995, pp. 34–51). How are these conflicts managed? Various ways in which media technologies are naturalised are considered as rearticulations of masculinity, as we saw in classical music (Green, 1997, p. 54). The electric guitar in post-punk music moves from being primarily a vehicle for individual expression, as in the blues/jazz/rock tradition, to a more impersonal sound source. Sound, rather than being 'authored', becomes increasingly 'authorless' ('white noise'). A resulting ideology of impersonality is also enacted through other technologies: the increased use of reverberation and the drone/jangle of the guitar taking precedence over the vocals – apparently distancing and problematising the male subject. But authority is reasserted indirectly, through the resultant 'wall of sound'. Finally, the idea of incompetence (failure to use technology correctly) is identified as an important means in post-punk music by which technology can be employed, but authorship disavowed. Again the question arises as to whether this practice is subversive or functions rather as a spectacle of male deviance, with its 'special' association with creativity (Green, 1997, p. 200). Incompetence also connects to McLuhan's ideas about the accessibility of new media and the death of 'specialism' (1964, p. 12).

Technology and masculinity are not just about 'boys and toys' (Lohan and Faulkner, 2004, p. 319). Technology can be more broadly defined as systems of organisation that make modernity possible – activities of rationalising, instrumentalising, ordering, hierarchising, prioritising, 'abstract systems' like money and information technologies such as hypertext – mediated 'action at a distance' (Thompson, 1995, p. 100). These may be defined as 'soft' as opposed to 'hard' technologies (rather like the distinction of computer software and hardware) but they are crucial to the maintenance of masculine hegemony (Hearn, 1992, pp. 140–207; Lister et al., 2003, p. 391). This leads towards practices based on the dissemination, organisation and hierarchisation of information, most relevantly on pop culture. Activities of archivalism and canonism, attitudes to listening to and collecting records are also significant here, and the degree to which they confirm or question masculinity. Technologies of reproduction are as important as those of production.

This chapter investigates the relationships between musical technologies and masculinities in indie. I'm going to propose a traditional three-part argument (thesis/antithesis/synthesis) which delineates a set of oppositional relationships and a possible way that indie synthesised these opposing tendencies. Of course, this paradigm may need some adjustment – we might even have to throw it out altogether. But it does provide a starting point. In Chapter 2, I wrote about classical music as a prediction of the forms of industrialised society – rational organisation, formal notation, a hierarchical division of labour – and related them to a masculinity marked by its rational control through mental process. While this instrumental approach seems the antithesis of rock culture, I suggested that it has continued to be significant to the way in which masculine authority is asserted in relation to all kinds of culture, popular and high. Such an approach includes, but is not limited to, the consideration of specific musical technologies, for example the electric guitar, the recording process, means of reproduction which have a clearly delineated and traditional relationship to gender – the 'men and their machines' discourse – but also includes the idea of technology as 'a process that includes the socially constructed knowledges and discourses that enable the technology to function' (Lister et al., 2003, p. 391). Technology is allied with masculine control, but also ultimately with a high cultural discourse of the artist (which masks to some degree the role played by technology).

Against this discourse of technological masculinity there is a counterdiscourse of folk primitivism, hugely important in rock. The influence of African-American culture has been one way in which this folk primitivism has been theorised. This folk primitivism also relates to how rock masculinity was seen as a kind of instinctive power or presence, which technological mediation threatens to dilute or vitiate (see Chapter 2). Masculinity here is more like a primitive force, which technology cannot control. I argued that this discourse of primitivism was significant to punk/ indie, although the association with blackness and sexuality was downplayed (see Chapter 3).

Rock discourse tries to balance these opposed elements. Steve Waksman suggests that 'adherents of the electric guitar saw the instrument as a means ... of blending "primitive" simplicity with "technological" complexity' (1999, p. 4). Waksman goes on to suggest that 'there is also a racial subtext here within which the primitive stands for African American influence upon electric guitar performance, whereas the technological stands for white contributions' (p. 4). But maintaining the balance has always been controversial: for example, progressive rock privileged the technological to the point where it became vulnerable to accusations of elitism. The folk discourse within rock has always been Luddite or technologically dystopian, desiring to minimise technological mediation between performer and audience. Such a view depends on the assumption that some sorts of technology are more 'natural' than others – for example, the electric guitar, which 'is used to invest the body of the performer with meaning, to confer upon it a unique identity whose authentic, natural appearance works to conceal its reliance upon artifice and technology' (Waksman, 1999, p. 5).

While tracing the history of the electric guitar from its invention to the mid-1970s, Waksman does not, however, address how punk rock and its offspring used the guitar. In one sense this chapter is a continuation of Waksman's project, but post-punk rock music may also have diverged in some important ways from Waksman's paradigm. The folk discourse in indie was reasserted through articulating primitivism in non-ethnic terms – as amateurism, infantilism, purism, irony and incompetence. But although ethnicity is less important, I argue that gender continues to be crucial. Punk/indie attempts to reconcile two contradictory modes of masculinity in relation to technology.

Having reviewed indie attitudes towards technology, I then want to look at indie musical practice – how different techniques and technologies create an indie 'sound' – use of electric guitar drone and jangle, buried vocals, lack of syncopation, reverberation, 1960s song structures, but kind of smothered. The first point is that despite defining itself against the homogeneity of the mainstream, indie guitar rock is, in sonic terms, quite homogenous. This is not entirely surprising – a minimalist aesthetic, a restricted set of musical and technical possibilities. But on the other hand, it does sit rather uncomfortably with indie as 'independent' – we might expect alternative music to be a bit more diverse. The contention here is that sonic orthodoxy is perhaps indicative of a normative or hegemonic expectation of what indie sound should be – this in turn may relate to the values of a dominant group. Finally I read this sound as synthesising the folk/modernity opposition set out above – as a sound which references both folk music and a particular reading of rock music history, but can also be heard as modern or even postmodern. A revised indie version of the rock canon privileges certain types of rock masculinities, whose keynote is not their physical presence as performers, but rather the 'sound' they create. This leads towards a consideration of indie masculinity as 'indirect' in the sense of both rejecting an obviously sexual machismo, instrumentality and aggression, but also redirecting these tropes through the use of sound and technology.

Ironic amateurism, technological infantilism

Warhol is a significant precursor here. His basic approach was to let the technology do the work – at the same time, he accepted that this might produce unintended consequences. He combined a McLuhan-esque enthusiasm for the possibilities of media with an implicit recognition that they problematised authorship. As a film director, Warhol's approach was to set the camera rolling and leave it (Smith, 1988, p. 251). Whatever happened was up to the performer. There was no editing apart from joining the separate reels. We see an echo of this in Lou Reed's *Metal Machine Music* (1975) – Reed set up a feedback loop between microphone and speakers, pressed the 'record' button and left the room. That noise, albeit edited and copied, was the record (Morley, 2003, p. 310). This aesthetic of non-intentionality idealises the role of technological productivity and tends to disparage the idea of artist as creator. I want to examine two theorisations of alternative incompetence that influenced 1980s alternative music – Lester Bangs and Brian Eno – focusing on how they discuss gender, specifically how they imagined an alternative to rock in the sense of another set of gender possibilities. At the same time they were obviously different: Bangs was American, Eno English, Bangs loved rock and roll, Eno wasn't so sure. But for both, questions of musical technique and technology were central to how they imagined rock.

Bangs thought 1970s music (and musicians) elitist and pretentious, and its emphasis on technical mastery alien to his vision of an inclusive musical community. He proposed replacing 'musos' with amateurs who would re-infuse rock with passion: 'Apparently nobody ever bother to inform nine/tenths of musicians that music is about feeling, passion, love, anger, joy, fear, hope, lust, EMOTION DELIVERED AT ITS MOST POWERFUL AND DIRECT IN WHATEVER FORM, rather than whether you hit a clinker in that third bar there' (Bangs, 1987, pp. 373–4; pp. 326–7, capitals in original). By this he meant musical amateurs using basic musical resources (electric of course) to make an almighty, freeform racket. Failure and incompetence became precious because they reversed the normative emphasis on technique and mastery. He codified this approach as an emergent punk aesthetic, combining minimalism, amateurism and assault, several years before punk rock formally began (Gendron, 2002, pp. 233–5). Drawing on recordings of 1960s US garage rock (exemplified by *Nuggets*, the work of another punk archivalist, Patti Smith's guitarist Lenny Kaye), The Stooges and The Velvet Underground, Bangs prophesied a music 'that would retain the primordial rock and roll drive whilst shattering all the accumulated straitjackets of key and time signature which vanguard jazz musicians had begun to dispose of almost a decade before ... a truly free music, where the only limits were the musician's own consciousness and imagination' (1987, p. 41).

The perversity of Bangs' stance is both its great strength and weakness – while empowering to amateur musicians, it also depends on a highly idealised view of musical creativity as necessarily opposed to learned techniques and structures. The contradiction becomes clearer when we consider how Bangs (1987, pp. 41–6) regarded free jazz as the incarnation of his musical ideal. But free jazz musicians were not untutored geniuses – they had spent years playing more formal and structured music, and that knowledge and technique was fundamental to the emergence of the 'freer' form. Or, as Toynbee puts it, 'the practice of free music cannot be exempted from ... the inevitability of genre' (2000a, p. 108). At the very least, it will be constrained by the fact that 'freedom' is inevitably constrained by the necessity of avoiding references to other genres. The jazz identification also suggests a strong Beat legacy – Beats idealised blackness as spontaneous creativity, and while Bangs didn't necessarily agree, the utopianism of his vision suggests the rearticulation of a primitive, idealised folk creativity through white punk.

Another paradox of Bangs' position is that his theory is based on listening to recordings, but was translated into live musical practice, a tension that informs indie culture's ambivalent relations with technology. His emphasis on natural, untutored creativity overlooks the importance of knowledge and investment in music (whether his own or that of musicians) and how these are used to create a construction of what the natural should be (or how certain musical practices become 'natural' in a given genre). Bangs' repeated emphasis on the physical and visceral: 'Rock and roll is not an artform – it's a raw wail from the bottom of the guts' (1992, p. 104) suggests natural creativity and the immediacy of the 'live', physical experience. But this affirmation of rock culture's repeated emphasis on the superiority of live to recorded performance hides the multifarious ways in which the 'new' is constructed from a revoicing of traditional and generic elements. It also seeks to naturalise ideological and intellectual elements such as canon within alternative culture in a way that preserves the myth of their spontaneity and originality. Bangs was also an important role model for the 'record collectors' whom I argue later in this chapter have an essential (but mostly invisible) role in educating nascent indie musicians.

Eno started his career with 1970s UK glam rockers Roxy Music, initially embracing a spectacular visual androgyny. 'Paradoxically, Eno's visual persona changed from "feminine" to "masculine" during the same period around 1975 that his musical style underwent a marked shift from "masculine" to "feminine"' (Tamm, 1995, p. 90). Like Bangs, Eno is offended by 'technological excess', the flaunting of technological power or musical virtuosity, and seeks a more minimal approach, and like Bangs, his vision of creativity ultimately hinges on a vision of 'innocence'. But his version of incompetence is more cerebral. For Eno, making music is a profoundly technological process, but he tries to minimise his own role in the process and basically let the machines do more of the work: inventing systems and setting them in motion, like Warhol (Tamm, 1995, p. 8). Eno insists that he is not a musician because this implies a degree of authorship and intentionality that makes him feel uncomfortable: 'lack of technique … makes one confront one's vulnerability' (Tamm, 1995, p. 48).

This vulnerability is, he argues, essentially feminine: 'The world is in science. I use that word in a limited sense: deification of rational knowledge … the western version of masculinity opposes rational man against intuitive woman … the part of my being that interests me has always been my intuition' (Tamm, 1995, pp. 88–9). For Eno the idea of authoring work is basically masculine; accordingly, most rock music is marked, rather tediously, he feels, by its all too obvious authorship – expressive singing, lyrics, a purposive beat. In contrast he posits a music characterised by a lack of control and presence: generative music that comes about through letting technological systems run and produce new and unexpected sound formations. Eno defeats technology (and the Western rational project), then by insisting that he is not in control – he just lets things happen. Again, he justifies this to some degree by a kind of creation myth – he wants to create a music that has a feeling of innocence: 'I'm interested in feeling like a very young child, but I'm not interested in feeling like a teenager' (Tamm, 1995, p. 54).

Tamm comments that Eno has a paradoxical relation with technology: 'Eno may have been eager to admit his instrumental incompetence; but in the studio he sits at the centre of a sophisticated body of music-making machinery, just as the traditional composer does when he is writing for an orchestra, and in each case what the mind is able to conceive and the ear to hear is the result of training and discipline as well as imagination' (1995, p. 164; see also p. 70). Tamm compares him to a classical composer; the other obvious analogue is the producer and sound engineer. Eno's argument seems to be that if he doesn't play the instruments (or tell the musicians what to play) then he is not controlling the process. But he is in charge: 'my role is to co-ordinate them, synthesize them, furnish the central issue which they all will revolve around' (Tamm, 1995, p. 99) – it's still an Eno album that results, and presumably he gets the royalties, not the musicians. By this argument, Phil Spector (whom Eno frequently mentions) was not in control either; after all, he neither necessarily wrote the parts nor played them. Yet we still talk about the Spector sound, not the Ronettes or the Righteous Brothers or the Hal Blaine or the Ellie Greenwich sound. The question of agency – who did what – which Eno emphasises, is less important than who is in overall intellectual control; who owns the music-making process.

Eno's theorisation of gender is pretty weak. While appearing to acknowledge the historical specificity of gender, his adoption of a feminine 'passivity' is simply reheated Freud. Besides, his own rhetorical habits suggest a highly cerebral form of intellectualism (his favourite word, according to Tamm (1995, p. 16), is 'interesting'). He proceeds by empirical methods, and though he disclaims rationality, it is very much part of his process, albeit producing irrational results (Tamm, 1995, p. 119). Moreover, his music, if it can be called that, doesn't seem to be about emotion at all, rather it is supposed to be 'interesting' or for 'thinking'. What this suggests is a strong mind/body split and especially an avoidance of any kind of sexuality. Ultimately Eno is not so much androgyne as android.

Rather than viewing Eno as a 'soft man' (as in Reynolds and Press, 1995, pp. 205–7) I would view his intellectuality as masculine; he is very much at home with his machines. Broadly we might say that in problematising his authorship of technology, he simply transforms *techne* as art or skill into technology as instrumentality. His aesthetic minimises human interaction or involvement. Tamm ascribes to him 'a point of view which is detached almost to the point of being chilling' (1995, p. 91). Eno seems like a very solitary figure – he avoids interacting with fans because they might stifle his creativity (Tamm, 1995, pp. 183–4). Some of his 'practices' are simply precious. Tamm comments of one of Eno's guitars: 'he never changed the strings, and when the top one broke he decided not to replace it'

(1995, p. 71). So how would Eno feel if some mere musician, not seeing the bigger picture, had picked up the guitar, replaced the string and tuned it? Would he accept it as 'an accident'? Or would (perish the thought) Eno be angry?

However, Eno is certainly useful because he demonstrates more clearly than any other musical practitioner the replacement of direct by indirect forms of control. His control is not in his participation; it is in the way his non-participation allows him to stand back and see the whole process objectively. If Foucault talked about the panopticon as a system of normalisation 'a power [which] has to qualify, measure, appraise and hierarchise, rather than display itself' (1978, p. 144), Eno operates a kind of 'panphonicon' in which sound is invisibly regulated – we might call it instrumental irrationality (Foucault, 1984, pp. 206–13).

Eno is also influential on indie music in terms of his persona; the part of him which presumably he would wish to minimise. His self-professed neutrality and indifference place him close to David Byrne (with whom he has frequently col-laborated), while his affectless, determinedly neutral singing voice affects a kind of naivety which many indie practitioners have sought to emulate (Gans, 1985, pp. 52, 56–61). His avoidance of the body in his music certainly also had an impact on indie musicians – as suggested elsewhere, the 1980s was a period in which performing sexuality was seen as problematic, especially for men – Eno provided some clues as to how to turn disembodiment into musical practice.

We can sum up how Bangs and Eno theorise technology (and how we might critique their theories) as follows.

- Musical creativity is equated with amateurism – technique and mastery with redundancy. Skill is compromising as it implies that one has been 'taken over' by technology or sees technique as an end in itself – the virtu-oso. If you can't play, the argument goes, you can't 'play' by the rules. What this promises is that the performer's 'use' of technology has not com-promised his integrity, because we can't tell whether the effect is intended or not. But this disavows the extent to which any musical performance is mediated through technology and cultural codes.
- Because the amateur 'doesn't know' what he is doing, this questions the intentional relationship of meaning to author and, by extension, of tech-nique to intentionality – incompetence proves that, far from being a godlike 'star', you're just an ordinary guy, like the audience. Mistakes are precious because they prove this. But although mistakes can enhance crea-tivity, this does not mean that they're necessary or somehow superior to 'authored' work – clearly it takes an author to recognise the value of a mistake.
- If you're not 'in control', then you're somehow feminised – problematising authorship is a way of problematising masculinity, the assumption being that authorship assumes an autonomous patriarchal subject, and that the frag-mentation of the subject necessarily feminises it. As I argued in Chapter 1,

I think this is reductive. Gender (or indeed any social meaning) cannot be read off style in isolation from a broader social context.

- Warhol's passive power is re-enacted in Eno – the artist controls through the act of observation.
- Both offer an aesthetic of deviance or resistance to the norm. As Green (1997, p. 133) points out, deviance and rule breaking can be annexed to a discourse of superior creativity – 'the similitude of genius' – which can confirm masculinity. This is obvious in Bangs' pugnacious, confrontational approach. In Eno it is more codified and formalised – consider, for example, his Oblique Strategies, a set of 'cue cards' which offer ways of subverting 'standard' musical practice (Gans, 1985, p. 66; Tamm, 1995, pp. 77–8). However, both can also be read as hierarchical in their implicit claim to the aesthetic 'superiority' of practitioners of their approach. The pursuit of subversion can become a new orthodoxy: Bangs' punk aesthetic was codified and formalised, becoming a standard by which other practice was judged, even a form of homosocial policing (Bannister, 1999, pp. 102–3; Gendron, 2002, p. 234). In the same way, while few would dispute the novelty value of Eno's approach, it could in time become limiting, and a confirmation of the producer's rather than the musician's agency (Gans, 1985, pp. 85–7). The final point is that Eno's strategies are mainly for studio, not live performance. Although designed to increase spontaneity, they are mainly applicable to fixed systems with fixed variables. (Bangs is similar to Eno here because, as I pointed out, his ideas of 'liveness' and spontaneity were based on an archive of recordings that supposedly incarnated these qualities.)

Indie and technology

At Flying Nun, Chris Knox combined Bangs' Luddite punk and Eno's non-intentional amateur aesthetic ('Honour thy error as a hidden intention' (Tamm, 1995, p. 49)). In performance, Knox (still) often highlights his performance errors, emphasising his fallibility and breaking down, in a quasi-folk manner, the 'illusion' of performance and the division between performer and audience: 'If I can do it, anyone can!' (Knox, 1990). This can also be read as a Brechtian self-consciousness – the highlighting of error alienates the audience, inviting them to reflect on the 'constructed' nature of performance. Knox claims that he likes to record as 'live' as possible, minimising technological intervention: 'I use only one mike and my only effect is an antique plate reverb ... used very sparingly' (Knox, 1991). And, of course, computers are cheating (Knox, 1989a). Low production values, lack of overdubbing, cheapness and DIY amateurism also mark the recording as being uncommercial and therefore uncompromised. Flying Nun band The Gordons (now recording for Matador Records as Bailter Space) recorded their self-titled first album with instruments they'd made themselves (McKessar, 1988, p. 27).

Such approaches were common in other indie scenes. Hüsker Dü's early albums seem to have been recorded in little more than the time it took to play them (Azerrad, 2001, pp. 166, 169, 171). Indeed drummer Grant Hart notes, 'In our whole oeuvre ... there's probably not five second takes' (p. 169). Of course, that little boast reminds us that that the 'live' approach also has a competitive edge – are you man enough to 'cut it live'? Similarly, Knox's idealisation of immediacy and amateurism is rather disingenuous, given his bountiful performance and song-writing abilities and his (wonderful) voice. He's not as bad as he makes out. So there's a certain amount of pose in the whole amateur schtick. Similarly, Paul Westerberg (of The Replacements) comments: 'When some people go to rock shows ... they want to be taken by the hand and told, "Sit back, don't worry, we'll take over". And our attitude has always been, "Help!"' (Arnold, 1995, p. 107). But again this was calculated – the group saved their worst performances for their most important gigs (Azerrad, 2001, p. 214). Why? One reason was that The Replacements, far more than their contemporaries, actually had a lot of commer-cial potential. They played a brand of classic Springsteenesque, air-punching, anthemic US rock'n'roll; hence their exaggerated need to prove their 'authentic-ity' to their punk roots by 'fucking up'.

The Jesus and Mary Chain were another indie act whose 'incompetence' was a bit of an act. Their early gigs were legendarily awful, but in the studio the band were anything but slapdash – the 'raw' fuzzy sounds of *Psychocandy* were created by laborious overdubbing of layers of distorted guitar (Robertson, 1988, p. 45). Citing the precedent of Phil Spector, the band wanted to create 'masterpieces', replicating Spector's Wall of Sound. This suggests again that authenticity has nothing to do with 'liveness' or the minimisation of mediation. Kevin Shields's (My Bloody Valentine) painstaking approach to recording is similar, and similarly Spectoresque in its sound and ambition (Cavanagh, 2000, pp. 340–43, 413–16, 423–8). And, as Eno points out, Spector 'understood better than anyone that a recording studio could do things which could never actually happen' – that is, things that could never be 'live' (quoted in Tamm, 1995, p. 30). Bands who want 'liveness' are faced with the paradox that rawness and spontancity do not simply happen – they are effects created (or at the least enhanced) in the studio (Toynbee, 2000a, pp. 104–5).

Robert Forster of The Go-Betweens comments on live performance: 'At the time [the late 1970s] the prevailing belief was that if you've got eight tons of equipment, you must be a better band than someone who's got four tons of equip-ment. I was immediately into the aesthetic of *as little equipment as possible*. Always look like you're completely undernourished in terms of equipment. Just to upset people ... but also I liked the sound of it' (Nichols, 2003, p. 34).

One way to read this, as I've already suggested, is as a reaction to 1970s 'excess'. If 1970s metal bands had too much gear, they were also 'too much' in their performance – too much gesturing, too many pointless solos, too much noise, too macho. There was obviously a class angle in all this – metal was perceived as working-class music, and indie was basically more middle-class and intellectual, saying, effectively, we don't need all that gear, it's in *bad taste*. So indie alters the terms of the discourse (or perhaps more accurately, reverses them). I think that's a very middle-class thing to do – if you don't like the game, you change the rules to suit yourself. It bespeaks a certain confidence in your own intellectual worldview.

The 'difference' of New Zealand music (particularly Flying Nun) was persistently associated with extreme amateurism. The Clean were lauded by New Zealand rock writer Campbell Walker as having 'no background, bugger all gear, no singing ability' while Dunedin Sound bands were characterised by low-fi sound, lack of image and lack of political and social comment – an aesthetic of 'lack' (Mitchell, 1996, p. 218). Jamming econo indeed. On the other hand, minimalism has been a prominent modernist/avant-garde discourse since the Bauhaus – it cannot be simply read as a guarantee of spontaneity. Indie draws on a history of (canonical) recordings of this type – The Velvet Underground's first two albums, for example (Heylin, 1993, pp. 3–15).

Straw (1997b, p. 497) notes that indie culture was suspicious of the perceived rate of change (technological and other) in black music, which served as damning evidence of its technologisation and commodification, very much like the folk music critique of mass culture. This discourse of indie technological dystopianism can, again, be read in terms of purity – 'the old (that is, 1960s) ways are the best' – and archivalism, for example the use of 'old' technology – classic guitars (Fender, Gibson, Burns, Hofner), amps (Fender, Vox), keyboards (mellotrons, Jansen organs), four-track tape recorders, tape echo, plate reverb, analog over digital (effects, recording, synthesisers), valve technology over transistors (Knox, 1989a). This can be glossed as both necessity (old gear *may* be cheaper and more accessible) and more authentic – the sounds produced are non-commercial and therefore better. However, such a conservative approach calls into question the extent to which indie can be seen as innovative and 'different'. Indie musicians were largely bound by their use of existing musical technology and, as Attali (1985, p. 35) suggests, old technology tends to support traditional styles of music making. In the context of the early 1980s, with synthesisers, sampling, electronic music and hiphop, indie's concentration on good old-fashioned electric guitars can be read as a kind of rock classicism, a return to tradition.

Representations of indie masculinities in sound

In this section I am concerned with the (re)production of gender ideologies through sound technology and abstract systems. Proletarian male pride traditionally had to do with the display of masculine physical and sexual prowess, and this ideology was important to early rock. But this connection of physicality and masculine authority in rock has eroded. Authority has become less a matter of physical effort or bodily presence, and more a matter of the way in which performance is framed, the shaping of the overall aesthetic or epistemological system in which we hear or see a musical performance. Critical Theorist Herbert Marcuse states that 'The ever-more-complete mechanisation of labor in advanced capitalism, while sustaining exploitation, modifies the attitude and status of the exploited ... the proletarian of the previous stages of capitalism ... was the living denial of his society. In contrast, the organised worker in the advanced areas of technological society lives this denial less conspicuously' (1991, pp. 26–7). The 'garage' bands of the 1960s and 1970s became the 'bedroom' bands of the 1980s. Such a retreat from the public sphere represents a break from traditional rock masculinities' association with 'the street'. In indie musical performance, masculine power is expressed indirectly, not as machismo, but as technical incompetence, implying aesthetic superiority; as knowledge from archivalism (see below), a knowing invocation of past musical texts and practices; and through sound – usually that of electric guitar.

To extend the terms of my hypothesis to sound, I hear indie sound (white noise drone) as representing a synthesis of opposing folk and modern attitudes to technology: the folk tradition of timeless authenticity achieved through minimal technological means, and the modern or perhaps postmodern position, of sound as noise – as the message rather than the medium. Mediation through technology is ubiquitous in popular music, but some types of popular culture and music comment on and amplify the implications of mediation, and these effects ('hypermediacy', 'cultural noise') are achieved through technology and other apparatuses of modernity. Whereas pop music often aims to hide the effects of its mediation by positing a direct, intimate relationship between singer/song and listener, in indie guitar rock, this relationship is always in some way being questioned. Perhaps the buzz of distortion can be seen as analogous to the continual background noise of an overcrowded, industrialised, mediated society – indie rock seems to say that we never hear one voice speaking to us alone, but always a multitude of possible, possibly phantasmagorical voices. This may lead towards postmodernism – 'the waning of affect', but is equally assimilable to a folk discourse – an impersonal tradition that belongs 'to the people'. The Byrds were an influential precursor of this fusion of folk and technology (see below).

The electric guitar in punk/indie

The electric guitar's centrality to rock continues in indie/punk, but not as a vehicle of personal, expressive virtuosity. Punk took a more confrontational approach, approaching the guitar more as an impersonal noise generator, designed to blast the audience out of its apathy. Virtuosity was now denigrated. Indie guitar bands drew on the sound of punk and 1960s groups like The Byrds and The Velvet Underground, based around the guitar as a sound source, tending to play full sustained chords, droney, continuous lines or simple, modally inflected solos. The electric guitar was central to the structure and sound of the music, but was not featured primarily as a vehicle for individual expression – it was more about creating a context or atmosphere.

The drone/jangle of electric guitar in indie can be read as:

- a primitive or folk musical device; as an invocation of the musical past
- technologically generated noise – an expression of modernity
- a confrontational device for signalling difference (through excessive volume, distortion, opposition to conventional ideas of music as 'nice')
- a mediation or intervention between performer and audience, as an invocation of the musical past; as a problematisation of conventional models of musical meaning (through the masking of lyrics or harmonic structure)
- a way of breaking down the boundaries of the subject.

The drone has a dual polarity – it can be beatific ('folk') or sinister ('modern'). In the former case, punk/indie minimalism as expressed through electric guitar continues the Romantic ideology of a return to folk primitivism. It also refers back to a 'golden age' – the 1960s – and the artists associated with these sounds. In the latter case, modern or modernist classical music, for example, has frequently used 'primitive' musical devices to shock, to reject Western master narratives of harmonic complexity or to represent 'the return of the repressed' (for example Stravinsky's *The Rite of Spring*). The technology of industrial capitalism produces huge amounts of regular, monotonous sound as a by-product – this unwanted excess or abject is a reminder of the material reality that underlies Western narratives of progress. Punk/indie united primitivism and modernism by valorising amateurism as 'more real', but also by emphasising that today's 'folk reality' is not a primitive, rural society but a largely manmade, industrial, urban environment. An example would be Iggy Pop's description of how the sound of The Stooges was influenced by Detroit car assembly lines (*Dancing in the Street*, 'No Fun', 1996). Sound is thus related to discourses of technology and industrialisation.

The next two points relate to the sound of the electric guitar in indie as a way of making two different types of non-verbal meanings. The first is as a 'sound barrier' – a mode of social exclusion, signalling 'difference' (media simultaneously communicate and mark social boundaries). Warhol emphasised mediation as a way of keeping people at a distance (Koch, 1974, p. 28). Of course, turning up the volume amplifies the effect: Bangs' notion of assault. For example, Flying Nun band The Gordons claimed to be 'the loudest band in the world', clearly allying volume with domination (Bannister, 1999, p. 139). US bands like Dinosaur Jr. also used this approach – 'The one sort of statement that J [Mascis] had was, "We're going to be really fuckin' loud,"' – often to the extent that other members of the band were unable to hear what they were playing (Azerrad, 2001, p. 352). After Dinosaur's 1987 UK tour, 'a whole wave of English groups, dubbed "shoegazer bands" sprang up in their wake, playing folk chords through phalanxes of effects pedals to make swirling, deafening music' – Ride, Lush and My Bloody Valentine, the latter especially: 'They hit the first note and it was so loud it sent the glass hurtling. The beer didn't shake – the glass flew off' (Azerrad, 2001, p. 366; Cavanagh, 2000, p. 492).

But the performances of groups like My Bloody Valentine eschewed traditional gestures of rock machismo: no posing, no solos, just a painful throbbing in the ears. Aggressive then, but an indirect form of aggression: the musician as a source of noise, a domination mediated by technology rather than physical display. Clearly this formed an extreme contrast with the spectacle (or non-spectacle) of the group itself, who in person were extremely soft-spoken and self-effacing (Cavanagh, 2000, p. 315). Kevin Shields of My Bloody Valentine says: '[It's] because we know that once you get above one hundred decibels, that causes a physical change in people. Endorphins get released into the system because the body can sense imminent damage' (Cavanagh, 2000, p. 315; see also pp. 426–7). A key idea, then, is that volume reintroduces the element of physicality, of embodiment into the musical experience, although paradoxically this can only be achieved through battering it (and the audience) into submission (Cavanagh, 2000, pp. 492–3). 'Increasingly, what's most appropriate is *immobility* before a bombardment ... of noise' (Reynolds, 1989, p. 246). The idea that the body can only be experienced through pain seems to derive from hardcore – albeit that here violence is now achieved through indirect means (Azerrad, 2001, pp. 45, 49). Again, we look back to Warhol's Exploding Plastic Inevitable for an adumbration of this 'sensory overload' approach – an approach that was supposed to 'destroy the egos' of the audience.

The use of reverberation may add to the effect. Of course, 'reverb' has always been a feature of recorded music, but usually used selectively, on vocals especially. Spector used it on everything, creating that muddy, apocalyptic, slightly anachronistic grandeur that characterises his work. For indie musicians, it not only had that 'authentic' 1960s ring, it also had other advantages:

> Reverberation achieves a sense of distance and vastness, at the expense of personality. It creates majesty, at the expense of intimacy. It is cool, rather than warm. It is cerebral, rather than visceral. It's like the big picture, but at the expense of detail ... the attraction of distance to young men is not hard to understand. It sounds impressive, and you can hide the messy details. (Bannister, 1999, p. 72)

Reverberation combined with a full instrumentation has an obvious archival connotation – the 'wall of sound', employed by 1960s producers like Phil Spector and Brian Wilson. Reverb literally denotes distance in space, but it can also connote distance in time – 'the past' (for example, it is often used on film soundtracks for flashback episodes) thus linking to archivalism – not only were reverby 1960s sounds influential on indie, but arguably these same sounds were already marked by nostalgic references that simultaneously also invoked canons and past authorities – hence Spector's references to his works as 'little symphonies for the kids'

(Pareles and Romanowski, 1983, p. 516). Reverberation can be read as a mediation that encourages the listener to hear the past in the present, imparting authority – it has a 'patina of authenticity' – while at the same time distancing the listener from precise articulations and specific meanings. For reverberation also 'muddies' the sound, de-emphasising individual elements and tending towards a total, enveloping, homogeneous noise. This approach was taken to an extreme by groups like The Jesus and Mary Chain and My Bloody Valentine. The effect tends towards disembodiment: 'the sound literally isn't all there. It's actually the opposite of rock'n'roll. It's taking all the guts out of it … just the remnants, the outline' (Kevin Shields, quoted in Reynolds, 1990, p. 121). It creates a flattening effect. As such there again seems to be a connection to Warhol, for whom distance and decay were central preoccupations.

Timeless flight – The Byrds

While I've already discussed The Velvet Underground and Spector in some detail as forming part of an alternative 'art-rock' history of popular music masculinities, of all indie influences, The Byrds come closest to predicting the forms of indie music (Hesmondhalgh, 1999, p. 46; Larkin, 1995, p. 3; Reynolds, 1990, p. 37). Their use of jangle and drone, studio effects and psychedelic curlicues, the way they addressed and identified with McLuhan's technological utopianism, while also referencing 'folk', all provide a useful case study of a proto-art-rock band: 'The Byrds – do they even count as rock and roll? Probably not, but neither did the Velvets, and that's what so important about them?' (Thompson, 2000, p. 2). Both the Velvets and The Byrds were distant in space and time from indie scenes, so clearly identification has to be based around the affect of their recorded performances. In fact, I argue that it was precisely their understanding and articulation of distance that makes them so germane. Both used electric guitars to generate drone/jangle and reverberation, as well as assuming certain subject positions within texts. In doing this, they articulated masculinities in new ways.

The Byrds emphasised jangle: McGuinn's 12-string was effectively the lead instrument, but it did not necessarily play solos, rather it was a constant throughout the song. The Byrds were 'the product of a self-conscious sonic conception', suppressing individuality and spontaneity in favour of a formalist, some would say formula-ised, approach (Miller, 1980, p. 228, Weiner, 1972, p. 10). They favoured musical style over content, suppressing individuality in favour of a communal, harmony-based approach (Hardy and Laing, 1990, p. 111). Vocals had an impersonal, abstract quality, 'an effete, susurrating murmur' (Reynolds and Press, 1995, p. 165) even when the texts dealt with social issues ('The Bells of Rhymney', The Byrds, 1965). Leader Roger McGuinn compared The Byrds' sound to specifically technological discourses – at one point they were called the Jet Set (Pareles and Romanowski, 1983, p. 78) – 'The sound of the airplane in the Forties was a rrrrrrooooooaaaahhhhh sound and Sinatra and other people sang with those sort of overtones. Now we've got the krrrriiisssshhhhh jet sounds, and the kids are singing up in there now. It's the mechanical sounds of the era: the sounds are different and so the music is different' (quoted in James, 1965). Traditional ideologies of rock as physical, spontaneous, creative expression are supplanted by a more intellectualised, reflexive self-positioning in relation to existing musical and social discourses.

The continuity of sensation of drone/jangle combined with emotional detachment may give an affect that can perhaps best be compared to travel, a defining experience of modernity. McGuinn continually compared the band's sound to machinery of transport: emphasising mobility, lack of ties to any particular time or place, and internationalism ('Eight Miles High', 'CTA-102'). The idea of continual movement connects to young men, associated in modern culture with fast cars, just as rock music and counterculture is associated with 'the road'. Locale (which also stands for tradition) is displaced by the eroticism of continual motion (Reynolds and Press, 1995, pp. 51–2). In 'Turn! Turn! Turn!' (1966a), The Byrds cunningly conflated this motion discourse with traditional ideas of seasonal change and the Christian concept of mutability. By placing Pete Seeger's setting of Ecclesiastes 3:9 in a rock context, they made it seem like McLuhan's prophecies about the mythic, 'tribal' properties of new media were coming true: 'the medium is the message'. Like the 'pure information' of McLuhan's electric light, drone and jangle can function to obliterate time and space by bringing diverse locales together under the umbrella of the all-embracing indie sound (McLuhan, 1964, p. 15). Thus it can offer a common 'identity' to social groups diverse in time and space. The band's synthesis of nature and technology is probably best heard on *Notorious Byrd Brothers* (1968).

The Byrds saw themselves as prophets of an 'international music' (James, 1965) – they were, to paraphrase one of The Beatles' most Byrds-like songs, 'nowhere men'. This 'freedom' from location could also work to assuage male Oedipal anxieties within indie about influence and paternity, not only from the black roots of popular music, but from any 'roots' music. For example, whereas, say, Creedence Clearwater Revival or The Kinks are both pretty obviously American and English respectively, drawing strongly on local, historic musical traditions (rockabilly and New Orleans, English music hall), The Byrds, by contrast, came out of the sky. Although clearly indebted to folk and country, their ideology of 'international music' worked to disavow such influence and identify instead with the 'now' of technology, so it was possible for, say, young male musicians in a post-colonial culture like New Zealand to be influenced by them without the Oedipal anxiety attached to a more specifically located music (Abrams, 1988, p. 84). Just as technological modernity bursts the bounds of the nation state, so The Byrds and the Velvets played with a cosmopolitanism that defied any single site of origin. The local or specific functions as an 'idiom or spectacle' which masks wider transnational structures of power (Appadurai, 1990, pp. 306–7). Indie as a global phenomenon reproduces some of these assumptions – apparently local in its origins, but global in its connotations. In a globalised and dislocated world, authority is no longer constituted through presence, but, paradoxically, through absence: 'our experiences of self and others, meaning and identity, have been increasingly subject to the specifically dislocatory logic of capitalism … making our experience of these phenomena far more disseminated than they once might have been' (Gilbert, 1999, p. 35).

The Byrds' influence on indie, I argue, partly stems from their rearticulation of authority through discourses of indirection. They synthesised 'folk' and techno-logical discourses by the idea of personal anonymity. However, as I have argued elsewhere, as far as gender is concerned, both these discourses emanate from a similarly masculinist position. As such, they produced new masculinities – the articulation of masculine hegemony was achieved differently, but was still con-trolling in its 'knowingness'.

Archivalism and canonism

The 1980s saw the emergence of 'a globally diffuse subculture of consumption' – middle-class men with time on their hands, pop culture on their minds and (increasingly) a computer in their bedroom (Eng, 2002). This formation was first recognised in accounts of Japanese 'otaku': a term which basically means 'home' but came to refer to detached, isolated, socially retarded young men 'obsessively interested in the details of a single field … that was generally considered useless from a professional perspective, such as computer games or TV stars' (Eng, 2002). Also referred to as 'information elitists', 'elite fans' and 'hyper consumers', otaku and their Western equivalents (think of the Comic Book Guy in *The Simpsons*, the conspiracy theorists of *Slacker*, any of Hornby's anti-heroes) are characterised by a detailed knowledge of aspects of pop culture such as comic books and music. Once regarded as geeks and even as a social threat (after otaku 'characteristics' were discovered in a Japanese child murderer), otaku have become increasingly respectable – even credited with 'a pioneering role in the information society' (Eng, 2002). This suggests that this group of 'reluctant insiders' can convert their knowledge into cultural capital.

Much otaku interaction takes place in mediated forms, especially online, is highly competitive and centres around the trading of 'valuable' information about one's chosen speciality 'in the hopes of finding and/or producing high value infor-mation that could be traded for power and influence' (Eng, 2002). Eng likens their community to the online scientific community, where he suggests that new infor-mation has a similar premium: 'Appropriators of scientific culture … the otaku adopt the social practices of scientific culture in their everyday lives and as partici-pants in an information economy' but employ this mainly to cultural ends, giving rise to William Gibson's characterisation of otaku as 'the passionate obsessive, the information age's embodiment of the connoisseur' (Gibson, 2001).

Similarly, if the pop/rock canon, as Motti Regev (2002, p. 261) suggests, represents the claims of a 'knowledge'-based, post-industrial middle class to a distinctive cultural capital, then indie rock, to some extent, was perhaps a means for some of its lower, more bohemian strata to convert some of their intellectual capital into social status. At the end of the film version of Nick Hornby's *High Fidelity*, the protagonist sets up his own indie record label. Hornby's books *High Fidelity* (1995) and *Fever Pitch* (1994) describe a 'subculture' of career-challenged young men who identify with mediated, impersonal, abstract systems based on aspects of pop culture, which supply them with a sense of belonging while at the same time distancing them from more direct forms of social engagement (Giddens, 1990, pp. 140–41).

Both works play out a similar gendered conflict in which a male protagonist has to negotiate between the culture he loves (soccer in *Fever Pitch* and popular music in *High Fidelity*) and the people (family, women) in his life. In both books popular culture is figured as a homosocial world of male bonding, to which women are opposed (literally and figuratively). Popular culture supplies a depersonalised routine or structure which supplies security for men: in *Fever Pitch* the recurrent structure of the football seasons; in *High Fidelity* the fact that the narrator is not only a music fan but also a record shop proprietor. Both main characters find comfort in the world of statistics: in *Fever Pitch* the endless calculation of goal differences, the recitation of scoring statistics, home and away records and so on – the whole body of knowledge of soccer – and in *High Fidelity* the obsessive listing – ten greatest guitar solos, ten greatest first tracks, ten greatest break-ups, the ordering of one's record collection, the search for obscure catalogue numbers. 'Hornby suggests that ... boys define themselves by relation to their interests ... while girls define themselves by their relations to other people' (Thurschwell, 1999, p. 298). The male characters find safety within this numerical, mathematical world – it is a place of symbolic authority, a world from which subjectivities are exiled. They can also participate vicariously in 'goal-oriented behaviour': Arsenal winning the championship, the comparison of 'greatest recorded performances'. Both music and football, conceptualised as abstract systems of statistics, are areas where the male characters can imaginatively participate in a world of 'pure' achievement (Faludi 1999, p. 113).

Lists of the 'top' albums, singles, singers or artists were increasingly common in 1980s rock media, in *NME*, *Rolling Stone* and more recently *Q* and *Mojo*. They are also examples of connoisseurship and canonism. In turn, Western canonism is often critiqued as representing a 'privileged, elite group of white male critics', and this holds for popular and high culture alike (Childers and Hentzi, 1995, p. 37). Canon-related practices such as archivalism are not simply a cataloguing of the past – they are political and selective. Foucault views them as discursive practices which shape the way we 'know' (1972, p. 131). Emblematic of the highest social aspirations and artistic achievements of a given social group, canon provides a means of proving intellectual superiority.

Indie did not simply arise organically out of developing post-punk music networks, but was shaped by media (particularly print), and was not just collective, but also stratified, hierarchical, parochial and traditional. Canon (articulated through practices of archivalism and connoisseurship) is a key means of stratification within indie scenes, produced by and serving particular social and cultural needs for dominant social groups (within indie scenes, for example, journalists, scenemakers, tastemakers, record company owners, some musicians). David Buckley suggests that 'By 1979 ... pop history was not so much progressing in linear time but folding in on itself' (2002, p. 4). That is, post-punk revivals of older musical styles (ska, for example) highlighted the increasingly reflexive nature of music making: 'there was such a variety of genres and styles ... that making new music was, for some, an act of musical archaeology as opposed to innovation ... A great rock group ... needed not just a sexy singer, a great virtuoso, or a sussed marketing scam ... It needed a pop *historian*' (Buckley, 2002, p. 5). In R.E.M.'s case, they had just such a rock aficionado, reader, listener and archivist with 'presumably ... one of the largest record collections in Georgia' – guitarist Peter Buck (pp. 5, 7). In the UK, Hornby's *High Fidelity* and Giles Smith's *Lost in Music* (1995) focus on the increasing centrality of record collecting and secondhand record shops to pop music culture in the late 1970s and early 1980s.

Indie is usually represented in terms of musicians, bands and scenes. I suggest it could be rewritten as a history of record collectors. Indie had a huge investment in a version of the past, in its own voicing of 'rock tradition' (Arnold, 1995, p. 7; Buckley, 2002, p. 4). To find a Velvet Underground or a Byrds album in New Zealand (or Minneapolis, or Manchester) in 1980 would have taken effort, commitment and a lot of hanging around (usually secondhand) record shops. This was not casual consumption – it was a mission (Buckley, 2002, pp. 3–7). Such awareness of the past was (at the time) subversive. To uncover a 'lost' 1960s classic from the bin of a secondhand shop represented a small victory against the forces of modern capitalism, which were only interested in selling you the latest Dire Straits album.

The aforementioned shops were sometimes staffed by knowledgeable ex-hippies who had actually been there (the 1960s), had huge private record collections and who sometimes took a more than proprietorial interest in the young musician types who hung around their shops. Some wanted to 'educate' their customers; some were starting their own little record labels: in New Zealand, record shop owner Roger Shepherd of Christchurch (Flying Nun); in London, Geoff Travis (Rough Trade). In Scotland, Orange Juice was being given 'a crash course in [Postcard Records] Alan Horne's "magical hipness", absorbing the best pop, rock and soul records from the sixties and seventies which Horne had been collecting since his early teens' (Cavanagh, 2000, p. 28; see also pp. 37–42 and Kruse, 2003, pp. 51–5). A little later, Alan McGee would be doing the same with Creation (Cavanagh 2000; Hesmondhalgh, 1999, pp. 45–50). In Dunedin, Roy

Colbert of secondhand shop Records Records encouraged young musicians to listen to The Velvet Underground, 1960s garage rock and psychedelia, much like McGee and Horne (although Horne also liked soul) (Bannister, 1999, p. 21; Cavanagh 2000, p. 37). In Minneapolis, record shop owner Peter Jesperson educated young local bands, notably The Replacements, making sure 'they were aware only of the finest musical influences' (Jesperson also co-ran an independent label, Twin/Tone) (Azerrad, 2001, p. 200). Wuxtry Records in Athens, Georgia provided a focus for emergent bands such as the B-52s and R.E.M. – Peter Buck would 'spend hours in listening sessions, dissecting, analyzing, categorizing, and playing' with store co-owner Dan Wall (Buckley, 2002, p. 11). R.E.M.'s manager Jefferson Holt was another record shop owner (Buckley, 2002, pp. 40–1). In Brisbane, Australia, The Go-Betweens released their first two singles on Able, a label run by Toowong Music Centre proprietor Damien Nelson (Nichols, 2003, pp. 53–5).

Secondhand record shops and their owners performed a broadly educative function for indie musicians, broadening (selectively) their awareness of musical history. The canon is not a list, but rather a tool of education and a means of distributing cultural capital. Of the literary canon, John Guillory writes that:

> Where the debate speaks of the literary canon, its inclusions and exclusions, I will speak of the school, and the institutional forms of syllabus and curriculum … how works are preserved, reproduced, and disseminated over successive generations and centuries. Similarly, where the debate speaks about the canon as representing or failing to represent particular social groups, I will speak of the school's historical function of distributing, or regulating access to, the forms of cultural capital. (1993, vii–viii)

The problem with Sneaky Feelings was that we knew too much, and thus were not apt pupils, as Colbert wrote in his review of my book:

> Self-appointed rock critics are endemic to record stores the world over. They hold court in voices loud enough not only to silence whoever they're with, but also to let those behind the counter know they are in the presence of people who know the Right Stuff … Imagine my surprise … when … I found five of them up onstage in the same band. And a sixth was mixing their sound. Sneaky Feelings. Can you have six self-appointed rock critics in one band? (Colbert, 1999)

Colbert's rhetorical question suggests a distinction between 'critics' and real musicians who 'just do it', with the implication that we were too intellectual to play rock and roll (or perhaps more precisely that we challenged his version of the rock canon). This illustrates a thesis that I will presently develop – that rock's perceived anti-intellectualism naturalises certain forms of influence through discourses of spontaneity and originality. Colbert's preference was for punk rock, following Lester Bangs. As I already noted, Bangs' punk aesthetic downplayed the importance of archivalism to his own practice by foregrounding live performance, without acknowledging how deeply archival his vision of punk really was. Punk scenes took him at his word – in the UK especially, where the past was utterly dismissed (Gendron, 2002, p. 265).

In his account of gender and connoisseurship, 'Sizing Up Record Collections', Will Straw suggests that 'record collections, like sports statistics, provide the raw materials around which the rituals of homosocial interaction take shape ... each man finds, in the similarity of his points of reference to those of his peers, confirmation of a shared universe of critical judgment' (1997a, p. 5). However, 'there is an ongoing anxiety over whether the most valorised forms of masculine mastery are social or asocial' (1997a, p. 7). Peter Buck of R.E.M. comments: 'I'm not one of those anal types of collector ... that wants every different matrix number. I play records at parties when I'm drunk' (Buckley, 2002, p. 6). In other words, record collecting can be seen as a feminine activity (as consumerism often is), private, 'nerdy', 'geeky' and 'subservien[t] to the terms of a symbolic order' (Straw 1997a, p. 7). The collector 'depends' for his identity on things outside himself, and this is incompatible with public ideals of masculinity as self-sufficient, instinctual power (Hornby, 1995, pp. 73, 137). To resist the passive consumer/fan tag, male record collectors often adopt a bohemian, anti-commercial stance, typically by 'valorising the obscure' and transgressive. They contest hegemony, then, by setting up their own canon of 'great work' (Straw, 1997a, p. 10). Because many indie labels were initially more ideologically than commercially driven, the aesthetic preferences of the owner(s) were central to the style of music produced: 'the whole thing is just my taste' (McGee, quoted in DeRogatis, 1996, p. 221; see also Hesmondhalgh, 1999, p. 46). In the USA, Homestead Records (now Matador) head Gerard Cosloy (also editor of influential 1980s indie fanzine *Conflict*) was notorious for the vehemence of his views about what constituted correct musical practice (Arnold, 1995, pp. 37, 118–21; Azerrad, 2001, pp. 326–7). Such figures not only enabled indie production – they also played an important role in 'policing' the purity of the genre.

Many indie musicians were record collectors too: 'collecting and studying old rock bands is a rite of passage for young men entering the "scene"' (Hesmondhalgh, 1999, p. 47). But in public performance, young male musicians would want to avoid such potentially feminising identifications, so the archival aspects of the culture would disappear. Musicians wouldn't necessarily want to talk about their influences because it would compromise their cool, their originality. In Straw's words, 'hipness' is a 'controlled economy of revelation, a sense of when and how things are to be spoken of' (1997a, p. 9). 'Males police themselves ... in the ways they "wear" and release the knowledges they have cultivated' (Straw, 1997a, p. 7; see also Sedgwick, 1990, p. 185). The notion of control connects to power – a man who talks too much about what he 'knows' becomes feminised – selective silence is 'cool' and hides the effort of acquiring knowledge under a veil of 'instinctuality'. So musicians 'just do it' and disparage those who 'talk about it' (Robertson, 1991, pp. 9, 55). So while canonism is essential to understanding indie, at the same time it is also problematic because it compromises scenes and musicians' perceived independence, originality and subversiveness. Hence it is often downplayed. Of course, now that indie is over 20 years old, relatively institutionalised and extensively written about, the indie canon is frequently cited, but my point is that this was not and indeed could not always be the case.

Conclusions

I discussed how technology in rock music is positioned between a folk discourse of unmediated authenticity and a McLuhanite enthusiasm about the possibilities of new media, between technological dystopian and utopianism, and between different ideas of masculinities as articulated through the folk and art discourses. I looked at Lester Bangs and Brian Eno as major influences on technology's role in alternative rock, Bangs tending towards the folk model of technological minimisation, Eno identifying more with technology and against traditional humanist values. Both claim a problematisation of conventional rock masculinities through their emphasis on amateurism and non-intentionality. However, in doing so they disavow their own intellectuality – Bangs' aesthetic and Eno's cerebral control of the musical process. Their relinquishment of direct control is replaced with an overall intellectualisation. I went on to discuss how a similar dynamic is played out in the sound of indie – the guitar-dominated jangle/drone, which references both folk and technological discourses, creates an international folk music for aspiring white bohemians, working through an aesthetic of ironic amateurism, combining the immediacy of white noise with a withdrawal of the body. We might say that the sound of indie gives rise to ambiguity and irony, but not that it is necessarily therefore subversive of gender. Instead, I would suggest the sound of indie is of quiet men making loud noises. Male aggression (repressed through feminism) is rearticulated through sound as either offensive (excessive volume) or defensive (creating a sound 'barrier' between audience and performer) (Sutton, 1997, p. 529). It might be possible to hear this sound as a form of passive aggression.

A masculinised direct control of technology is replaced by identification with systems and theories of knowledge – a rationalisation and embourgeoisment of rock through the soft technologies of rationalisation. I then discussed how rock fans' and musicians' investment in abstract systems, and a scientised, technologised worldview is played out in the field of popular culture, identifying some key examples such as otaku, computer nerds, record collectors and the influence their culture had on indie, suggesting that such activities as archivalism, canonism and collecting, while influential, are often downplayed in accounts of indie scenes because they compromise its originality and authenticity. This partly explains the seeming anomaly of globally diverse indie scenes producing generically similar styles, apparently independently. More broadly this chapter has been about how knowledge produces cultural capital, and how masculine production of subcultural capital is imbricated with technological paradigms. As such, some men have an inside track, however reluctantly taken, to positions of power in an unashamedly technocratic society. In the final chapter, I will discuss some of the psychological and sociological ramifications of these subject positions.

Chapter 6

What will I do if she dies? Music, misery and white masculinities

'The unhappiest people I know ... are the ones who listen to pop music the most.'

(Hornby, 1995, p. 27)

Images and sensations of cold, sleep and death predominate in The Chills' 'Pink Frost' (1986), an evocative soundscape in which the velvety softness of Martin Phillipps' guitar tone, achieved through reverberation and attenuation of treble frequencies, creates a sumptuous 'bed' that is inviting and perilous, like hypothermia. The lyrics anxiously repeat questions: 'What will I do if she dies? What will I do if she's lost? Just the thought fills my heart with pink frost'. The 'she' is not characterised except in terms of the possibility of her death, which is associated with the narrator's death by guilt: 'How can I live when you see what I've done?' The idea of culpable loss combines with the seductive murmur of the guitar: in a word, melancholy, which Kristeva says is the 'most archaic expression of the non-symbolisable, unnameable narcissistic wound', that is, the loss of the mother, initiating the Oedipal phase (quoted in Reynolds and Press, 1995, p. 214).

The predominant emotional tone of 1980s indie music was pessimistic, marked by an overall sense of loss – of innocence, of love and (arguably) of traditional masculine power. Celebratory community gave way to dystopian isolation or regression into childlike fantasy. Clearly there are a number of reasons for this, not all to do with the state of mind of the participants. Art rock, punk and then indie all emulated high art 'seriousness', in line with their increasingly exclusive appeal, and as a way of highlighting their superiority to more commercial pop and rock. Abandoning both the obligatory optimism of pop and the sexual directness of earlier rock, alternative rock's distinctive angst (admittedly sometimes enhanced by its painful amateurism) acted to align it with other forms of exclusive, avant-garde or simply high culture in 'rejecting the generic, i.e. *common*, easy and immediately accessible' (Bourdieu, 1984, p. 32). Its gloomy outlook on the present and idealisation of past innocence confirmed its legitimacy as art. But, as I outlined in the introduction to this book, there were also some legitimate reasons why young white men in the early 1980s were feeling sorry for themselves.

This chapter looks at the causes, effects and remedies of melancholia in indie guitar rock and its association with various indie masculine personae. It argues a dialectical relation between indie masculinities and melancholia – while neither can be reduced to the other, each may incite it. There may be specific social circumstances that bring on melancholia, but, equally, I think there is also a gendered component in that the forms of hegemonic masculinity so far examined actually make it easy and sometimes profitable for some men to be miserable. We need to distinguish between the reality of male depression as a social problem and the extent to which the association of mental illness and the discourse of the artist act to legitimise and reify certain types of suffering – misery is not just a psychic state, but also a form of cultural capital.

Freud defines melancholia as a process by which a lost love object 'is set up within the ego' – cathexis or desire is withdrawn from the world and introjected (Freud, 1953–74, vol. 14, p. 249; vol. 19, p. 28; see also Butler, 1990, p. 61). To put it more literally, the melancholic, by withdrawing his energies and desires from direct relation and interaction with 'real' people and things, reinvests that energy within his psyche, endlessly replaying the drama of rejection and loss in a narcissistic vicious circle which excludes real relationships with others (Butler, 1990, p. 58). The verb 'replay' is no accident: media – TV, films, pop music – provide the melancholic soul with a potentially infinite series of replayable, mediated moments for him to masochistically relive and aestheticise his pain. 'What came first, the music or the misery? Did I listen to music because I was miserable? Or was I miserable because I listened to music?' (Hornby, 1995, pp. 26–7).

However, such lonely passivity is only half the melancholic story – for this lost object also functions 'as a critical voice or agency' (Butler, 1990, p. 61). The savagery of the accusing superego can lead to suicide (Butler, 1990, p. 62). This suggests that the other side of melancholy is introjected aggression – depression, understood in this way, is also an act of violence that is not externalised but instead becomes a form of self-punishment or masochism. Freud's model suggests a persecutory structure being set up in the psyche, which may be partly due to accusing voices in the world outside (for example, feminism in the case of masculinities) but also suggests more broadly a potentially schizophrenic oscillation between victimisation and accusation.[1] We will see this point amply demonstrated in the representations of white masculinities in this chapter. I argue that these polarities can only be worked out by moving away from Freud and towards Jessica Benjamin's (and, I argue, R.D. Laing's) concept of intersubjectivity, which views schizophrenic or sadomasochistic 'splitting' in terms of a more general model of dysfunctional identity development. Such splitting relates most obviously to problems of relationship, especially between child and parent, but also to how such problems may be exacerbated by modern society's masculinist devaluation of 'feminine' immanence and nurturance, its emphasis on individual autonomy and its rationalist bias. For example, despite Freud's diagnostic brilliance, he is unable to propose a satisfactory remedy for melancholia, other than finding a new love object to cathect.[2] He overlooks the thorny question of how such a process would occur, something impossible to envisage unless his intra-psychic model is set in a wider frame of reference – in terms of a much higher valuation of forms of social interaction and relationship than is found in Freud. Only in this way is any 'solution' to the problem of melancholia to be found.

What are some of the reasons for, and manifestations of, contemporary male melancholia? I will look at broad social trends and indie masculinities before focusing on examples of indie male melancholy, specifically Morrissey and Kurt Cobain.

Feminism

> Much might be said ... about the production and deployment ... of an extraordinarily high level of self-pity in nongay men ... In more intimate manifestations this straight male self-pity is often currently referred to (though it appears to exceed) the cultural effects of feminism ... this vast national wash of masculine self-pity is essentially never named or discussed as a cultural and political fact. (Sedgwick, 1990, p. 145)

Sedgwick argues that heterosexual male depression is essentially a self-interested ruse, part of the 'backlash' against feminine empowerment. While there is clearly some truth to this (see below, where I discuss male masochism and the 'suffering artist'), Sedgwick's summary rejection of men's emotional life seems little more than a reversal of the conventional male disparagement of female subjectivity. Indeed it may simply encourage perceptions that 'the disorder itself is seen as unmanly. Depression carries, to many, a double stain – the stigma of mental illness and also the stigma of a "feminine" emotionality ... Depression in men ... goes largely unacknowledged by both the men who suffer and by those who surround them. And yet the impact of this hidden condition is enormous' (Real, 1997, p. 22; see also Clare, 2000, pp. 23–4).

Feminist accounts, while displaying some perfectly righteous anger at men, need to avoid stigmatising them, because depression has such bad outcomes for society – most obviously in the form of violence (for example, the murder/suicide), but also more subtly in the way in which emotionally or physically absent fathers often hand on a legacy of depression to their offspring (Clare, 2000, pp. 2–3). While I don't want to get into psychoanalysing individual performers, it is notable that such family problems recur in both Cobain and Morrissey and clearly inform their work (Cross, 2001, pp. 1–39; Rogan, 1992, pp. 85–7).

Feminism's influence on indie is most clearly implied in themes of male guilt and apology: 'sorry', far from being the hardest word, has become one of the commonest (R.E.M.'s 'Southern Central Rain (I'm Sorry)', 1984; Hüsker Dü's 'I Apologise', 1985; The Go-Betweens' 'Apology Accepted', 1986; Nirvana's 'All Apologies', 1993). Guilty, 'suffering' men become a central trope. Clearly this emphasis has continued into 1990s indie, with songs like Beck's 'Loser' (1994) and Radiohead's 'Creep' (1993). Indie is 'the sound of the male voice struggling towards woundedness' (Sutton, 1997, p.528), a kind of 'moral masochism' (Silverman, 1992, p.191). Of Henry Rollins, Azerrad comments that '[i]n his diary, lyrics and performance Rollins would flagellate himself for being an ogre, then revel in being an ogre so he could flagellate himself some more ... Instead of lashing out, it was lashing in.' Rollins wrote: 'I hope I get bashed up soon ... I need the pain to play' (Azerrad, 2001, p. 49).

Rollins presents a sadomasochistic persona as both the perpetrator and receiver of violence: 'Instead of seeing a therapist and trying to rejoin the human race, he has founded his career on roaring like a wounded beast about how lonely he is, whilst simultaneously making it plain that he will still strike out at anyone who attempts to get near' (Collins, 2000). Reading this in terms of gender, we could surmise that men have internalised many of the feminist accusations about sexism and bad male behaviour. But withdrawal into isolation may exacerbate the problem (Azerrad, 2001, p. 49). Rather than mourn, they brood. Their confessions are suspect – indeed they may even display a kind of masochistic pleasure in baring their souls (Foucault, 1984, pp. 303–4). Deleuze suggests that male masochism is a 'strategy by which [he] manipulates the woman into the ideal state for the performance of the role he has assigned to her' (1989, p. 107).

Some other masculine appropriations of supposedly feminine subject positions I have already critiqued – most saliently that postmodern fragmentation of the subject, ego death and *jouissance* simply reify a Freudian concept of feminine subjectivity as opposite to masculine unity and autonomy. This is obviously to suggest that male masochism – men taking weak, fragmented, victim positions – does not challenge patriarchy (see Chapters 1 and 2). Instead the trope of male suffering allows men to have feelings without being responsible for them, because they are being 'made' to feel by somebody or something else. War or conflict make expressions of male emotion permissible, because in both men are not in control – some force outside them is making them do this. But Terri Sutton argues that this is not an advance – it's simply role reversal: 'a sexier hybrid in the martyrdom family – Admit you're an asshole, blame it on somebody else, plead for punishment ... what they are saved from is any ... responsibility' (1997, p. 531). For Lauren Goodlad, alternative rock masculinities represent:

> a kind of antisexist sexism ... postpunk music culture was ... dominated by male musicians, prone to appropriating 'femininity' as a male aesthetic credential, rather than to empowering women ... Through a familiar pattern in which traumatic loss ... finds expression in androgyny (as the lost female is replaced by a cathartic experience of 'femininity') normative male subjectivities were disrupted, refigured, and – to a certain extent – restored. (2003, p. 138)

However, indie rock does name the problem of male depression several years before it became a broad social concern, and this is significant. At the same time, the ways in which indie can be culturally and commercially valued as rock art may actually add fuel to the fire through the aestheticisation of male pain. In turn this aestheticisation legitimates masculine splitting and reproduces schizophrenia as a norm for masculine artistic production – being 'fucked up' becomes a kind of prerequisite for authenticity, especially in a genre that foregrounds its difference from mainstream culture.

The suffering artist

Mental illness, as Foucault (1984, pp. 125–6) reminds us, may be used as a way of categorising and containing deviant social elements. Against that, or perhaps on the same continuum, is the association of mental illness with uniqueness, individuality and creativity, and the extent to which this has reified the identification of emotional and social dysfunction with artistry. Laing (1965, p. 89) points out that many artists are schizoid, and that the development of inner phantasy that artists cultivate can exacerbate mental problems.

In a broader way, the idea of mental illness is deeply linked to Romantic discourses of the artist as unworldly and consumptive: Bangs' characterisation of the punk as 'sick', the artist as psychopath, to modern perceptions of GenX as a 'Prozac' nation, as autistic or passive/aggressive. The suggestion is that the artist or art articulates what normal society represses – if normal society appears healthy, the artist expresses its hidden sickness – the canary in a coalmine hypothesis. A not unrelated view is that the artist has a superior awareness, a heightened sensitivity and a prophetic function – as in Shelley's *A Defence of Poetry*. The implication is that his visionary insights may appear as madness in the eyes of contemporary society. 'Madness' in turn can legitimate an identification of artistry with feminine sensitivity and emotional expressiveness. However, in music, such terms usually apply to the male artist whose feminine sensibility is part of his genius: 'Masculinity is often most revered when marked by the discursively constructed feminine characteristics which characterise the genius. Then the masculine meaning of music may ... conjure up feminine attributes in a genius; but it will never conjure up that aberration, a female genius' (Green, 1997, p. 133).

The subtext of the 'genius' discourse is that patriarchal society suppresses emotional, individual expression, as for example in Kristeva's notion of the semiotic as a subversion of patriarchal language (Butler, 1990, p. 79). However, such a model may also lend itself to more traditional gender readings: for example, that the artist has a superior awareness or intellect, that he is 'standing out from the crowd' – in other words, Western individualism. (Also, the 'genius is pain' discourse tends to underplay the degree to which the pain is actually suffered by other people, usually the artist's family and friends). In this light we would have to see this Romantic conception of the artist as arising in tandem with the emergence of modernity – his opposition to 'the system', just like the opposition of his art to commerce, keeps the system running, like the positive and negative poles of a dynamo. Finally, in Mailer's *The White Negro* we have a model of artistic creativity hugely influential on rock music of the artist as male psychopath (combining a feminine sensitivity to stimuli with a narcissistic rage if he is denied personal gratification) (Mailer, 1957). I think in all these representations of madness certain kinds of underlying binaries are present – archetypally the Freudian notion that 'true' individuality is impossible in society because of the repressive demands of socialisation, and that accordingly the true artist and his/her art will always stand apart from 'the mass'. This is a model I have already critiqued elsewhere – ultimately the gender identity of the subject under such a scheme is irrelevant, because the scheme itself is patriarchal. The very isolation of the artist, if taken as proof of his authenticity, becomes indistinguishable from a paranoid-schizoid position in which 'no one knows what's going on but me'.

The general point here is that there is a fairly clear correspondence between emotional dysfunction, hegemonic masculine values and the discourse of the solitary 'genius'. The figure of the artist incarnates and apparently unites these contradictions.

Nostalgia, the 1960s and infantilism

Melancholics are obsessed with the past, a point relevant in a number of ways to indie masculinities. It helps explain their fascination with the 1960s, both as a time of literal childhood memories, but also as the golden age of pop culture, a salutary contrast to the grim realities of the present. Sixties psychedelia had given rise to 'child-men', notably Syd Barrett of Pink Floyd, a clear influence on the faux naif personae of Martin Phillipps of The Chills and Robyn Hitchcock of The Soft Boys (Brown, 1984b, p. 22; Colbert, 1985; DeRogatis, 1996, pp. 155, 160–65). Such regression was also present in the style and apparel of some scenes – Cavanagh writes of UK indie that 'words such as "cutie" or "charming" were used to underline the infantilism of the songs and personalities. The favoured garment was the anorak – the clothing of primary school. "The anorak was a style statement," says Stephen Pastel [of Creation band The Pastels]. 'It was saying: "…we've got to get back. Closer to the start of things. Being children"' (Cavanagh, 2000, p. 190). Similarly, Reynolds defines indie style as 'a mixture of pre-permissive, virtually pre-youth culture clothes and children's garments … it conceals the signs of sexual difference and of adulthood' (quoted in Frith and Horne, 1987, p. 178).

New Zealand indie also had a fascination with childhood. The Chills' songs (written by Phillipps) suggest child-like naivety: 'Kaleidoscope World', 'Pink Frost', 'Juicy Creaming Soda' (unreleased), 'Green-Eyed Owl' (1986), 'Sixteen Heartthrobs', (1987), 'Rolling Moon' (1986), 'Bee Bah Bee Bah Bee Boe' (1984). The Clean's song titles tell a similar story: 'Fish', 'Flowers', 'Slug Song' (1982). Lyrics feature nursery rhyme-like patterns: "I go up dadda up dadda up dadda up" ('End of my Dream', 1982); 'One o'clock, two o'clock, three o'clock, it's time to go' ('Sad Eyed Lady', 1981); 'This little boy [...]', 'Billy-oh, Billy-oh, Billy uh-huh' ('Billy Two', 'Thumbs Up', both on *Boodle Boodle Boodle* (1981). The Clean's and The Chills' cover art consists of doodles and childlike scrawls. The Bats provide another example of infantilism in their deliberately simplistic, repetitive songwriting and 'naive' vocalising. Boyhood innocence and its loss became a recurrent theme in indie, as did writing about children – 'Cattle and Cane' by The Go-Betweens (1983), 'Suffer Little Children', 'Reel around the Fountain' by The Smiths (1984a). For a more mainstream example, see U2's *Boy* (1980).

The flamboyant sexual androgyny that was a leading theme of 1970s art rock was replaced by regression to a pre-sexual, virginal state (the androgyny of the child), for example the 'straight' or 'nerd', as in Jonathan Richman (also an influence on Michael Stipe; Buckley, 2002, p. 28), David Byrne, and The Feelies (Gans, 1985, p. 43). The Go-Betweens' 'Robert and Grant just seemed like these completely androgynous types who would never be interested in the opposite sex' (Nichols, 2003, p. 80). Keightley (2001, p. 124) suggests that indie rock's fascination with childhood in some ways reflected its increasingly bourgeois Romantic outlook (the obverse of the suffering artist trope discussed above). Of course, this 'desexualisation' can also be read as a response to feminist critique of rock sexism.

Although the idealisation of childhood connoted masculine melancholy by referencing nostalgic high art Romantic visions of Arcadia, at the same time there was a counterdiscourse of 'childhood gone wrong'. Youth consumption by the 1970s had started to be seen as unhealthy and dependent, resulting in a re-imagining of youth consumption as sickly or vampire-like, and youth themselves as diseased or even moronic, as in the pinhead, cartoon-like punk rock of bands like the Ramones: 'Gabba gabba hey', 'One two three four, cretins gonna rock some more' ('Cretin Hop', 1977) – the fulfilment of Bangs' prophecy of the cretinous wretchedness of punk (Latham, 2002, p. 70; Carson, 1996, p. 108, Bangs, 1987, p. 273). The Replacements' legendary sloppiness (on and off stage) was redolent of small boys (Arnold, 1995, pp. 92–5; Azerrad, 2001, pp. 211ff). Gina Arnold describes it as engendering an almost maternal instinct: 'the feeling you get when you see a person get embarrassed, and you reach out a hand ... to help them through their humiliation' (1995, p. 94). In the USA especially, regressiveness has become equated with the resistant male stupidity of Homer and Bart Simpson, MTV's Beavis and Butthead and films like the Farrelly Bros' *Dumb and Dumber*, *There's Something About Mary* and so on (Savage, 1997, p. 396). However, infantilism in rock and elsewhere is mainly a male prerogative – female infantilism tends to become sexualised through the male gaze and thereby riskier for the practitioner (Courtney Love's *kinderwhore*, for example). In this, punk/indie participants reproduced the Foucauldian model, wearing social and media classifications of them as 'failures' as perverse badges of honour. This model also reproduced a binary logic – pathetic victims, who were also potentially criminal and deviant (or in Carson's terms (1996, p. 102), heroic losers.

Infantilism is continuous with a melancholic disengagement from social and emotional relations (especially sex) and a compensating concentration on 'fantasy' (Reynolds, 1989, p. 247). Reynolds notes recurrent references to states of entrancement and abandonment in UK indie: 'swooning' or being 'hypnotized' (1989, p. 247). This may relate to drug use but could also relate to indie discourses of regression to a passive, enwombed state. However, the dreamer motif also highlights the bipolar structure of melancholia: both passivity and the possibility of psychosis. David Lynch's *Blue Velvet* (1986) offers a relevant example: when Dennis Hopper's character sings Roy Orbison's 'In Dreams' while torturing Kyle McLachlan, the effect is more than a bizarre juxtaposition of romantic pop song with extreme violence, there is a closer connection between Orbison's persona in the song and Hopper's in the film – they are both 'dreamers': 'Frank is somewhere in Roy Orbison's dreams, too; he is part of the cost of dreaming' (Marsh, 1987, p. 8). Orbison's 'intense dreams and daydreams, which at times appear totally delusional, border on ... "possession"' (Lehman, 2003, p. 133). Peter Lehman argues that Orbison opened rock up to the expression of intense masculine vulnerability and fear, a new kind of rock masculinity marked by personal anonymity, fantasy and a strong preoccupation with dreaming, loneliness and failure (2003, pp. 24–5, 87). At the same time, a feminist commentary might point out how the intensity of Orbison's fantasy visions borders on a 'stalker' persona ('Pretty Woman', for example (Orbison, 1976)). There is a schizoid aspect to Orbison's persona (Lehman, 2003, pp. 101–4). The passive dreamer may be just one step away from psychotic violence.

The sadistic intellectual (the auteur)

If indie music isn't regressing to childhood, then it goes to the opposite extreme: dark, dystopian, nightmare scenarios, characterised by extreme distortion and aggression, as we hear in the music of Nirvana, hardcore, Big Black, Nick Cave, The Birthday Party, Butthole Surfers, Sonic Youth and Nine Inch Nails. Sometimes the two are present in the same moment: as in The Jesus and Mary Chain's desecrations of Phil Spector or My Bloody Valentine. Pain and suffering, far from being denied, are insisted upon. This sadism may be imagined as attacking the self (masochism) or the other. To refer back to Butler's interpretation of the Freudian model of melancholy (1990, p. 62), sadism is associated with the superego and the father. This is reproduced in rock culture in the way that 'sadists' tend to also represent themselves as intellectuals and advocates of high culture, a strategy that also counters accusations of intellectual effeteness through the 'compensation' of violence and psychosis, reaffirming distance from conventional high culture.

Sadistic rock intellectuals (historically Bob Dylan, Frank Zappa, Lou Reed, Leonard Cohen, but in indie Nick Cave, Henry Rollins, Steve Albini, Graeme Downes) typically construct themselves as cerebral observers of excess and debauchery, reproducing a traditional division of 'high' aesthetic awareness (mind) with a view of the body as abject, and violated. They replace sex with violence, or combine the two. Typically such artists (usually solo artists, which seems apt, given their personae) are also published poets and authors. Others work off high culture associations.

Nick Cave, originally singer of Melbourne's The Birthday Party, fashioned a persona built around high culture (poetry and novels) and rock excess and decadence (he based himself for some years in West Berlin). 'Australia's darkest son has made a well-documented career of his fixation with the sordid details underlying all facets of human life. Building his persona from equal parts fractured troubadour and epic poet, Cave has assembled a body of work that's as compelling for its literary narrative as it is for its brooding musical sensibilities' (Hreha, 2003). Any possible adverse connotations of Cave's high culture associations are offset by his lifestyle and lyrical preoccupations with violence against women: 'I've always enjoyed writing songs about dead women' (quoted in Reynolds and Press, 1995, p. 28). Reynolds traces a trail of female blood from The Birthday Party (his first band)'s 'She's Hit' through 'From Her to Eternity' to 'Your Funeral ... My Trial', which could be extended to his more recent *Murder Ballads* (1996). His persona is that of a psychopath who is absolved of worldly responsibilities by his artistic vocation.

Steve Albini was a well-known fanzine writer before he became a musician. His work in Big Black is notable for its preoccupation with extreme sounds and subject positions such as racists, sex criminals and psychopaths. Reynolds comments that 'in "Kerosene" the narrator combines the town's two forms of amusement (blowing things up and fucking the town slut) into a single blast of catharsis' (Reynolds and Press, 1995, p. 30). This is combined with an extremity of sound and presentation: the band's *Headache* EP (1987) features a photograph of a man's head after suicide by shotgun (at least that's what it looks like). Albini's band after Big Black, Rapeman, seemed calculated to offend, and succeeded (Azerrad, 2001, pp. 342–3). Albini's confrontational approach was double-edged – in effect, he invited people to despise him. Hence his aggression was also a kind of victimhood – 'Hate me please!' At art college, Albini 'planned to stand behind a Plexiglass wall and taunt people while inviting them to throw things at him; the wall and the objects would then become the sculpture' (Azerrad, 2001, pp. 314–15).

Of course, the very extremity and excess of these visions invites an alternative reading in terms (again) of camp: 'Today, the most advanced forms of bad taste vanguardism are located in a loosely defined nexus of cultish interests that have granted the most anti-social features of "sick" humor on to an attenuated paranoia about the normality of the straight world ... conspiracy theories ... bodily disorders and etiologies, religious cult tracts, mass murderer folklore, the psychopathology of atrocities' (Ross, 1989, p. 155). (See also Butthole Surfers, Jim Foetus, Sonic Youth and so on.) In New Zealand, this undercurrent of sick humour was most obvious in the Auckland indie scene, with bands like the Headless Chickens and This Kind of Punishment, and in the artwork of local musicians like Chris Knox of the Tall Dwarfs and David Mitchell of the Exploding Budgies, Goblin

Mix and the 3Ds, which reference 1960s comic styles and the standard preoccupation with death and violence.

A more high art approach was taken by Graeme Downes of the Verlaines, whose persona was half 'hoon' (New Zealand slang for a male working-class troublemaker) and half tortured artist. He presented his lyrics as poetry, claiming they were the most important part of his work, a line which most commentators reproduced without question: 'the words ... make nearly every other lyricist in the country look silly' (Brown, 1983b). Similarly Downes's work features high cultural identifications with classical music and literature (as is evident in his choice of band name) along with a mythologisation of the artistic vocation. High culture references included 'Baud to Tears', which quotes poems by French Symbolists/ decadents Baudelaire and Rimbaud, 'CD Jimmy Jazz and Me' (Claude Debussy and James Joyce – the latter featured on the cover of the 'Death and the Maiden' single) and the 'Ballad of Harry Noryb' (Noryb is an anagram of Byron). 'In "Phil Too" he even envisions himself as Julius Caesar: "the day that you left I sang 'Et tu Brute'"' (Verlaines, 1988; Bannister, 1999, p. 139). In live performance, Downes played the role of the 'poet maudit' to the hilt: 'Where Martin [Phillipps] was winsome and dreamy, Graeme was smouldering and Byronic. On stage, he whipped himself into an expressionistic frenzy' (Bannister, 1999, p. 44). Against these high cultural pretensions was set identification with the ferocity and energy of punk, allied with a 'hoonish' delight in pub culture:

> On *Hallelujah All the Way Home* [Flying Nun, 1986], eight out of the nine songs mention cigarettes. Nine out of nine if you include 'For the Love of Ash Grey'. Almost every song mentions pubs and drinking. Graeme was keen to display his 'earthiness', perhaps because in Kiwi eyes it made his excursions into 'art' look more credible. Violent extremities are another characteristic: ice and blistering heat, 'blood on my pickups' etcetera. This last was at least true – Graeme was always cutting his fingers on the strings while playing ... Then there's hell and madness, choking, kicking etc. It's not hard to see why some condemned Dunedin bands as gloom junkies ... As one would expect in a culture built around rugby, brutalisation is seen as a necessary part of any transcendent experience. (Bannister, 1999, pp. 138–9)

Downes was careful to maintain his credibility by mixing high cultural references with intimations of boozy camaraderie and dissolute bohemianism.

This combination of aestheticised intellectualism and violence demonstrates de Sade's idea that 'reasoning itself is a form of violence', performing 'a demonstration related essentially to the solitude and omnipotence of its author ... the reasoning does not have to be shared by the person to whom it is addressed any more than the pleasure is meant to be shared by the object from which it is derived' (Deleuze, 1989, p. 18; see also Reynolds and Press, 1995, p. 148). It is a demonstration: 'endless repetitions again and again retracing the thousand circles of an irreducibly solitary argument' (Deleuze, 1989, p. 20). Of course, the sadistic viewpoint implies a masochistic opposite, and many indie artists combine these two perspectives – Morrissey is a pertinent example.

Masculine splitting and schizophrenia – broader theories

In *Taking it like a Man* (1998, p. 5), David Savran traces the emergence of a similarly dualistic model of US white masculinity which began to surface in the 1970s, in response to feminism, civil rights, lesbian and gay rights, the Vietnam war and, most importantly, 'the end of the post-WWII economic boom and a resultant and steady decline in the income of white working- and lower–middle-class men' (Somerson, 2004, p. 216). White men used the trope of blackness and marginality (which emerged especially in the rock counterculture) as a way of starting to understand themselves as victims. Wendy Somerson comments that Savran describes 'A new white male "fantasmatic" emerging that responded to these changes "by encouraging the white male subject's simultaneous embrace and disavowal of the role of victim"'. The white male subject is split. 'On one hand, he takes up the "feminized positionality" of the victim, but on the other hand, he enacts fantasies of "hypermasculinized heroism"' (Somerson, 2004, p. 216, quoting Savran, 1996, p. 128). Such 'reflexive sadomasochism functions in the service of conservative ideology to consolidate … white masculinity in times of … crises' (2004, p. 216).

We see this dualism played out in media representations of masculinities. On the one hand, men are victimised, childlike and helpless: 'soft' masculinities, the 'feminised' man, the SNAG (Sensitive New Age Guy), the house husband. Robert Bly writes at some length about 'soft men' who represent a reaction against the traditional sexist 'Fifties man' and lack a strong male role model (usually a father), and he links these changes to social change in the post-war period, like Savran. He argues that although there is much commendable in this 'feminisation' of men, there is also a dangerous (in his view) lack of vitality (Bly, 1990, pp. 2–3). This feminisation theme was expressed in indie both through male masochism and through fetishisation of 'feminine' or childish 'weakness'.

On the other hand, media representations of male madness and men 'out of control' are becoming increasingly frequent in Western culture. Psychotic males on violent rampages, fathers who kill their families and themselves are in the news almost every day. Since *Taxi Driver* (1976) the male psychopath has become a stock and not unsympathetic figure in cinema. In Hollywood film, Michael Douglas has become representative of the type of white, middle-class man, victimised by women or the world (*Fatal Attraction*, 1987; *Basic Instinct*, 1992; *Disclosure*, 1994) who 'snaps' and goes on the rampage (*Falling Down*, 1993). The key here is that these figures in both TV and film increasingly invite identification, from *Henry – Portrait of a Serial Killer* (1989) to Tony of *The Sopranos*, to the films of Quentin Tarantino. We are shown that these killers are 'ordinary' – mafia bosses who cry and consult psychoanalysts about their mental problems. Similarly, the psychotic sadist has become, since punk, a standard persona, particularly in alternative rock of the type under discussion. Intrinsic to the melancholic model is therefore its 'split' personality. It is related to schizophrenia. But is there any way to cure it?

Remedies

Butler argues that, for Freud, melancholia is intrinsic to identity formation. Just as we have discussed elsewhere how Freud saw internalisation of prohibition as part of identity formation, so the process of losing desired objects and internalising them is 'character-building' (Butler, 1990, p. 58). This was typical of Freud's gloomy assessment of human nature, based on his autonomous model of the psyche, which results in the conflation of distinct subject positions, such as infant and psychotic (Laing, 1965, pp. 19–25). More broadly, melancholy can only be escaped by transferring cathexis onto a new external love object. But it is not clear how the locked-up melancholic soul would come to such a state. Thus we have to say that although Freudian psychology describes the problem of melancholia well, the antithetical terms of his system do not offer a ready synthesis. We can only achieve this by re-viewing its internal splitting mechanism in terms not just of itself but of states of relation to others – that is, as a schizophrenic state mediated through the insights of relational psychoanalysis.

R.D. Laing is careful to distinguish his approach to self from Freud. For Laing, self is relational – it is constituted through its relations with others – it is not a becoming-autonomous monad that gradually individuates from regressive attachments. Attachment is the very essence of existence (Laing, 1965, p. 26). In contrast, schizophrenia is a state of non-existence realised through a withdrawal from creative relations with others: 'The term schizoid refers to an individual the totality of whose experience is split in two main ways ... there is a rent in his relation with his world and ... a disruption of his relation with himself.' Not at home in the world, 'he experiences himself in despairing aloneness and isolation' and 'as "split" ... perhaps as a mind ... tenuously connected to a body, as two or more selves' (1965, p. 17). The point is that internal splitting is predicated upon a further split between self and world. Laing describes how the schizoid subject tries

> to be omnipotent by enclosing within his own being, without recourse to a creative relation with others, modes of relation that require the effective presence to him of other people ... The imagined advantages are safety for the true self, isolation and hence freedom from others, self-sufficiency and control [but] ... this shut-up self ... is unable to be enriched by outer experience, and so the whole inner world comes to be more and more impoverished. (1965, p. 75)

The schizophrenic is unable to sustain the paradox that relatedness is a precondition of identity, imagining instead that 'if one experiences the other as a free agent, one is open to the possibility of experiencing oneself as an *object* of his [*sic*] experience' (1965, p. 47). Other people are a threat to identity.

One can see the general similarities to Freud's position, but also the crucial distinction that a 'healthy' self is defined not just in intra-psychic terms, but in terms of its relations to others.[3] Benjamin expands Laing's position by connecting it to the problem of domination, thus leading further towards a gender critique (there is also an implicit gender critique in Laing's refusal of Oedipalisation as an adequate paradigm (1965, p. 56)). Benjamin argues that the problem of domination is insoluble in Freudian terms (superego mastering id): 'either we accept the necessity of some rational authority to control our dangerous natures, or we maintain naively that our better nature is dangerously repressed by the social order. But this opposition between instinct and civilization obscures the central question of how domination actually works', because of its absolute dichotomy of desire, subjectivity and the rational social order. 'Some kind of domination is inevitable; the only question is which kind?' (Benjamin, 1988, p. 4). This domination/submission dialectic is also reproduced in relations with the self as self-mastery:

> Internalization of authority proceeds by turning the frustrated wish for power inward: we may not be able to affect the world, but we can at least control ourselves; we may not be able to truly achieve independence ... but we can distance ourselves ... so that we appear completely autonomous. That this acceptance of powerlessness in the guise of autonomy may deny our responsibility to care for others is rationalized by the notion that we can ... do nothing to help them. This compact with the reality principle was expressed most eloquently by Descartes: 'My third maxim was to try to conquer myself rather than fortune, and to change my desires rather than the order of the world, and to generally accustom myself to believing that there is nothing entirely in our power except our thoughts'. (Benjamin, 1988, pp. 179–80, quoting Descartes, 1968, p. 47)

Thus the Cartesian splitting of object and subject is emblematic of a masculine mode of representing the world (Keller, 1985). It is related to a larger scheme of submission and domination, which is socially produced through instrumentality/rationalisation (or axiomatisation, as Deleuze and Guattari call it). This rationality, Benjamin argues, is patriarchal (1988, pp. 183–98).

But this same rational splitting also produces melancholia:

> The impasse of rationalism, analogous to the impasse of omnipotence, in which the subject completely assimilates the outside ... runs throughout western thought ... as the rational subject of thought became increasingly separate from the object, he internalized the qualities of that lost object, and attributed to himself all that was once part of the objective world. (Benjamin, 1988, p. 190)

Benjamin argues that the masculine rationalist position is marked by an alternation between domination and submission – a sadistic/masochistic continuum. It is schizophrenic because the other cannot be creatively envisaged, its existence is basically a threat, and as such the shut-up schizoid can only envisage relationship in terms of omnipotence or victimhood.

Unlike Freud, relational psychoanalysis does not view identity in terms of an agonistic model in which individual identity emerges through repression – rather, human subjects can interact in ways that construct personal identity as a negotiation between self and other, based on mutual recognition and epistemic negotiation. As such relational psychoanalysis sees identity as social construct but also as a felt subjective reality, that is dependent on recognition of the other and being recognised by the other as subjectively real. The parent/infant relationship (radically underrepresented in the theories so far examined) is seen as a key site for the emergence of a mutually shared subjective reality, a sense of agency and authentic 'sense of self'. Identity is not viewed as objective and autonomous, but as nevertheless in some sense real. This implies a different kind of epistemology to that operating in the public sphere and media – Øystein Holter's theorisation of domesticity provides a useful counterexample here.[4] It suggests that men need to embrace and understand this alternative epistemology if they are to come to a better self-understanding, but that the primacy of the public over the private sphere means that there is little obvious incentive for them to change. But the price of not changing may well be higher, as I will demonstrate with reference to two of indie's best-known 'sons', Kurt Cobain and Morrissey.

Grunge, Nirvana and the postmodern subject

In the early 1990s, Nirvana, grunge and the Seattle scene burst into public awareness. For many indie commentators, Nirvana's commercial 'triumph' represented the vindication of indie's years of struggle in the 1980s. But grunge drew on different influences to 1980s indie, in particular 1970s metal. As a result it was 'angry' in a way that was novel to indie (Nehring, 1997, pp. 79–86). The combination of 'rage' and commercial success meant that grunge was much more extensively covered in the media, and in discussions of Nirvana's music and its main author, Kurt Cobain, we find more evidence of polarised media discourses on white masculinity. Nirvana and Cobain were seen to express both psychotic 'rage' and extreme victimhood and abjection. The psychosis of this rage was in its 'meaninglessness'. The *New York Times*, commenting on the Lollapalooza 1991 tour, claimed that 'the rage of [the music]' is 'as inarticulate as it is widespread' and thus the audiences 'don't much care who or what that "rage" is aimed at. All they want to feel is that someone is as angry as they are' (Jon Pareles, quoted in Nehring, 1993, p. 328). The implication is that rage does not lead to constructive action, or alternatively that in the modern media environment, rage is just another marketing tool.

Even more sympathetic accounts of Nirvana tend to stress the chaotic: 'All of it communicated anger, maybe loathing, definitely passion, no matter how inchoate' (Handy et al., 1994). On the other hand, media discourses also paint Cobain as a humble saint who was unprepared for and ultimately destroyed by fame, a 'soft' man who wore dresses onstage and denounced homophobia. Cobain certainly hated the 'jocks' who supposedly bullied him at school, and was profoundly disturbed by the idea that such un-PC types might actually enjoy the band's music: 'If any of you … hate homosexuals, people of different colour, or women, please – leave us the fuck alone' (Cobain, *Incesticide* liner notes, 1992).

Neil Nehring strongly rejects the 'meaningless rage' thesis as a postmodern depoliticisation of rock: '[the] dismissal of any association between rock and rebellion offers ... the clearest evidence that the ... basis of postmodern theory is an abandonment of political agency' (1997, p. 86). However, the 'devaluation' of the subject which Nehring attributes to postmodern theory is clearly there in Nirvana (presumably this is why Nehring never discusses Cobain's lyrics, because they would contradict his thesis about agency). The subject *is* devalued – by itself. On the other hand, I don't think the postmodern 'schizophrenic' position is tenable either, because simply substituting a multiple fragmented subject for a whole unified one misses the way in which identity is constructed through meaningful relations with others. It is reasonably easy to speculate that this was part of the reason for Cobain's problems – he clearly had an awful childhood, and when he got famous it destroyed him, because he simply lacked the sense of self necessary to survive all the projections, interpretation and representations being placed upon him (Cross, 2001, pp. 1–39).[5] 'Kurt Cobain is not a person ... He's turned in to something that represents different things for different people ... he had no life, no peace, constant chaos. He had become a freak' (Daniel House, quoted in Powers, 1995, p. 787).

Cobain's subject positions alternate between extreme passivity and anger. Victimisation, masochism and sadism recur – 'Bipolar opposites attract' ('Pennyroyal Tea', 1993) – as do references to childhood neglect (and trauma), for example 'Paper Cuts' (1989) and 'Sliver' (1992). 'All Apologies' (1993) presents a persona whose subjectivity is literally 'all apologies'; that is, if you took them away, there would be nothing left. The subject simultaneously imagines himself as omnipotent and victimised – he is to blame for everything. Of course, this is only the flip side of 'you are to blame for everything'.

Rape is almost a leitmotif of Cobain's writing – for example 'Rape Me' (1993) and 'Polly' (1991) (sung from the point of view of a rapist): one is either a rapist or raped, and this is presented as routine. The implication is that rape is a metaphor for all human relations – one is either servant or master ('Serve the Servants', 1993). Even where there is not a literal rape, images of violation and consumption abound – 'Drain You' (1991), 'Dive' (1993) – or of eating or consuming the other (again with the implication that all relationships are parasitic) – 'Milk It' (1993), 'Drain You' (1991). The connection to sadomasochism is clear. One possible interpretation is that many of the above songs are about Cobain's victimised relation to his audience. This invites speculation as to the extent to which the discourse of the star reproduces a culturally sanctioned schizophrenic split, in which the star persona becomes public property (Dyer, 1986, p. 13). Laing suggests that the schizophrenic's relation to visibility is complex: 'he may *need* to be seen and recognised, in order to maintain his sense of realness and identity. Yet, at the same time, the other presents a threat to his identity and reality' (1965, p. 113). This is because 'one is threatened with the possibility of becoming no more than a thing in the world of the other' (Laing, 1965, p. 47; see also Hector, 1998, p. 64).

Typically Cobain's songs oscillate between sadism and masochism, domination and submission in the schizoid manner. If the above suggests the former, there is also a great deal of passivity and evocation of infant 'bliss'. A particular focus is the mother–child relationship. Tellingly, mother and lover are often conflated in Cobain. 'Dumb' (1991) (which means 'happy') suggests regression towards a pre-Oedipal state of original innocence, a scenario that also occurs in the medicated la-la land of 'Lithium' (1991), a medication prescribed for bipolar disorders. 'Drain You' (1991) mixes images of a perfect Edenic reciprocity (only possible because both characters are 'babies') with allusions to the mother/infant dyad (hence 'draining' could be read as 'suckling'). The intimacy of physical connection and the images of exchange of bodily fluids suggest total dependence on the love of a maternal other (udder?) ('Scentless Apprentice', 1993) or climbing back into the womb ('Pennyroyal Tea', 1993). Failing that, castration removes the 'pain' of sexuality – 'Beeswax' (1992), 'On a Plain' (1991). Relationship is thus imagined in terms of absolutes – either child or parent, either powerful or exploited.

The schizoid worldview articulated in Cobain's lyrics finds its structural parallel in the arrangements of the songs, which typically alternate between quiet dreamy verses and screaming, angry, distorted electric choruses (Stubbs, 1999, p. 101). This use of extreme contrasts (first popularised by the Pixies) was not only influential, but also echoed the bipolarity of emotional states in schizophrenia – oscillating between helpless despair and narcissistic rage. 'Smells like Teen Spirit' (1991) is probably the best example, moving from vague *anomie* in the verses to a sudden outpouring of demands from the other in the anthemic chorus. Likewise, Cobain's melodies tend to move from repetitive syncopations on the verses, which give a feeling of somnambulistic disconnection, to a punchier approach on the chorus, as do his vocals: from nasal, slurry and offhand to rough-edged howls and the occasional Lennonesque grunt, the stylistic extremism of *Plastic Ono Band* (Lennon, 1970) being perhaps Cobain's most obvious influence – apt, given Lennon's preoccupations with childhood pain and psychic therapy.

It might be possible to hear Nirvana as a half-protest against patriarchal domination. It could be argued that Cobain was a 'sensitive new age guy' type: 'They [Nirvana] were letting down their guard, expressing their vulnerability and admitting that, like the rest of us, they were all scared geeks and "losers"' (Kitts et al., 1998, p. 18). Cobain, not only in his lyrics but also in his cross-dressing and statements about gender, was identifying not so much with women, but with a model of femininity that is essentialising and ideological – women are subalterns, and we should feel sorry for them. 'For all Cobain's vocal defense of gay and women's rights, it was clear who the real victim was. It was the guy wearing the dress, pretending he had no power, no responsibility, no effect – and the guys in the auditorium, pretending along with him' (Sutton, 1997, p. 530).

Morrissey, Warhol and narcissism

I understand narcissism as a condition that is closely linked to schizophrenic dissociation and its absolute model of power relations, but also one that is by implication more active, more performative. It shares with schizophrenia the notion of 'dividing the self to obviate the threat of needing others … in its pathological form, it seeks to evade the immediacy of forbidden need by reducing it to … a spectacle in which one is both actor and audience' (Koch, 1974, pp. 117–18; see also Symington, 1993). Similarly Laing suggests, following Hegel, that 'the schizo avoids the act, except as a performance' (1965, pp. 86–9; Hegel, 1949, pp. 349–50). There is continuity between the schizoid, the narcissist and the artist – they are essentially performers, and this can be a way of avoiding engagement. But for the narcissist, this performative aspect takes on a special importance – making the world the stage on which one's inner fantasies are played out (again, this relates to the role of media as I suggested in Chapter 2, using the example of Phil Spector). Other people are not real, because they simply represent externalised aspects of the narcissist's inner drama. Narcissism provides a clue as to how inner fantasy affects other people. Again it is not hard to see how closely these paradigms work in with common understandings of the artist – creator of a fantasy world which is then objectified in the form of a text. Azerrad's account of J Mascis (2001, pp. 346–75; see Chapter 4) presents an almost textbook male narcissist – a sadistic voyeur who although apparently passive and blank, causes others to act out and injure themselves mentally and physically. This in turn relates to Mascis's position in the band as 'the artist' – because the rest of the band deferred to him, he could play out his most destructive fantasies while all the time pretending he was somewhere else.

In a world where mediated relations repeatedly take the place of direct interpersonal contact, narcissistic delusions are likely to become more common. Probably the classic example of this is the 'deranged' fan and the media superstar: Mark Chapman and John Lennon come to mind. Fan and star play out a drama of dominance and submission. But clearly the artist, who has such a strong investment in media, is as likely to be prey to such delusions as any fan. In relation to the art rock tradition in particular, I have discussed the way in which musicians have created sound 'worlds' that clearly compensated them to some degree for their social ineptitude.

In Chapter 2 I discussed Warhol's aesthetic and its influence on rock masculinities, an aesthetic that has been described as narcissistic (Koch, 1974, pp. 115–21). Warhol took up the position of observer, marked by an all-seeing gaze, but in general minimising his own authorship or agency of the work. 'Warhol's … solution to the narcissistic dilemma is … to absent himself as conspicuously as possible' (Koch, 1974, p. 120). By doing this, he was creating a stage in which other people would enact his fantasies. Discussing Warhol's film career, critic Henry Gedahzler comments 'a sadist-voyeur is exactly the right consolidation of psychological qualities

150   WHITE BOYS, WHITE NOISE

[for being a film-entrepreneur]. I mean, he doesn't go round hurting people, but they do get hurt' (quoted in Smith, 1988, p. 185). In this he inverted the mass cultural critique, identifying himself both as passive and feminised by glamour, as the kind of 'blank' consumer/voyeur of the Adornoesque nightmare, but also as a media 'star', an object, if you like, of his own gaze (Dyer, 1986, p. 5). As such Warhol was producing an aesthetic of self-alienation. Of course the advantage of Warhol's approach was that it allowed the artist to work through personae, an option that was not available to Cobain, whose participation in a more traditional rock discourse demanded a more personal style of authenticity. Rock discourse is in general suspicious of a too obvious self-aestheticisation – it smacks of homosexuality. As such there was arguably not enough of a separation between Cobain's life and work – both were continuously seen in terms of the other. Warhol had the advantage that his personal life (if he had one) was 'off limits'. Morrissey also suggests a 'successful' balancing of these discourses.

Morrissey is the British Warhol. Like Warhol, he is obsessed by fame and glamour, to the extent that 'nothing else is real' (camp aesthetic). He pretends to have no sex life, and like Warhol insists that true happiness can only be found in mediated relations (Rogan, 1992, pp. 1–5). Like Warhol he has a carefully fashioned public image. And finally, he's a miserable bugger. Clearly there are also a number of resemblances between Cobain and Morrissey – their 'sensitiveness', their identification with feminism, their exploration of the misery of the male victim, and their status as frontmen for iconic indie bands and as 'spokesmen' for a generation of disaffected youth. Obviously there are also differences – Morrissey is still alive for example, he courts the media in a way that Cobain didn't and, of course, there are cultural differences, as they come from different sides of the Atlantic. It could be said that Morrissey cultivates a persona to a greater degree than did Cobain – we never hear about the messy details of his life, and many of his autobiographical details remain relatively obscure compared with Cobain, although an unhappy childhood does seem to be a common bond between them (Reynolds and Press, 1995, p. 215). Morrissey reflects the typical UK preoccupation with style and artifice, Cobain in comparison offers a rather more traditional style of US rock 'authenticity'.

Much has been made of the influence of non-musical figures on Morrissey, especially Oscar Wilde's combination of witty paradox, personal flamboyance and androgyny, and aestheticism (Hawkins, 2002, p. 68; Watney, 1995, p. 595). The central paradox of Wilde was his insistence that art and artifice are not inferior to, or dependent on, life, but are, in contrast, an enhancement of it. Wilde was reacting against the moralism of Victorian literature by asserting the superiority of art to ethics (for example the Preface to *The Picture of Dorian Gray*). Morrissey, however, seems to see art not as an enhancement of, but as a replacement for, life: 'When young I instantly abandoned the human race in favour of pop music' (quoted in Bret, 1994, p. 9). In conversation with Simon Reynolds, when asked about his 'ambitions', personal and artistic, Morrissey replied 'Artistic. Nothing else counts' (Reynolds, 1990, p. 21). The obvious similarity is to Warhol, who practised a similar absolutism. It further suggests Morrissey's renunciation of 'life', something that Wilde would never have endorsed. It could be argued, then, that it would be a mistake to 'read' Morrissey psychologically, as if his lyrics had anything to do with the 'real world'. But how else are we to read them? Given the consistency of his persona, what he says in his songs and interviews, however calculatedly 'artificial', is all we have to work with. So while his utterances may not necessarily reflect the 'real' Morrissey, at the same time his persona has an inner consistency that can be analysed, irrespective of its relation to the 'author'.

The second point about Wilde and Morrissey is that they are both concerned, on some level, with male narcissism, with the virtue of being 'selfish'. On one level this is confirmation of their fondness for paradox, inverting conventional (Christian) values of selflessness and concern for others. Sedgwick states that, in Wilde, this selfishness can be read as a coded reference to male homosexuality (as with his 'camp' insistence on artifice). *The Picture of Dorian Gray*, for example, can be read in terms of a (tragic) story of male self-love (Sedgwick, 1990, p. 160). Again citing the establishment of homosexuality as a scientific 'category' in the late nineteenth century, Sedgwick argues that this made explicit a binary of acceptable and unacceptable sexualities, so that what could no longer be represented explicitly (male/male love) was represented instead as male self-love (as with Gray and his portrait), the collapsing of homosexual/heterosexual definitions with the self/other: 'I do not *love* him. I *am* him' (Sedgwick, 1990, p. 164). The development of what Sedgwick describes above as 'male self-pity' can be partly explained, therefore, as a form of sublimated homosexuality. The plethora of homoerotic images and discourses in Morrissey and The Smiths' work suggest that such a concept may prove useful. We might enquire, however, as to how far the equation of selfishness and homosexuality, arguably necessary in Wilde's time, was still relevant in the 1980s. I would be more inclined to read *Dorian Gray* as a moral parable about the deleterious effects of narcissism.

Morrissey provides a complementary example to Cobain of indie male suffering. Like Cobain, his worldview is bipolar, alternating between extremes of masochism and sadism. The other in his songs is often not named or particularised; rather, it is androgynous, protean and usually all-powerful. In contrast, the singer's persona is usually passive – things are done for him or to him. Like Cobain, a number of his songs deal with child abuse ('The Headmaster Ritual', 1985; 'Suffer Little Children', 1984a; 'Reel Around the Fountain', 1984a). Morrissey's fondness for the imperative ('That Joke Isn't Funny Anymore', 1985) seems to indicate command, but typically he asks to be acted upon – often in the opening lines of the song, as in 'There is a Light That Never Goes Out', 'Shoplifters of the World', 'Half a Person', 'Asleep', 'This Night Has Opened My Eyes' (all 1987a), or in the title or hook ('Ask', 1987a; 'Accept Yourself', 1984b, 'Please Please Please Let Me Get What I Want', 1984b). Morrissey typically imagines himself as a supplicant or victim. Sometimes he imagines inflicting violence on the other (as in the infamous 'Margaret on the Guillotine' (Morrissey, 1988) or 'Heaven Knows I'm Miserable Now', 1984b) but he 'destroys the other only in fantasy ... his rage is turned inward ... the masochist despairs of ever holding the attention or winning the recognition of the other, of being held securely in the other's mind' (Benjamin, 1988, p. 72). Just as the schizoid is split, Morrissey imagines himself as 'half a person' – any assertion of identity is always immediately qualified ('How Soon Is Now', 1985; 'Unloveable', 1987a; 'Shoplifters of the World', 1987a), the implication being that only the other can fill the void of his being, but since this other is only approached in fantasy, such a consummation is always deferred. Laing suggests that for the schizophrenic, 'love is ... feared more than ... hatred' (1965, p. 45), because love implies a relationship with the other. The consummation that Morrissey imagines can only be approached by extreme violence – repeatedly he imagines the achievement of love in terms of self-destruction ('There is a Light', 1987a; 'What Difference Does it Make', 1984b) or apocalypse ('Ask', 1987a). This is because for the schizophrenic, love is violence, not just in the sadomasochistic sense but in the sense that admitting the other would constitute an intolerable threat to his own identity: 'In so far as he feels empty, the full, substantial, living reality of others' threatens to engulf him 'as gas will obliterate a vacuum ... He can only relate to depersonalised persons, to phantoms of his own phantasies ... perhaps to animals' (Laing, 1965, p. 77).

Another reading of this trope of self as lack is that Morrissey identifies with women. Morrissey tends to imagine women (where named as such) in the familiar bipolar fashion as either powerful – 'Sheila Take a Bow' (1987a), the antagonist of 'William It Was Really Nothing' (1984b) – or helpless victims – 'Girlfriend in a Coma' (1987b), 'Girl Afraid' (1984a). This ambivalence also comes across in his remarks about women: 'I think women have become very open about their needs and desires, and this was entirely due to feminism. By women being open about sex, it has made life much easier for men' (quoted in Reynolds, 1990, pp. 17–18). In this women are figured as powerful, but there's also a self-serving aspect – woman's action enables men to be passive. This is a distortion of feminism, although one that is consistent with the bipolar worldview in which one party is always powerful, the other powerless.

Masculinity in Morrissey is imagined as other to the self – sadistic, physical and violent. 'I'm enormously attracted to people who can look after themselves. I'm obsessed by the physical, in the sense that it always works. It's a great power to be very physical' ('Rushholme Ruffians', 1985; 'Sweet and Tender Hooligan', 1987a; 'Handsome Devil', 1984b quoted in Reynolds, 1990, p. 18). But he disavows 'physicality' himself, thereby taking up a basically masochistic relation to it. In this sense he is similar to Cobain, who likewise imagines 'men' in terms of a stereotype of powerful 'grunt' working-class masculinity ('In Bloom', 1991; 'Son of a Gun', 1992; 'Floyd the Barber', 1989). The difference is that Morrissey eroticises the relationship, while Cobain does not (although Nirvana acted out homoeroticism in other contexts). Morrissey often employs camp – 'feminine' modes of hyperbole, typically reminiscent of the mother – 'The Queen Is Dead' (1986), 'William It Was Really Nothing' (1984b), 'Heaven Knows I'm Miserable Now' (1984b) – and comes across as a scolding but ineffectual mother figure – 'What Difference Does it Make' (1984b). This raises the question of whether camp can be read politically as a statement against hegemonic gender discourses. The argument, as set out by Judith Butler (1990, pp. 31–3), is that camp can be liberating because it highlights the construction of gender as a performance rather than a natural innate disposition. This may be true, but many women find camp insulting because it represents a parody of femininity as essentialised by men (a view that Butler has subsequently endorsed (1993, p. 237)). In other words, camp tells us more about men's (and thereby society's) view of women than it does about women per se.

Both Morrissey and Cobain display a loathing for the body. This is articulated through ambivalence about sex, through images of violence inflicted on the body. This loathing is socially mediated in the sense that feminism was extremely criti-cal of traditional 'macho' male sexuality, and subsequently in indie rock, certain modes of 'masculine' performance were no longer deemed acceptable. However, if the response of men is to simply withdraw themselves from their bodies and disavow agency, then we can see again how this does not in any sense overcome the problem – rather it merely 'switches' from one extreme to the other, from sadistic action to masochistic denial. It is characteristic of the schizophrenic to be 'disembodied': *'The body is felt more as one object among other[s] ... than as the core of the individual's own being ...* the body is felt as the core of a *false self'*, which the 'inner', 'true' self observes (Laing, 1965 p. 69). This also explains why in the schizoid world, all action is performance – because of the distance between the 'true' self (mind) and the 'false' (the body).

The schizophrenic false self is structured similarly to Sartre's concept of 'bad faith' in that it does not serve as a vehicle for fulfilment or gratification (of the self); rather it is primarily a means of compliance: 'a negative conformity to ... the other's standard ... a response to what others say I am' (Laing, 1965, p. 98). The false self becomes that thing for the other. This false self becomes identified with the body (because the body is present in the world) but is reviled by the inner self, which sees it as a charade or performance that has nothing to do with it: 'All that you can see is not me' (Laing, 1965, p. 37). It is interesting to relate these observations back to the figure of the star, whose body is in the public arena, and is subject to projections and expectations, a situation which has schizoid possibili-ties, especially for someone who is ontologically insecure in the first place. Arguably the most iconic stars are those who are represented as tragically split in exactly this way – Marilyn Monroe, Elvis Presley, James Dean, Kurt Cobain (Dyer, 1986, pp. 22–3).

Many of Morrissey's lyrics are about the star/audience relationship, either explic-itly ('Paint a Vulgar Picture' (1987b), a song about marketing a 'dead star') or implicitly: the traditional pop music I/you, lover/loved subject/object relationship becomes analogous for fans' relationships to Morrissey. In this sense, the inaccessibility of the loved one (object) in his work ('I Want the One I Can't Have', 1985; 'Please, Please, Please, Let Me Get What I Want', 1984b) – mediated, fantastical relationships which can never be consummated – is very appropriate: 'look but don't touch'. Of course, in his curious way, Morrissey 'keeps faith' with his audience – his avowed celibacy, for example, and disdain for sexual relations: 'I can't imagine my body feeling sexual excitement. I don't reject sex. I don't accept it either. It simply doesn't exist' (quoted in Rogan, 1992, p. 91). This suggests not only that he values mediation above direct contact, but also that he is 'saving himself up' for that impossible moment when he meets his audience. This in turn keeps fans' fantasies intact and the dream alive. Accordingly it is apt that Morrissey is always miserable and lives in fantasy – because he is always deferring happiness for that moment when he meets you (the fan), a moment that will never occur (Reynolds, 1990, pp. 27–8).

Andrew O'Hagan (2004) points out that another part of Morrissey's appeal is how he presents himself as a fan: 'The fans were outfanned by the object of their fanaticism: here was a pop phenomenon made up of pop phenomena – Morrissey's influences were the whole point of him, it seemed, and he understood hero-worship in such a manner as to make him a new sort of hero.' We could say here also that Morrissey's persona is 'split' between fan and star positions, between adorer and adored. By acknowledging his own worship of other stars, he reminds us that however much we love him, he will always love another more – we gaze at Morrissey, but his gaze is always elsewhere: precisely because he is like his fans, we can only relate to him to the degree that we share his obsession. Essentially we are always caught in the position of adoring someone who adores someone or something else. There is a fairly obvious homosocial angle on this: our relation with Morrissey is always mediated by a third party; it is a triangular structure. This is not to say that it is not available to female fans as well, of whom Morrissey clearly has many, but it is the act of adoration that is key, not the gender of the gazer or recipient of the gaze – and because this gaze is always directed towards an unattainable other, there is no chance that it will ever be returned, which would force us to recognise the homoerotic content of our own desire.

On one level, the discourse of the star can be read as an exemplar of how in modernity the subject/object split that is the basis of scientific objectivity has been reproduced in all our relations as alienation: 'the transformation of all relationships into objective, instrumental, depersonalised forms' (Dyer, 1986, p. 13; see also Benjamin, 1978, pp. 35–6; Weber, 1970, pp. 15–16). This reproduces patriarchal logic – 'the instrumental orientation and the impersonality that govern modern social organization and thought should be understood as masculine. This means that male domination, like class domination, is no longer a function of personal power relationships … but something inherent in the social and cultural structures' (Benjamin, 1988, pp. 186–7), in other words, Weber's 'disenchanted world'. Morrissey clearly accepts this paradigm; indeed he positively encourages it – it produces the alienated subject and constructs it to participate in an asymmetrical structure of subordination and domination. Clearly there is no space in Morrissey's world for 'recognition of the other'. This comes across strongly in his media statements on a range of issues, from Margaret Thatcher ('Margaret on the Guillotine', 1988) to racial minorities. Violence, while deplored in relation to animals, is condoned in human relations, because it is preferable to the reciprocity of intimacy. Even biographer Johnny Rogan, who is unstinting in his praise of Morrissey and The Smiths' artistic achievements, remarks of the singer: 'There is an insatiable ego at work here … When he sings "I would sooner just be blindly loved", he is, alas, not exaggerating' (1992, p. 5).

Conclusions

I have argued in this chapter that representations of hegemonic white masculinity in popular culture can be usefully described in terms of a melancholic model. That is, such masculinities' non-relational and therefore non-negotiable structure is similarly structured to other modes of masculine representation. Masculinities have traditionally been identified with images of the tough, impermeable male body or ego as a castle or fortress that resists all influence and incursion (Easthope, 1986, pp. 37–44; Jeffords, 1994; Rutherford and Chapman, 1988, p. 11). Such a 'warrior' masculinity doesn't need other people – he can survive in 'the wild' if necessary. But the key aspect is his self-sufficiency and autonomy, and it seems to me that melancholics incarnate a very similar discourse of masculinity defined as a mode of non-relation: they don't need other people either, or else they claim the terms of the interaction to be too threatening to their own identity. The opposition of 'soft' and 'hard' men is a binary discourse which preserves masculine hegemony.

A constant theme throughout this book has been the association of hegemonic masculinity with systems of binary opposites. For example, in Chapter 1, I argued that the object/subject separation was central to systems of observation, power and control. The contradictions of this approach become manifest, however, when masculinities take themselves as an object of investigation, introducing an element of reflexivity in which such distinctions are no longer tenable. In this chapter I have looked at how binary systems produce binary possibilities – rock masculinities are structured around divisions, between mind and body, self and other, aggressor and victim, reason and irrationality, masculine and feminine, star and fan. Morrissey and Cobain play within this system, but without really challenging its basic tenets. They play with 'feminised' subject positions; they play with madness and the other, but never enter into a 'real' relation. The 'choice' between activity and passivity, between Oedipal empowerment through prohibition and pre-Oedipal regression and *jouissance* reproduces a masculine experience – 'going back to the womb' is an option only for men. 'Whatever the choice – aping "strong" masculinity or "weak" femininity – neither is risking physical exposure as a man' (Sutton, 1997, p. 532).

Recognition of the other is predicated on self-recognition – that is, that we can disentangle our desire from what we see: 'the distinction between my fantasy of you and you as a real person is the very essence of connection' (Benjamin, 1988, pp. 70–71). This is a distinction that Cobain and Morrissey are not interested in or able to make – they prefer the fantasy. This accounts for their pessimistic world-view, which reifies the suffering of the Romantic artist as a monadic, isolated individual in a lonely fantasy world: art, far from being the negation of the capitalist system, is the ultimate expression of its ideological agenda – the atomisation of society into a myriad separate subjects, endlessly pursuing phantasmic desires. In this chapter I have emphasised how the attempt to set up the subject as an autonomous, pure entity, independent of relations with the world, produces schizophrenic dissociation – depression and madness. Some postmodern commentators have argued that schizophrenia is a defining feature of Western society today; Deleuze and Guattari (1983) even suggest that schizophrenia offers a way of resisting Oedipal (and by implication, patriarchal) structures of power. But I have argued that embracing schizophrenia, indeterminacy and fragmentation doesn't work if it means simply moving from one pole of extreme paranoid rationality to schizoid irrationality, order and chaos. It is not enough to 'stop making sense'. Rather, a different kind of sense is needed.

I have also looked at how binaries can work apparently in contradiction of dominant models of gender. This is to suggest that class and ethnicity complicate gender positioning, for example in the ways that adoption of a 'camp', ironic aesthetic can increase (sub)cultural capital. Middle-class concepts of purity and refinement work in tandem with homosociality to create 'purity', whether imagined as folk authenticity or aesthetic *jouissance* and indeterminacy, as in Chapter 3. In Chapter 5 I looked at indie 'white noise' as an example of this: problematisation of authorship (incompetence) united technologically dystopian (folk) and utopian (progressive, high art) positions. But these positions are in themselves unreal – there is no 'original' immanent place (whether imagined as the womb, Eden, 'pure' folk culture or 'pure' noise) and no transcendent, utopian destination either.

Notes

1. Butler's model of gender formation through melancholy I do not find convincing, precisely because it accepts Freud's intra-psychic model as a sufficient paradigm. Laing and Benjamin argue otherwise (Benjamin, 1988; Laing, 1965, p. 22–3).

2. His inability to explain why trauma and loss may be obsessively repeated intra-psychically led towards his formulation of the controversial theory of the 'death instinct' (Freud, 1953–74, vol. 19, pp. 40–46).

3. This position may be fruitfully compared with Freudian/Lacanian definitions of schizophrenia as described in Fredric Jameson: 'the failure of the infant to accede fully into the

realm of speech and language' – pre-Oedipal, refusing 'loss' (1983, p. 118). Jameson's model of postmodern schizophrenia is deficient to the degree it relies on Freud.

4. Holter understands the family scene as invoking a different kind of epistemology to the outside world, which he refers to as 'a centripetal process, a movement towards a centre. I may think of lines moving into, and out from, this centre. The movement may also be termed prismatic.' What this family centre consists of, he suggests, is a kind of collective identity to which all the I's contribute – 'the relationship between the "us" and the "I's" is connective ... the I's are not positions defined by themselves, isolated and opposed, as in exchange relations where the one reflects the value of the other. Rather each refracts the whole and thereby expresses and extends the whole' (Holter, 1995, p. 110).

5. Of course, such experiences are not exclusive to men, but women rarely get the opportunity to market their pain in this way, without suffering severe critical consequences – consider for example, Cobain's wife Courtney Love, Alanis Morissette and Christine Aguilera. Male mental dysfunction has aesthetic status; women are simply 'crazy'.

Conclusion

... white noise

I want to summarise what I've said and relate it back to the title of the book: looking at how white boys and white noise interact, and suggesting some more positive possibilities for masculinities arising out of my study.

Noise is a central aspect of our lives: whether cable hum, traffic sound, tape hiss or TV or radio interference, it is a perpetual reminder of modernity. So it should not be surprising that indie was preoccupied with it. But it is necessary to distinguish between different types of noise, or different ways in which the concept of noise can be used. It is also necessary to point out that its potential is ambiguous – a point that many cultural commentators, in their keenness to identify 'subversion', have overlooked.

First, there is noise as sound, the white noise that many commentators have constructed as central to the difference of indie. Indie's supposed oppositionality was related to its increasing use of white noise and volume as parts of its sonic arsenal, a tendency that references both punk rock but also the 1960s traditions of psychedelic drone and Spector's Wall of Sound. It was theorised as a kind of 'absolute music', in which all direct references to human authorship and representation (voice) have been removed. White noise came to represent a kind of space of *jouissance*, a free play of meanings devoid of authorship that was quintessentially postmodern and fragmented. One can see how this relates to how white noise is usually defined: sound in which all frequencies have equal amplitude – hence there is no pattern in it except that which one chooses to discern (a bit like the white dots that used to appear on the TV set after the end of transmission). It exemplifies indeterminacy. Alternatively it replaces conventional signification with a visceral experience, particularly if noise relates to the use of excessive volume. Second, there is the more general concept of 'cultural noise': a break or discontinuity between sender and receiver, highlighting the tendency of the process of mediation towards indeterminacy (Goode and Zuberi, 2004, p. 7). Finally, there is Attali's concept of noise (1985), which seems to take a little from both of these definitions. However, there has been a tendency to conflate these distinct concepts of noise, and this has led to simplifications.

For Attali, noise is the predictor of new cultural possibilities, a prophecy of a new social order and the breakdown of an old one (1985, p. 19). Many accounts of indie conflate white noise and Attali to suggest that if you use or highlight noise, then you must be subversive: 'with music is born power and its opposite: subversion' – that is, noise (Attali, 1985, p. 6). However, even if we accept Attali's binary scheme, there is obviously a difference between Attali's noise and noise per se. For example, Attali insists that noise equates to the development of new music technology, so rap would have to be understood as a much more subversive noise than anything indie has produced (1985, p. 35). In indie, 'pure' white noise has become reified as a mark of resistance. I demonstrated how this determination to read noise as subversion produced readings of noise as 'feminine', which were based on exactly this conflation of different concepts of noise.

However, while I argue that indie's radical potential is thus attenuated, indie noise still has a power to mark social difference and exclusion. Media both communicate and exclude (underline social difference). The degree of exclusion is linked to the degree of noise in the message – understood here as cultural misunderstanding, the difference between the cognoscenti who 'get it' and the ordinary folk who don't, or those who can 'stand it' and those who can't (again, an approach that may produce gender as a category of difference). However, cultural noise can refer to both 'accidental' noise and noise added or left in at the production stage. It can be both intentional and non-intentional. Part of my point in Chapter 5, then, was to suggest in which indie played with this ambiguity through discourses of amateurism – it became impossible to tell whether the noise of indie was intentional or not. This was one way in which indie negotiated the problem of technology's link to masculine power, by questioning the authorship of noise (can noise be said to have an author?). So cultural noise, as marking social exclusion and difference, relates not only to literal sound, but also to indie use of a veil of self-protective irony and ambiguity to problematise 'presence' and relationship.

Ambiguity is a form of cultural noise that invokes categories of interpretation only open to a select few. Its cool indeterminacy becomes a way of singling out those who can still get the message through the layers of static. As such, indie actively invites misreading. Its irony and ambiguity refer to a high art discourse, in which noise is heard as avant-garde – an irruption of 'reality' (often pain) into the sound world, more broadly the way that indie invites an 'art' reading, but also Warhol's camp aesthetic, which emphasised cultural noise – the effective impossibility of limiting readings of a text, the consequent irrelevance of authorial intention and the power of the consumer to make sense of media in their own way. Camp 'ambiguity' – the aestheticisation of mass culture – became another strategy that could be employed to assert a superior aesthetic awareness. The power of the audience to create meaning is annexed to the power of the artist, who, in modernity, asserts his control through an aestheticising gaze. It is a simplification to read the camp insistence on style and artifice, so beloved of UK critics, as producing a feminine counterdiscourse to male rock authenticity. Reversing the terms of the mass culture critique, as Warhol did, simply produces a new set of essentialisations. The cultivation of style over substance simply reified the capitalist patriarchal binary.

For me, the ambiguity of indie is linked to particular strategies of masculinity. Its open-endedness is closely linked to the way that it 'can't be bothered'. Communication is just too much of an effort. The distance created through these strategies is self-imposed. It's about a passive–aggressive approach that asserts presence negatively – 'I am too cool to communicate with you, but don't ignore me either'. The supposed polysemy of white noise also connects to Deleuze and Guattari's concept of productive schizophrenia – capitalism as 'unlimited semiosis' – literally in that noise is one of the most obvious waste products of industrial capitalism (Holland, 1999, p. 14). Arguing against this model, but also against Fredric Jameson's gloomy schizoid dystopia (1983), I'd suggest that schizophrenia, while it may be literally productive, does not offer an escape from, or transcendence of, conventional systems of meaning. Its irrationality is simply an inversion of, rationality, reproducing patriarchal binaries of reason and unreason, masculine and feminine, aggressor and victim. I would compare it with Laing's post-Freudian definition of schizophrenia as the self in radical isolation, split off from the world and accordingly split within itself. Laing (1965, p. 23) sees the problem as epistemological – Freud, by dividing the mind into 'bits' was doing the very thing that the schizophrenic does to him- or herself. This vicious circle is reinforced by the scientific gaze. Self in isolation goes mad, but Western masculine epistemology, in positing autonomous individualism, is in itself schizoid. Accordingly it is characteristic of masculinities to oscillate between extreme positions – I looked at how this self-hate self-love dichotomy was played out in Morrissey and Cobain, noting how both regularly flipped poles, obviating the possibility of connection and equality with others. The discourse of the 'star' in media then exacerbates the effect by emphasising sado-masochistic relationships like star/fan. Morrissey, of course, does not use white noise as such, but his insistence on mediation as life's true meaning opens up a similar kind of hall of mirrors to the indeterminacy of 'pure' sound.

White boys use white noise to make themselves heard – whether they have anything to say, however, other than the fact that they are there, and they are different from you, remains a moot point. White noise does not communicate; it merely asserts. Essentially my argument is that arguments about noise as schizophrenic *jouissance* are forms of postmodern pimpery – white guys getting a taste of the other (Moore, 1988). Their notions of femininity as masquerade and artifice are a devaluation and distortion of femininity.

Noise ends up confirming male autonomy and power, because its indeterminacy can be used equally for subversive or conservative ends. Noise is power, for good or ill. Originally interpreted to indicate the purity and authenticity of the music, it was increasingly 'added at source' through the use of volume, distortion, the power chord and feedback, albeit that in indie such resources are used indirectly – a discourse of quiet men making loud noises. The removal or minimisation of the performer's presence or body, rather than being seen as questioning his power, should be read as demonstrating how in modernity power is manifested indirectly, through technology. Of course, if such power is indirect, then this raises the question of why other social groups, for example women, cannot also use such resources. One only has to listen to the music of Sleater-Kinney, Hole or PJ Harvey to realise that there is no necessary or exclusive association between guitar power, white noise and masculinity. Yet at the same time, these bands have something that only a few male indie groups have – expressive singers. To sing is to put yourself and your body on the line in a way that few indie groups attempt. Their singing also has a definite blues or emotional edge to it that is generally lacking in indie music. I know this insistence on the voice may seem regressive, but as basically a populist, I believe that vocal presence is an essential part of good pop music (where would Nirvana be without it?). Also, in terms of audience, modes of relation and conditions of performance, we would have to say that indie is not particularly welcoming to women. Indie's characteristic mode of negation, its insistence on extremity and denial of community and body (consonant with Adorno) are aspects that few women are comfortable with, unless they are hell-bent on being 'one of the boys'. I'm not saying here that woman should not or cannot participate in alternative music making – rather that it exacts a high price.

To briefly indicate how white noise relates back to each of the chapters, in Chapter 2 I discussed how problematisation of meaning worked as a strategy for white masculinities to identify themselves as avant-garde and intellectually superior. The whiteness of noise, cultural and otherwise, came to signify a kind of cleansing of rock music from its necessary association with body and sex. I discussed the implications of this for indie's relation with black music, drawing a historic model in which black culture's perceived marginality was rearticulated as a folk or youth-based 'purity'. I argued that, like camp, black cool became a resource for white masculinities seeking to define themselves as oppositional – the 'White Negro', whose binary formulation both reproduced hegemonic values and demonstrated an increasingly schizoid and unembodied worldview of masculine asociality. It produced white rock masculinities split between essentialised positions of victimhood and aggression, as children or child molesters, as varieties of deviance, but subject to an overall intellectual control that mediated these personae, making them subject to a Foucauldian gaze.

Various kinds of noise, both cultural and literal, became signifiers of this difference – the author died, but was resurrected as a disembodied voyeur. White noise, articulated as purity, becomes reified, and in Chapter 3 I traced how indie gradually marginalised music that did not conform to this ideal. In Chapter 4 I discussed how commentators have attempted to rationalise indie music as presenting a homosocial purity that is problematised by the insertion of an audience, setting an idea of pure music – authentic hardcore/punk – against the cultural noise created by the insertion of the band into media. The white noise of punk is posited as a musical absolute or singularity that is analogous to hard homosocial masculinity. Any falling off from this white noise ideal is due to the introduction of influence – from audiences, from media, from past musical practice, from the feminised mainstream.

So far undiscussed, but essential for the overall argument is Chapter 1's theorisation of masculinities, which argued that the male body is misidentified as masculinities' main object of study, because masculine power is not primarily embodied but is more in the intellectual modes of apprehension that frame such studies. Power consists not in representations but in how those representations are organised. I reviewed the Frankfurt School's discussion of instrumental rationality as an example of male power that has lost its gender associations, become disembodied and instead works instrumentally and invisibly. This model is reproduced in the way indie rock culture increasingly values 'detachment', 'irony' and purity. This is an embourgeoisment of rock – alternative music is increasingly functioning as a form of high culture. This point has already been made by Hibbett (2005), although I believe that I have set the issue in more of a historic context. Also I have addressed in more detail the question of who exactly benefits from the cultural capital created – white men.

The missing link in the white noise/white boys paradigm, and in theories of masculinity more generally, is the idea of relationship. For example, noise functions well as an idea of disruption and slippage, but not so well as a means of connection. Similarly theories of masculinities or masculine theories have been stymied by a persistent sense of alienation, power and domination which always perceives the other as an object or threat. Freud was obsessed by the idea of killing the father, and of the potentially negative and disruptive power of the subconscious, which could only be controlled though repression. Human culture, as Freud understood it, was basically individualistic and agonistic. Modern capitalism similarly produces a culture based on the desiring individual, increasingly unrestrained by social convention, tradition or family ties. Its insistence on perpetual novelty is reproduced especially in popular culture, whose constant turnover of new styles and fashions seems bent on reproducing an eternal present without memory. This infantilisation of the consumer is represented in the seeming 'dumbness' of alternative rock masculinities – conflating the rock discourse of youth with the mass culture critique. As such, it confines rock masculinities to basically childlike, socially dysfunctional or at most adolescent states of mind. As such, rock culture is generally hostile to adult masculinities and rejecting of rock culture's obvious 'father figures' – the black man and the hippy.

Rock culture's masculinism is articulated in its Freudian antagonisms: its model of rebellion always sets father against son (and roots for the son). But this model also obviates the possibility that there may be creative relationships between them, past and present – that there is rock 'tradition' (indeed, in general, this aspect of rock culture generally works to hide rock's archivalism, as we saw in Chapter 5). For example, when Johnny Rotten (or was it Malcolm McLaren?) announced that he wanted to kill hippies, the media and rock culture were ready to heed the call, not literally of course, but with their pens and typewriters. The result of this is that, in post-punk rock culture, the hippy became an almost universally derided figure, or simply an absence. It is certainly remarkable the way in which neo-psychedelic critics like Reynolds, Gilbert and DeRogatis theorise psychedelia as if the counterculture never existed. By reducing psychedelia to a matter of semiotics (and drugs), they elided all the political agendas that the counterculture created, such as concern about the environment, alternative lifestyles, alternative religions, feminism – basically ways of challenging the post-industrial, postmodern, capitalist, polluted, global-warming mess that we are presently mired in. As I said in the introduction, rock culture's rejection of the counterculture makes me suspicious, because it seems as if hippies have always been fair game for the establishment too. They've become a kind of universal pariah (MacDonald, 1998, p. 3). This is unfortunate, because again the bearded hippy offers a genuine alternative masculinity, if only we could forgive him for 'failing' us the first time around.

Scratch a lot of punk/indie demagogues and you'll find a hippy underneath. Greg Ginn's favourite band was the Grateful Dead. Chris Knox was a longhaired folkie in the 1970s, and indeed his most obvious influence (especially vocally) is not Johnny Rotten but Robin Williamson of The Incredible String Band. John Peel was as inclined in 1969 to rave about prog as he was later to rave about punk. It seems to me that these men need to rediscover their younger self, or at least ask themselves why they find it so necessary to destroy aspects of their past. As discussed in Chapter 5, hippy mentors, father figures if you like, were a significant influence on indie music. Even hardcore band Minor Threat had hippy connections: Skip Groff, a record shop owner, 'happily lectured them on rock history' as did Inner Ear studio owner Don Zientera (Azerrad, 2001, pp. 122, 126). 'MacKaye's parents exemplified the best of what the sixties counterculture was about ... raised their kids in a tolerant, super intellectual, open-minded atmosphere. I think they're both real hippies – real-deal microbus be-in dropout hippies ... there wasn't "go do this and be all you can be" ... it was like "well son, let's listen to what you're listening to"' (Rollins, quoted in Azerrad, 2001, p. 135). MacKaye in turn was the driving force behind Fugazi, an interesting and innovative band both musically and in terms of their social practice – one of the few to forge a career totally outside the grip of the majors. Although I know that I criticised US indie's obsession with independence elsewhere, MacKaye has at least taken it from a stance to an actual cthos, an ongoing, community-based cultural initiative.

When I look at the various alternative music subcultures and associated models of masculinity, it strikes me that, of all of them, only the counterculture offered any kind of serious threat to establishment values. Punk rock was simply too pessimistic to offer much in the way of positive alternatives, and 1980s indie rock culture seemed too obsessed with infantile child-men (either innocents or psychopaths) to offer any models of masculinities that could operate in the real world. Another unique aspect of the counterculture (in terms of rock culture) was its concern with spirituality and its quest for religious enlightenment. Although I am not religious myself, I can increasingly see the point of believing in something larger than oneself. It is of course very easy to point out where the hippy dream went wrong, and how open it was to exploitation by hucksters and nutters alike (Manson, for example). It's easy if not de rigueur, to be sceptical.

One obvious hippy ideal was that of egalitarian cooperation and communality. Although I have talked a lot about the negativity of indie rock, it does seem to me that at specific moments some indie bands really do suggest positive possibilities. One of these is to break away from the hegemony of the individual voice that is so central to pop music, and instead posit the possibility of community or at least dialogue within a song. Traditionally such dialogue in popular music has largely arisen from the call and response patterns of black music. But in indie it occurs more commonly in the form of a dialogue between two singers. Some examples here would include The Go-Betweens, Hüsker Dü, R.E.M. and the Minutemen. These bands work because of the tensions between the approaches of the singer/writers and they way their work creates a kind of conversation; witness the combination of Michael Stipe's and Mike Mills's vocals, each a separate melody that intertwines with, and comments on, the eccentricities of the other (for example 'Fall on Me', 1985). In The Go-Betweens' case the tension is between McLennan's slightly fey but sincere pop/folk romanticism and Forster's histrionic campness, for example on the atmospheric 'As Long as That' (1983). The song starts with McLennan softly picking out a minor-key riff on the bass, then Forster wades in with a typical outburst. McLennan answers him by doubling the bass melody – when the two vocals come together for the chorus it's a great moment. 'Cattle and Cane' (1983) has a similar dialogue form in which McLennan sings the main body of lyrics about a half-remembered childhood in Queensland, but Forster adds a spoken monologue over the coda (the track is also lifted by drummer Lindy Morrison who masterfully negotiates the unusual 11/4 rhythm).

The greatness of the Minutemen was that they didn't play the indie game, a feat all the more remarkable given their long association with the extremely hardline SST. Of all the bands of the time, the Minutemen were the most musically unconventional and eclectic, combining the abruptness of Captain Beefheart and early 1980s political funk like The Pop Group with a thin, piercing, angular but vaguely Latin-inflected guitar style, writing impassioned lyrics about political injustice, covering Steely Dan *and* Creedence Clearwater Revival (Minutemen, 1984). They were everything you wanted alternative rock to be – risk-taking, different, engaged but always musical. Guitarist D Boon seems to have had a unique onstage presence. A kind of non-image, he looked more like a trucker than a rock star, but that was the point – no one was going to mistake him for Lou Reed. But more important was the overall musical and ideological chemistry – far more than any other indie band, the Minutemen seemed to have been a 'talk about it' band in which there was a reasonably free exchange of opinions on a wide range of issues (Azerrad, 2001, pp. 71–3). You can hear that in the way in which the musical elements in the band seem locked in a perpetual free-form dialogue. An indie band who saw musicianship as a way of expanding rather than limiting possibility (The Smiths being the other obvious reference here), the Minutemen are and were a breath of fresh air in the otherwise stultifyingly macho SST scene.

Hüsker Dü was another band with a fascinating clash of musical personalities – Mould the muso whose guitar playing drives the band almost singlehanded, but whose lyrical misery and anger can become oppressive, and Grant Hart, who is a lousy drummer, but sings like a (fallen) angel. If Mould supplies the energy, Hart supplies the soul with his engaging rasp, not dissimilar to Springsteen, Petty and also that other great indie vocalist Paul Westerberg. Such singers are not frightened of the occasional expressive blues twist. 'New Day Rising' (1985), title track of the LP, is a particularly good example of the vocal strength of the band – apparently no more than a repetitious one-chord chant with occasional screaming, it becomes, over its three-minute span, a vocal tour de force, as Hart and Mould spin around and embroider each other's passion. Some Hüsker songs suffer from a ridiculously murky mix (which was, after all, part of the indie ethos) but here the vocals cut through and touch you.

After the band broke up, Mould's solo work became well-known in indie circles, though personally I found it too dark, and much preferred Hart's *Intolerance* (1989). His 'All of My Senses' sounds like a man waking from a long, bad dream (the 1980s) and discovering that it's a new day outside. 'His surreal, free-associating lyrics are laden with metaphors of liberation; everything is a movement away from the pointless solipsism of suffering' (Levin, 2001). I guess what I'm saying is that I like music that has some kind of strong feeling to it that is not wholly dark. In New Zealand, I think the most consistent talent to emerge out of Flying Nun is David Kilgour, formerly of The Clean (I would say Bressa Creeting Cake, but they didn't emerge till 1996 unfortunately). Always a superbly rhythmic guitarist, Kilgour is also an underrated singer, someone who can sing out of tune without it mattering because they have a timbre or sonority (like, say, Burning Spear). Seemingly unburdened by the neuroses and personal problems that afflicted many of his more lauded contemporaries, Kilgour has gone on in his solo career to build a distinctive body of work in the genre of ambient, slightly twangy guitar pop (Kilgour, 1991, 1994, 2002, 2004). He has always shied away from the fuzzbox, eschewing the obligatory white noise alienation that distortion entails. And finally, he's actually a nice guy (in my experience), who's not a control freak. A final mention must go to Graeme Downes of the Verlaines, whose melodic and harmonic ambition always strove to break free of the repetitive minimalism of so much indie music.

And what of my own practice as a musician?

Compared with many indie groups, Sneaky Feelings were relatively democratic when it came to producing material and taking responsibility for the band's sound and music. Although David and I were the main songwriters, both drummer Martin Durrant and bassist John Kelcher contributed song material. Most other local indie bands tended to be more autocratic, with usually one or at the most two main songwriters and other musicians. In my experience, the more autocratic the band structure, the less fun it is, and the more likely it is to come unstuck. Autocracy and friendship simply do not go together. In retrospect, the relative equality of band members in relation to musical production is something that I feel proud of. We have all remained friends and stay in regular contact. At the same time, I think the commercial logic of the music industry favours bands with a clearly recognisable frontperson, so in some ways the democratic group format will always struggle in the marketplace.

That said, I have highlighted how Sneaky Feelings also had many of the classic problems of homosocial group interaction: a lack of honesty about emotions in personal interaction, a tendency towards musical perfectionism and a general lack of recognition and reward of the positive aspects and abilities we all saw in each other. Towards the end of our career we increasingly became each others' backing musicians, rather than a truly cooperative enterprise. The pressure and desire of 'making it big' impacted negatively on intra-band relations.

I still play in a band and have tried to apply some of the lessons I have learned about the importance of cooperation and mutual recognition. For me, the primary pleasure of playing music is that of cooperating and interacting in a structured group environment. The experience of playing together as a band is, for me, the one inalienable pleasure of music. As such, it makes sense to give each player a reasonably free rein to come up with their own parts. Once, I would tell other members what to play, acting pretty much like a classical composer would. I now avoid this where possible, as it is demeaning for the other players and minimises the creative possibilities that arise from a freer, less structured interaction. This approach also changes the emphasis from music as an idealised final product or commodity to a process – because process is where the main pleasure and reward of playing music lies.

I have also tried to simplify my songs. While I was brought up on the Beatles' sophisticated, complex and idiosyncratic song structures, I have found that in practice, playing with musicians of often modest abilities, it is better to avoid extensional complexity and focus instead on the power of repetition, intentional development and interaction, and thus leave more space for individual creativity ('jamming'). I have also changed my lyric writing in two ways: by avoiding too obviously negative or cynical sentiments and trying to write in a more positive way that still seems authentic to me, and also by simplifying my lyrics. Ironically, I have indie to thank for some of the above – writing my thesis, focusing on the use of simplicity and repetition in punk/indie, seems to have subconsciously influenced my own approach. But basically, I take a more hippy-like attitude towards the music – relaxed and informal.

Clearly all the above also relates back to the concepts of masculine artistry discussed. By giving up some control of the music process, my pleasure is enhanced. By envisaging music as a group process, I reject the patriarchal insistence on the autonomous individual or the commodity nature of a finished, discrete product.

By focusing on positive feelings, I resist the obligatory identification of art with pain and suffering which is too easily annexed to a masculinist worldview. Of course, it might be possible to object here that the reason I have become more relaxed and informal in my practices is that I don't actually have an audience. Let's face it; the world is not hanging on my every musical pronouncement. However, from my point of view, that is beside the point. True, music is more of a hobby than a career to me now, but that does not mean it is less important. Perhaps rather than a hobby, it would be more accurate to stay that playing music is a form of meditation, focusing on a meaningful activity in a way that gives me a sense of freedom and renewal. Viewed in this way, the question of an audience becomes irrelevant.

It could be objected here that while I have written at some length about the pleasure of playing music, I have offered little for music listeners. I would not deny that listening to music is still very important to me, but I have no recommendations on how to 'do it better'. I would, however, say one thing – the idea that musicianship is a special craft or ability is part of hegemonic discourse. Musical production and participation should be open to all. As Attali says, 'music is illustrative of the evolution of our entire society: deritualize a social form, repress an activity of the body, specialise its practice, sell it as a spectacle, generalize its consumption, then see ... it is stockpiled until it loses its meaning' (1985, p. 5). Like Attali, I would like to imagine a utopian final stage of this process – the democratisation of musical production. 'Performed for the musician's own enjoyment, as self-communication, with no other goal than his own pleasure ... Thus composition proposes a radical social model, one in which the body is treated as capable of not only production and consumption, and even of entering into relations with others, but also of autonomous pleasure' (Attali, 1985, p. 32). In some ways this was what punk/indie was supposed to be about, but it got hijacked by all the weight of pre-existing models of art, for example the insistence on autonomy, which is reproduced in Attali. I think Attali's model would have more resonance if it stressed the communal and social power of music making, rather than its solitary pleasure. So if you want to challenge patriarchy, my advice is to start singing and playing, ideally with other people. In this way, you might start to realise what punk and indie promised but failed to deliver, a true music by and for the people.

Bibliography

Books and articles

Abrams, M.H. (1988), *A Glossary of Literary Terms*, 5th edn, New York: Holt, Reinhart and Winston.

Adorno, Theodor (1998), *Beethoven: The Philosophy of Music: Fragments and Texts*, ed. Rolf Tiedemann, trans. Edmund Jephcott, Stanford, Calif.: Stanford University Press.

—— (1990), 'On Popular Music', in Frith, Simon and Andrew Goodwin (eds), *On Record: Rock, Pop and the Written Word*, New York, Pantheon, pp. 300–14.

—— (1973), *Philosophy of Modern Music*, trans. Anne G. Mitchell and Wesley V. Bloomster, London: Sheed & Ward.

Adorno, Theodor and Max Horkheimer (1994), *Dialectic of Enlightenment*, trans. John Cumming, New York: Continuum.

Alberti, John (1999), ' "I Have Come Out to Play": Jonathan Richman and the politics of the faux-naif', in Dettmar, Kevin J.H. and William Richey (eds), *Reading Rock and Roll: Authenticity, Appropriation, Aesthetics*, New York: Columbia, pp. 173–90.

Appadurai, Arjun (1990), 'Disjuncture and Difference in the Global Cultural Economy', in Featherstone, Mike (ed.), *Global Culture: Nationalism, Globalization and Modernity*, London: Sage, pp. 295–310.

Arnold, Gina (1995), *On the Road to Nirvana*, London: Pan.

Aronowitz, Stanley (2002), 'Introduction', in Horkheimer, Max, *Critical Theory: Selected Essays*, trans. Matthew J. Connell and others, New York: Continuum, pp. xi–xxi.

Attali, Jacques (1985), *Noise: The Political Economy of Music*, trans. Brian Massumi, foreword by Fredric Jameson, afterword by Susan McClary, Minneapolis: University of Minnesota Press.

Azerrad, Michael (2001), *Our Band Could Be Your Life: Scenes from the American Indie Underground 1981–1991*, Boston: Little, Brown.

Bangs, Lester (1992), 'In Which Yet Another Pompous Blowhard Purports to Know the True Meaning of Punk Rock', in Heylin, Clinton (ed.), *The Penguin Book of Rock'n'Roll Writing*, Harmondsworth: Penguin, pp. 103–5.

—— (1987), *Psychotic Reactions and Carburetor Dung*, New York: Vintage.

Bannister, Matthew (2005), 'Kiwi Blokes: Recontextualising White New Zealand Masculinities in a Global Setting', *Genders*, 42.

—— (1999), *Positively George Street: A Personal History of Sneaky Feelings and the Dunedin Sound*, Auckland: Reed.

Barthes, Roland (1990), 'The Grain of the Voice', in Frith, Simon and Andrew Goodwin (eds), *On Record: Rock, Pop and the Written Word*, New York, Pantheon, pp. 293–300.

Bayton, Mavis (1990), 'How Women Become Musicians', in Frith, Simon and Andrew Goodwin (eds), *On Record: Rock, Pop and the Written Word*, New York, Pantheon, pp. 238–57.

Beauvoir, Simone de (1972), *The Second Sex*, trans. and ed. H.M. Parshley, Harmondsworth: Penguin.

Beige, Davy (2000), 'Open Strings', *New Zealand Musician*, October/November.

Benjamin, Jessica (1998), *Shadow of the Other: Intersubjectivity and Gender in Psychoanalysis*, New York: Routledge.

—— (1988), *The Bonds of Love: Psychoanalysis, Feminism and the Problem of Domination*, New York: Pantheon.

—— (1978), 'Authority and the Family Revisited: Or, a World Without Fathers?', *New German Critique*, 13, 35–57.

Betrock, Alan (1982), *Girl Groups: The Story of a Sound*, New York: Delilah Communications.

Bloom, Allan (1988), *The Closing of the American Mind*, London: Penguin.

Bly, Robert (1990), *Iron John: A Book About Men*, Reading, Mass.: Addison-Wesley.

Bogue, Ronald (1989), *Deleuze and Guattari*, London: Routledge.

Bortle, Scott (2001), 'R.D. Laing as a Negative Thinker', *Colloquia*, Spring, http://laing-society.org/colloquia/philosophy/bortle.htm, accessed 8 December 2003.

Bourdieu, Pierre (2001), *Masculine Domination*, trans. Richard Nice, Cambridge: Polity.

—— (1990), *In Other Words: Essays Towards a Reflexive Sociology*, Cambridge: Polity.

—— (1984), *Distinction: A Social Critique of the Judgement of Taste*, trans. Richard Nice, London: Routledge & Kegan Paul.

Bourdieu, Pierre and Wacquant, Loïc J.D. (1992), *An Invitation to Reflexive Sociology*, Cambridge: Polity.

Bourke, Chris (1997), *Crowded House: Something So Strong*, Sydney: Macmillan.

Bradby, Barbara (1990), 'Do-Talk and Don't-Talk: The Division of the Subject in Girl Group Music', in Frith, Simon and Andrew Goodwin (eds), *On Record: Rock, Pop and the Written Word*, New York, Pantheon, pp. 341–68.

Brennan, Teresa (2004), *The Transmission of Affect*, Ithaca and London: Cornell University Press.

Bret, David (1994), *Morrissey: Landscapes of the Mind*, London: Robson.

Brown, Russell (1984a), review of *Send You*, Sneaky Feelings, *Rip It Up*, October.

—— (1984b), 'Of Chill and Frost', *Rip It Up*, April, 20–22.

—— (1983a), 'Growing up Tall', *Rip It Up*, July, 16.

—— (1983b), review of 'Death and the Maiden', The Verlaines, *Rip It Up*, July, 28.

—— (1983c), 'Stone Free', *Rip It Up*, June, 12.

—— (1982), 'Chills Defrost', *Rip It Up*, June, 12.

Buckley, David (2002), *R.E.M. Fiction: An Alternative Biography*, London: Virgin.

Burton, Graeme (1999), *Media and Popular Culture*, London: Hodder & Stoughton.

Butler, Judith (2000), 'Subjects of Sex/Gender/Desire', in *Psychoanalysis and Woman: A Reader*, ed. Shelley Saguaro, Basingstoke: Macmillan, pp. 309–22.

—— (1993), *Bodies That Matter*, New York: Routledge.

—— (1990), *Gender Trouble: Feminism and the Subversion of Identity*, New York: Routledge.

Cammick, Murray (1998), 'The State of the Music Nation: Part 1,' *Real Groove*, August, 14–15.

Carducci, Joe (1992), 'The Thing of It and the King of Thing', in Heylin, Clinton (ed.), *The Penguin Book of Rock'n'Roll Writing*, Harmondsworth: Penguin, pp. 124–50.

Carrabine, Eamonn and Brian Longhurst (1999), 'Mosaics of Omnivorousness: Suburban Youth and Popular Music,' *New Formations*, 38, 125–39.

Carson, Tom (1996), 'Rocket to Russia', in Marcus, Greil (ed.), *Stranded: Rock And Roll for a Desert Island*, New York: Da Capo, pp. 107–17.

Cavanagh, David (2000), *The Creation Records Story: My Magpie Eyes are Hungry for the Prize*, London: Virgin.

Chambers, Iain (1985), *Urban Rhythms: Pop Music and Popular Culture*, London: Macmillan.

Childers, Joseph and Gary Hentzi (eds) (1995), *The Columbia Dictionary of Modern Literary and Cultural Criticism*, New York: Columbia University Press.

Christgau, Robert (1991), 'Rock Music is Here to Stay', *Village Voice*, 18 June, www.robertchristgau.com/xg/bkrev/carducci-91.php, accessed 2 December 2004.

—— (1990), 'Decade: Rockism Faces the World', *Village Voice*, 2 January, http://www.robertchristgau.com/xg/rock/decade-89.php, accessed 2 May 2005.

—— (1973), *Any Old Way You Choose It: Rock and Other Pop Writing, 1969–73*, Baltimore: Penguin.

Chunn, Mike (1992), *Stranger than Fiction: The Life and Times of Split Enz*, Wellington: GP Publications.

Churton, Wade Ronald (2000), *Have You Checked the Children? Punk and Post-punk Music in New Zealand, 1977–1981*, Christchurch: Put Your Foot Down Publishing.

Clare, Anthony (2000), *On Men: Masculinity in Crisis*, London: Chatto & Windus.

Clarke, Gary (1990), 'Defending Ski-jumpers: A Critique of Theories of Youth Subcultures', in Frith, Simon and Andrew Goodwin (eds), *On Record: Rock, Pop and the Written Word*, New York, Pantheon, pp. 81–96.

Clawson, Mary Ann (1999), 'Masculinity and Skill Acquisition in the Adolescent Rock Band', *Popular Music*, 18 (1), 99–114.

Coates, Norma (1997), '(R)evolution Now? Rock and the Political Potential of Gender', in Whiteley, Sheila (ed.), *Sexing the Groove: Popular Music and Gender*, London: Routledge, pp. 50–64.

Cohen, Finn (2001), review of *Our Band Could Be Your Life*, http://www.indyweek.com/durham/2001-11-14/volume7.html, accessed 3 November 2004.

Cohen, Sarah (2001), 'Popular Music, Gender and Sexuality', in Frith, Simon, Will Straw and John Street (eds), *Cambridge Companion to Pop and Rock*, Cambridge: Cambridge University Press, pp. 226–42.

—— (1997), 'Men Making a Scene: Rock Music and the Production of Gender', in Whiteley, Sheila (ed.), *Sexing the Groove: Popular Music and Gender*, London: Routledge, pp. 18–34.

Cohn, Nik (1980), 'Phil Spector', in Miller, Jim (ed.), *The Rolling Stone Illustrated History of Rock & Roll*, New York: Rolling Stone, pp. 150–60.

—— (1969), *Pop From the Beginning*, London: Wiedenfeld and Nicolson.

Colbert, Roy (1999), 'Like a Complete Unknown', *New Zealand Listener*, 6 November, 43.

—— (1995), sleevenotes for CD reissue of *Split Seconds* (Bill Direen), Flying Nun.

—— (1990–91), 'Singing in my Sleep: Martin Phillipps and the Chills', *Music in New Zealand*, 58–64.

—— (1985), sleevenotes for *Tuatara* LP, Flying Nun.

Collins, Simon (2000), review of *The Portable Henry Rollins*, http://www.pixie-inc.demon.co.uk/littlethorn/issue2/rollins.html, accessed 2 October 2004.

Connell R.W. (2000), *The Men and the Boys*, Cambridge: Polity.

—— (1995), *Masculinities*, Berkeley: University of California Press.

—— (1987), *Gender and Power*, Cambridge: Polity.

Corsini, Raymond J. and Alan J. Auerbach (1996), *Concise Encyclopedia of Psychology*, New York: John Wiley.

Cosloy, Gerard (2005), review of *Back from the Grave Part 1*, Various Artists, originally in *Conflict*, date unknown, http://www.klangundkleid.ch/katalog/detail.asp?ID=619&SID=3, accessed 23 September 2003.

Coyle, Michael and Jon Dolan (1999), 'Modeling Authenticity, Authenticating Commercial Models', in Dettmar, Kevin J.H. and William Richey (eds), *Reading Rock and Roll: Authenticity, Appropriation, Aesthetics*, New York: Columbia University Press, pp. 17–35.

Crain, William (2002), 'Jonathan Richman', http://www.furious.com/perfect/modern-lovers.html, accessed 10 November 2003.

Cross, Charles R. (2001), *Heavier than Heaven: A Biography of Kurt Cobain*, New York: Hyperion.

Cutler, Chris (1991), *File Under Popular*, New York: Semiotext(e).

Dafydd, Rees and Luke Crampton (1996), *Encyclopedia of Rock Stars*, New York, D.K. Publishing.

Davey, Tim and Horst Puschmann (1996), *Kiwi Rock*, Dunedin: Kiwi Rock Publications.

Davies, Helen (2001), 'All Rock and Roll is Homosocial: The Representation of Women in the British Rock Music Press', *Popular Music*, 20 (3), 301–20.

Davies, Laura Lee (1996), 'Velocity Girls: Indie, New Lads, Old Values', in Cooper, Sarah (ed.), *Girls! Girls! Girls! Essays on Women and Music*, New York: New York University Press, pp. 124–34.

DeCurtis, Anthony (1999), 'Lost in the Supermarket: Myth and Commerce in the Music Business', in Kelly, Karen and Evelyn McDonnell (eds), *Stars Don't Stand Still in the Sky: Music and Myth*, New York: New York University Press, pp. 31–35.

Deleuze, Gilles (1989), *Masochism: Coldness and Cruelty*, New York: Tone.

Deleuze, Gilles and Felix Guattari (1983), *Anti-Oedipus: Capitalism and Schizophrenia*, trans. Robert Hurley, Michael Seem and Helen Lane, Minneapolis: University of Minnesota Press.

DeRogatis, Jim (1996), *Kaleidoscope Eyes: Psychedelic Rock from the 60s to the 90s*, Secaucus, NJ: Carol Publishing.

Descartes, Rene (1968), *Discourse on Method*, London: Penguin.

Deveaux, Monique (1994), 'Feminism and Empowerment: A Critical Reading of Foucault', *Feminist Studies*, 20 (2). Database: *Academic Search Premier,* http://weblinks3.epnet.com.ezproxy.auckland.ac.nz/citation.asp?tb=1

Dix, John (1988), *Stranded in Paradise*, Wellington: Paradise Publications.

Donaldson, Mike (2003), 'Studying Up: The Masculinity of the Hegemonic', in Towsen, S. and M. Donaldson (eds), *Male Trouble: Looking at Australian Masculinities*, Melbourne: Pluto, pp. 156–79.

Douglas, Mary (1970), *Purity and Danger: An Analysis of Concepts of Pollution and Taboo*, Harmondsworth: Pelican.

Downes, Graeme (1999–2000), review of *Positively George St*, Sneaky Feelings, *Music in New Zealand*, 36, 66–67.

Doyle, Jennifer, Jonathan Flatley and Jose Esteban Munoz (1996), 'Introduction' in Doyle, Jennifer et al. (eds), *Pop Out: Queer Warhol*, Durham, NC and London: Duke University Press, pp. 1–19.

Duff, Cameron (1999), 'Stepping through the Eye of Power: Foucault, Limits and the Construction of Masculinity', http://www.foucault.qut.edu.au/duff.html, accessed 10 April 2005.

Dyer, Richard (1986), *Heavenly Bodies: Film Stars and Society*, New York: St Martin's.

Easthope, Antony (1986), *What a Man's Gotta Do: The Masculine Myth in Popular Culture*, London: Paladin.

Eggleton, David (1994), 'The Bats: Hearing Secret Harmonies', *Music in New Zealand*, 26, 44–63.

Ehrenreich, Barbara (1983), *The Hearts of Men: American Dreams and the Flight From Commitment*, Garden City, NY: Anchor/Doubleday.

Eng, Lawrence (2002), 'Otak-who? Technoculture, Youth, Consumption, and Resistance', www.rpi.edu/~engl/otaku.pdf, accessed 1 December 2004.

Fabbri, Franco (1982), 'A Theory of Musical Genres: Two Applications', in Horn, David and Philip Tagg (eds), *Popular Music Perspectives*, Goteborg and London: IASPM, pp. 52–81.

Faludi, Susan (1999), *Stiffed – The Betrayal of the American Man*, New York: William Morrow.

Felder, Rachel (1993), *Manic Pop Thrill*, New York: Echo.

Firestone, Shulamith (1970), *The Dialectic of Sex: The Case for Feminist Revolution*, New York: William Morrow.

Flatley, Jonathan (1996), 'Warhol Gives Good Face: Publicity and the Politics of Prosopopeia', in Doyle, Jennifer, Jonathan Flatley and Jose Esteban Munoz (eds), *Pop Out: Queer Warhol*, Durham, NC and London: Duke University Press, pp. 101–33.

Fornäs, Johan, Ulf Lindberg and Ove Sernhede (1995), *In Garageland: Rock, Youth and Modernity*, trans. Jan Teeland, London: Routledge.

Foucault, Michel (1991), 'What is an Author?', in Mukerji, Chandra and Michael Schudson (eds), *Rethinking Popular Culture: Contemporary Perspectives in Cultural Studies*, Berkeley: University of California Press, pp. 446–64.

—— (1984), *The Foucault Reader*, ed. Paul Rabinow, New York: Pantheon.

—— (1983), 'The Subject and Power', in Dreyfus, H. and P. Rainbow (eds), *Michel Foucault: Beyond Structuralism and Hermeneutics*. Chicago: University of Chicago Press.

—— (1980), *Power/Knowledge: Selected Interviews and Other Writings, 1972–1977*, ed. and trans. Colin Gordon et al., Brighton, Sussex: Harvester.

—— (1979), *Discipline and Punish: The Birth of the Prison*, trans. Alan Sheridan, New York: Vintage.

—— (1978), *The History of Sexuality*, Vol. 1: *An Introduction*, trans. Robert Hurley, New York: Pantheon.

—— (1972), *The Archaeology of Knowledge; and the Discourse on Language*, trans. A.M. Sheridan Smith, New York: Pantheon.

Frank, Marcie (1996), 'Popping Off Warhol: From the Gutter to the Underground and Beyond' in Doyle, Jennifer, Jonathan Flatley and Jose Esteban Munoz (eds), *Pop Out: Queer Warhol*, Durham, NC and London: Duke University Press, pp. 210–23.

Freud, Sigmund (1953–74), *The Standard Edition of the Complete Psychological Works of Sigmund Freud*, ed. James Strachey, in collaboration with Anna Freud, assisted by Alix Strachey and Alan Tyson, London: Hogarth.

Frith, Simon (1996), *Performing Rites: On the Value of Popular Music*, Cambridge, Mass.: Harvard University Press.

—— (1992), *We Gotta Get Out of This Place: Popular Conservatism and Postmodern Culture*, New York: Routledge.

—— (1988), *It's a Sin: Essays on Postmodernism, Politics and Culture*, Sydney: Power Publications.

Guillory, John (1993), *Cultural Capital: The Problem of Literary Canon Formation*, Chicago: University of Chicago Press.

Habermas, Jürgen (1970), 'Towards a Theory of Communicative Competence', *Inquiry*, 13, 360–75.

Handy, Bruce et al. (1994), 'Never Mind', *Time Magazine*, 18 April.

Hardy, Phil and Dave Laing (eds) (1990), *The Faber Companion to 20th-Century Popular Music*, London: Faber.

Harrington, Joe S. (2002), *Sonic Cool: The Life and Death of Rock'n'roll*, Milwaukee: Hal Leonard.

Hartsock, Nancy C.M. (1983), *Money, Sex, and Power: Toward a Feminist Historical Materialism*, New York: Longman.

Hawkins, Stan (2002), *Settling the Pop Score: Pop Texts and Identity Politics*, Aldershot: Ashgate.

Hawthorn, Jeremy (2000), *A Glossary of Contemporary Literary Theory*, London: Arnold.

Hearn, Jeff (1992), *Men in the Public Eye*, London: Routledge.

Heartfield, James (2002), 'There is No Masculinity Crisis', *Genders Online*, 35, http://www.genders.org/g35/g35_heartfield.html, accessed 12 March 2005.

Hebdige, Dick (1979), *Subculture: The Meaning of Style*, London and New York: Methuen.

Hector, David (1998), *The Complete Guide to the Music of Nirvana*, London: Omnibus.

Hegel, Georg (1949), *The Phenomenology of Mind*, trans. J.B. Baillie, London: Allen & Unwin.

Hesmondhalgh, David (1999), 'Indie: The Institutional Politics and Aesthetics of a Popular Music Genre', *Cultural Studies*, 13, 34–61.

Heylin, Clinton (1993), *From the Velvets to the Voidoids: A Pre-punk History for a Post-punk World*, London and New York: Penguin.

Hibbett, Ryan (2005), 'What is Indie Rock?', *Popular Music and Society*, 28 (1), 55–78.

Hills, Matthew (2002), *Fan Cultures*, London: Routledge.

'History of the Pixies' (2004), http://www.baileyswalk.com/index.php, accessed 3 March 2005.

Hogg, Colin (2001), 'Easy Listening CD Coming Soon to a Holmes Near You', *Sunday Star Times*, 14 May, A1.

Hoggart, Richard (1957), *The Uses of Literacy*, London: Chatto & Windus.

Holland, Eugene W. (1999), *Deleuze and Guattari's Anti-Oedipus: Introduction to Schizoanalysis*, London and New York: Routledge.

Holter, Øystein Gullvåg (1995), 'Family Theory Reconsidered', in Borchgrevink, Tordis and Øystein Gullvåg Holter (eds), *Labour of Love: Beyond the Self-evidence of Everyday Life*, Aldershot: Avebury, pp. 99–131.

Holtz, Geoffrey T. (1995), *Welcome to the Jungle: The Why Behind 'Generation X'*, New York: St Martin's Griffin.

Horkheimer, Max (2002), *Critical Theory: Selected Essays*, trans. Matthew J. Connell and others, New York: Continuum.

—— (1992), *We Gotta Get Out of This Place: Popular Conservatism and Postmodern Culture*, New York: Routledge.

—— (1988), *It's a Sin: Essays on Postmodernism, Politics and Culture*, Sydney: Power Publications.

Guillory, John (1993), *Cultural Capital: The Problem of Literary Canon Formation*, Chicago: University of Chicago Press.

Habermas, Jürgen (1970), 'Towards a Theory of Communicative Competence', *Inquiry*, 13, 360–75.

Handy, Bruce et al. (1994), 'Never Mind', *Time Magazine*, 18 April.

Hardy, Phil and Dave Laing (eds) (1990), *The Faber Companion to 20th-Century Popular Music*, London: Faber.

Harrington, Joe S. (2002), *Sonic Cool: The Life and Death of Rock'n'roll*, Milwaukee: Hal Leonard.

Hartsock, Nancy C.M. (1983), *Money, Sex, and Power: Toward a Feminist Historical Materialism*, New York: Longman.

Hawkins, Stan (2002), *Settling the Pop Score: Pop Texts and Identity Politics*, Aldershot: Ashgate.

Hawthorn, Jeremy (2000), *A Glossary of Contemporary Literary Theory*, London: Arnold.

Hearn, Jeff (1992), *Men in the Public Eye*, London: Routledge.

Heartfield, James (2002), 'There is No Masculinity Crisis', *Genders Online*, 35, http://www.genders.org/g35/g35_heartfield.html, accessed 12 March 2005.

Hebdige, Dick (1979), *Subculture: The Meaning of Style*, London and New York: Methuen.

Hector, David (1998), *The Complete Guide to the Music of Nirvana*, London: Omnibus.

Hegel, Georg (1949), *The Phenomenology of Mind*, trans. J.B. Baillie, London: Allen & Unwin.

Hesmondhalgh, David (1999), 'Indie: The Institutional Politics and Aesthetics of a Popular Music Genre', *Cultural Studies*, 13, 34–61.

Heylin, Clinton (1993), *From the Velvets to the Voidoids: A Pre-punk History for a Post-punk World*, London and New York: Penguin.

Hibbett, Ryan (2005), 'What is Indie Rock?', *Popular Music and Society*, 28 (1), 55–78.

Hills, Matthew (2002), *Fan Cultures*, London: Routledge.

'History of the Pixies' (2004), http://www.baileyswalk.com/index.php, accessed 3 March 2005.

Hogg, Colin (2001), 'Easy Listening CD Coming Soon to a Holmes Near You', *Sunday Star Times*, 14 May, A1.

Hoggart, Richard (1957), *The Uses of Literacy*, London: Chatto & Windus.

Holland, Eugene W. (1999), *Deleuze and Guattari's Anti-Oedipus: Introduction to Schizoanalysis*, London and New York: Routledge.

Holter, Øystein Gullvåg (1995), 'Family Theory Reconsidered', in Borchgrevink, Tordis and Øystein Gullvåg Holter (eds), *Labour of Love: Beyond the Self-evidence of Everyday Life*, Aldershot: Avebury, pp. 99–131.

Holtz, Geoffrey T. (1995), *Welcome to the Jungle: The Why Behind 'Generation X'*, New York: St Martin's Griffin.

Horkheimer, Max (2002), *Critical Theory: Selected Essays*, trans. Matthew J. Connell and others, New York: Continuum.

—— (1992), 'The Cultural Study of Popular Music', in Grossberg, Lawrence, Cary Nelson and Paula A. Treichler (eds), *Cultural Studies*, London: Routledge.

—— (1988), *Music for Pleasure: Essays in the Sociology of Pop*, London: Basil Blackwell.

Frith, Simon and Howard Horne (1987), *Art into Pop*, London and New York: Methuen.

Frith, Simon and Angela McRobbie (1990), 'Rock and Sexuality', in Frith, Simon and Andrew Goodwin (eds), *On Record: Rock, Pop and the Written Word*, New York: Pantheon, pp. 371–89.

Gaar, Gillian (1992), *She's a Rebel: The History of Women in Rock & Roll*, Seattle: Seal.

Gallagher, Tom, Michael Campbell and Murdo Gillies (eds) (1995), *The Smiths: All Men Have Secrets*, London: Virgin.

Gans, David (1985), *Talking Heads*, New York: Avon.

Gelling, Randy (1999), 'Joe Carducci: Rock and the Pop Narcotic 1999', October, www. furious.com/perfect/carducci.html, accessed 26 November 2003.

Gendron, Bernard (2002), *Between Montmartre and the Mudd Club: Popular Music and the Avant Garde*, Chicago and London: University of Chicago Press.

Gibson, William (2001), 'Modern Boys and Mobile Girls', *Observer*, 1 April, http://www. observer.co.uk./life/story/0,6903,466391,00.html, accessed 1 April 2005.

Giddens, Anthony (1991), *Modernity and Self-Identity. Self and Society in the Late Modern Age*, Cambridge: Polity.

—— (1990), *The Consequences of Modernity*, Cambridge: Polity.

Gilbert, Jeremy (1999), 'White Light/White Heat: Jouissance Beyond Gender in the Velvet Underground', in Blake, Andrew (ed.), *Living through Pop*, London: Routledge, pp. 31–48.

Goode, Luke and Nabeel Zuberi (eds) (2004), *Media Studies in Aotearoa/New Zealand*, Auckland: Pearson Education.

Goodlad, Lauren M.E. (2003), 'Packaged Alternatives: The Incorporation and Gendering of "Alternative" Radio', in Squier, Susan Merrill (ed.), *Communities of the Air: Radio Century, Radio Culture*, Durham, NC and London: Duke University Press, pp. 134–63.

Goodwin, Andrew (1992), *Dancing in the Distraction Factory: Music Television and Popular Culture*, Minneapolis: University of Minnesota Press.

Gracyk, Theodore (1996), *Rhythm and Noise: An Aesthetics of Rock*, Durham, NC and London: Duke University Press.

Grajeda, Tony (2002), 'The "Feminization" of Rock', in Beebe, Roger, Denise Fulbrook and Ben Saunders (eds), *Rock over the Edge*, London: Duke University Press, pp. 233–54.

Gray, Marcus (1993), *An R.E.M. Companion: It Crawled from the South*, New York: Da Capo.

Green, Lucy (1997), *Music, Gender, Education*, Cambridge: Cambridge University Press.

—— (1988), *Music on Deaf Ears: Musical Meaning, Ideology and Education*, Manchester: Manchester University Press.

Greer, Germaine (1971), *The Female Eunuch*, London: Paladin.

Grossberg, Lawrence (1997), 'Another Boring Day in Paradise: Rock & Roll and the Empowerment of Everyday Life', in Gelder, Ken and Sarah Thornton (eds), *The Subcultures Reader*, London and New York: Routledge, pp. 477–93.

—— (1994), 'Is Anybody Listening? Does Anyone Care? On "the State of Rock"', in Ross, Andrew and Tricia Rose (eds), *Microphone Fiends: Youth Music and Youth Culture*, London: Routledge, pp. 41–58.

—— (1994), *Critique of Instrumental Reason*, trans. Matthew J. Connell and others, New York: Continuum.

Hornby, Nick (1995), *High Fidelity*, London: Gollancz.

—— (1994), *Fever Pitch*, New York: Penguin.

Horton, Marc (2002), 'Feels like the First Time: Sneaky Feelings and the Rest of the Best of the Flying Nun Sound', *Perfect Sound Forever*, http://www.furious.com/perfect/sneakyfeelings.html, accessed 2 April 2004.

Hreha, Scott (2003), review of Nick Cave and the Bad Seeds, *Nocturama*, http://www.popmatters.com/music/reviews/c/cavenick-nocturama.shtml, accessed 30 June 2004.

Humm, Maggie (1995), *The Dictionary of Feminist Theory*, Hemel Hempstead: Prentice Hall.

Huyssen, Andreas (1986), 'Mass Culture as Woman: Modernism's Other', in Modleski, Tania (ed.), *Studies in Entertainment: Critical Approaches to Mass Culture*, Bloomington: Indiana University Press, pp. 188–207.

Hyland, Matthew (1990), 'In Defense of Surreal Guitars', *Stamp*, 13 September.

James, Bev and Saville-Smith, Kay (1994), *Gender, Culture and Power: Challenging New Zealand's Gendered Culture*, 2nd edn, Auckland: Oxford University Press.

James, Billy (1965), sleeve notes, The Byrds, *Mr Tambourine Man*.

Jameson, Fredric (1988), *The Ideologies of Theory: Essays, 1971–1986*, vol. 2, Minneapolis: University of Minnesota Press.

—— (1983), 'Postmodernism and Consumer Society', in Foster, Hal (ed.), *The Anti-Aesthetic: Essays on Postmodern Culture*, Washington: Bay, pp. 111–25.

Jeffords, Susan (1994), *Hard Bodies: Hollywood Masculinity in the Reagan Era*, New Brunswick, NJ: Rutgers University Press.

Jensen, Kai (1996), *Whole Men: The Masculine Tradition in New Zealand Literature*, Auckland: Auckland University Press.

Jesson, Bruce (1989), *Fragments of Labour: The Story Behind the Fourth Labour Government*, Auckland: Penguin.

Johnson, Vivien (1992), 'Be My Woman Rock'n'Roll', in Hayward, Philip (ed.), *From Pop to Punk to Postmodernism: Popular Music and Australian Culture from the 1960s to the 1990s*, Sydney: Allen & Unwin, pp. 127–38.

Jones, Cliff (1996), *Echoes: The Stories Behind Every Pink Floyd Song*, London: Omnibus.

Jones, Steve and Kevin Featherley (2002), 'Re-viewing Rock Writing: Narratives of Popular Music Criticism', in Jones, Steve (ed.), *Pop Music and the Press*, Philadelphia: Temple University Press, pp. 19–40.

Joyce, James (1921), *A Portrait of the Artist as a Young Man*, London: The Egoist.

Kavanagh, Dennis (1990), *Thatcherism and British Politics*, Oxford: Oxford University Press.

Keightley, Kier (2001), 'Reconsidering Rock', in Frith, Simon, Will Straw and John Street (eds), *Cambridge Companion to Pop and Rock*, Cambridge: Cambridge University, pp. 109–42.

Keil, Charles and Stephen Feld (1994), *Music Grooves*, Chicago: University of Chicago Press.

Keller, Evelyn (1985), *Reflections on Gender and Science*, New Haven, Conn.: Yale University Press.

King, Michael (1999), *Being Pakeha Now: Reflections and Recollections of a White Native*, Auckland: Penguin.

Kitts, Jeff, Brad Tolinski and Harold Steinblatt (eds) (1998), *Nirvana and the Grunge Revolution*, Milwaukee: Hal Leonard.

Klein, Joshua (2002), 'Grant Hart (Hüsker Dü)', in *The Tenacity of the Cockroach: Conversations with Entertainment's Most Enduring Outsiders*, New York: Three Rivers.

Knox, Chris (1991), 'Uneffected Music', *New Zealand Listener*, 4 February, 72–73.

—— (1990), 'Wee Gems', *New Zealand Listener*, 26 February, 94–95.

—— (1989a), 'Digitised to Death', *New Zealand Listener*, 11 March, 57.

—— (1989b), 'Future Chic', *New Zealand Listener*, 3 June.

—— (1986), 'Top Tetanus', *New Zealand Listener*, 1 June, 53–54.

—— (1985a), 'Underground Resurfaces', *New Zealand Listener*, 4 May, 45.

—— (1985b), 'Rasta Nah Leggo', *New Zealand Listener*, 16 November, 75.

Koch, Stephen (1974), *Stargazer: Andy Warhol's World and His Films*, London: Calder and Boyars.

Kruse, Holly (2003), *Site and Sound: Understanding Independent Music Scenes*, New York: Peter Lang.

Laing, Dave (1997), 'Rock Anxieties and New MusicNetworks', in McRobbie, Angela (ed.), *Back to Reality: Social Experience and Cultural Studies*, Manchester: Manchester University Press, pp. 117–32.

—— (1986), *One Chord Wonders: Power and Meaning in Punk Rock*, Milton Keynes: Open University Press.

Laing, R.D. (1965), *The Divided Self: An Existential Study in Sanity and Madness*, London: Penguin.

Landau, Jon (1972), *It's Too Late to Stop Now*, San Francisco: Straight Arrow.

Larkin, Colin (1995), *The Guinness Who's Who of Indie New Wave*, London: Guinness.

—— (1998), *The All-time Top 1000 Albums*, London: Guinness.

Lasch, Christopher (1978), *The Culture of Narcissism*, New York: Norton.

Latham, Rob (2002), *Consuming Youth: Vampires, Cyborgs, and the Culture of Consumption*, Chicago: University of Chicago Press.

Law, Robin, Hugh Campbell and Ruth Schick (1999), 'Introduction' in Law, Robin, Hugh Campbell and John Dolan (eds), *Masculinities in Aotearoa/New Zealand*, Palmerston North: Dunmore, pp. 13–35.

Lazell, Barry (1997), *Indie Hits 1980–1989: The Complete UK Independent Charts (Singles & Albums)*, London: Cherry Red.

Leach, Elizabeth Eva (2001), 'Vicars of "Wannabe": Authenticity and the Spice Girls', *Popular Music*, 20 (2), 143–68.

Lehman, Peter (2003), *Roy Orbison: The Invention of an Alternative Rock Masculinity*, Philadelphia: Temple University Press.

Levin, Rick (2001), 'Heart to Hart: An Old Flame Burns Brightly', http://thestranger.com/2001-05-03/music.html, accessed 4 March 2005.

Levi-Strauss, Claude (1969), *The Elementary Structures of Kinship*, Boston: Beacon.

Lister, Martin, Jon Dovey, Seth Giddings, Iain Grant and Kieran Kelly (2003), *New Media: A Critical Introduction*, Philadelphia: Temple University Press.

Lohan, Maria and Wendy Faulkner (2004), 'Masculinities and Technologies: Some Introductory Remarks', *Men and Masculinities*, 6 (4), 319–29.

McCarthy, Thomas (1994), 'The Critique of Impure Reason', in Kelly, Michael (ed.), *Critique and Power: Recasting the Foucault/Habermas Debate*, Cambridge, Mass.: MIT Press, pp. 243–82.

MacDonald, Ian (1998), *Revolution in the Head: The Beatles' Records and the Sixties*, London: Pimlico.

McDonnell, Evelyn and Ann Powers (eds) (1995), *Rock She Wrote*, New York: Delta.

McDonnell, Evelyn (1995), 'Beyond the Tracks – Alternative Music – Music Column', *Interview*, October, http://www.findarticles.com/p/articles/mi_m1285/is_n10_v25/ai_17624803, accessed 3 March 2005.

McKessar, Paul (1988), 'Flying Nun Records', *Music in New Zealand*, Spring, 26–30.

McLeay, Colin (1994), 'The "Dunedin Sound": New Zealand Rock and Cultural Geography', *Perfect Beat*, 2 (1), 38–50.

McLuhan, Marshall (1964), *Understanding Media: The Extensions of Man*, London, Sphere.

McRobbie, Angela (1999), 'Thinking with Music', in Kelly, Karen and Evelyn McDonnell (eds), *Stars Don't Stand Still in the Sky: Music and Myth*, New York: New York University Press, pp. 37–49.

—— (1990), 'Settling Accounts with Subcultures: A Feminist Critique', in Frith, Simon and Andrew Goodwin (eds), *On Record: Rock, Pop and the Written Word*, New York, Pantheon, pp. 66–80.

Mailer, Norman (1957), *The White Negro*, San Francisco: City Lights (unpaginated: refs in the text are counted from the first page of the book).

Marcus, Greil (1999), 'Introduction: All This Useless Beauty', in Kelly, Karen and Evelyn McDonnell (eds), *Stars Don't Stand Still in the Sky: Music and Myth*, New York: New York University Press, pp. 17–27.

Marcuse, Herbert (1991), *One-Dimensional Man*, London: Routledge.

Marsh, Dave (1999), *The Heart of Rock and Soul*, New York: Da Capo.

—— (1987), 'All That You Dream', *Rock & Roll Confidential*, 69, January, 7–8.

—— (1985), *The First Rock & Roll Confidential Report*, New York, Pantheon.

Massumi, Brian (1992), *A User's Guide to Capitalism and Schizophrenia: Deviations from Deleuze and Guattari*, Cambridge, Mass.: MIT Press.

Merleau-Ponty, Maurice (2003), *Phenomenology of Perception*, trans. Colin Smith, London: Routledge.

Middleton, Richard (1990), *Studying Popular Music*, Buckingham: Open University Press.

Miller, Jim (1996), 'Presenting the Fabulous Ronettes Featuring Veronica', in Marcus, Greil (ed.), *Stranded: Rock and Roll for a Desert Island*, New York: Da Capo, pp. 40–48.

—— (ed.) (1980), *The Rolling Stone Illustrated History of Rock & Roll*, New York: Rolling Stone.

Millett, Kate (1970), *Sexual Politics*, New York: Doubleday.

Mitchell, Tony (1996), *Popular Music and Local Identity: Rock, Pop and Rap in Europe and Oceania*, London: Leicester University Press.

Moon, Michael (1996), 'Screen Memories, or Pop Comes From the Outside: Warhol and Queer Childhood', in Doyle, Jennifer, Jonathan Flatley and Jose Esteban Munoz (eds), *Pop Out: Queer Warhol*, Durham, NC and London: Duke University Press, pp. 78–100.

Moore, Allan F. (2001), *Rock: The Primary Text*, 2nd edn, Aldershot: Ashgate.

Moore, Suzanne (1988), 'Getting a Bit of the Other: The Pimps of Postmodernism', in Chapman, Rowena and Jonathan Rutherford (eds), *Male Order: Unwrapping Masculinity*, London: Lawrence & Wishart, pp. 165–92.

Moore, Thurston (1992), 'Stabb's Hand Touched Me and I Slept', in Heylin, Clinton (ed.), *The Penguin Book of Rock'n'Roll Writing*, Harmondsworth: Penguin, pp. 357–68.

Morgan, David H.J. (1992), *Discovering Men*, London and New York: Routledge.

Morley, Paul (2003), *Words and Music: A History of Pop in the Shape of a City*, London: Bloomsbury.

Mulvey, Laura (1989), *Visual and Other Pleasures*, Bloomington and Indianapolis: Indiana University Press.

Murray, Charles Shaar, (1992), 'What Have They Done to My Blues Ma?', in Heylin, Clinton (ed.), *The Penguin Book of Rock'n'Roll Writing*, Harmondsworth: Penguin, pp. 604–12.

Neale, Stephen (1980), *Genre*, London: British Film Institute.

Negus, Keith (1999), *Music Genres and Corporate Cultures*, London: Routledge.

—— (1992), *Producing Pop: Culture and Conflict in the Popular Music Industry*, London and New York: E. Arnold.

Nehring, Neil (1997), *Popular Music, Gender and Postmodernism*, Thousand Oaks, Calif.: Sage.

—— (1993), *Flowers in the Dustbin: Culture, Anarchy and Postwar England*, Ann Arbor: University of Michigan Press.

Nichols, David (2003), *The Go-Betweens*, Portland, Oreg: Verse Chorus.

O'Hagan, Andrew (2004), 'Cartwheels over Broken Glass', *London Review of Books*, 26 (5), 4 March, http://www.lrb.co.uk/v26/n05/ohag01.html, accessed 3 August 2004.

Pareles, Jon (1991), 'Now is the Summer of Discontent', *New York Times*, 25 August, 20–22.

Pareles, Jon and Patricia Romanowski (eds) (1983), *The Rolling Stone Encyclopedia of Rock'n'Roll*, London: Rolling Stone.

Peters, Guy (2002–2005), 'Frank Black (1993)', http://www.guypetersreviews.com/frankblack.php#fb, accessed 17 July 2004.

Pfeil, Fred (1995), *White Guys: Studies in Postmodern Domination and Difference*, London: Verso.

Phillips, Jock (1987), *A Man's Country? The Image of the Pakeha Male – A History*, Auckland: Penguin.

Poniewozik, James (2001), 'Talking About My Generation', *Time Magazine*, 20–27 August, 84.

Powers, Anne (1995), 'Never More', in Kureishi, Hanif and Jon Savage (eds), *The Faber Book of Pop*, London: Faber and Faber, pp. 786–95.

'Punk Rock City, U.S.A. – An Interview with Gina Arnold' (1993), *Stay Free!*, 5, http://www.bibiblio.org/pub/electronic-publications/stay-free/5/punk.htm.

Real, Terrence (1997), *I Don't Want to Talk About It: Overcoming the Secret Legacy of Male Depression*, New York: Scribner.

Regev, Motti (2002), 'The "Pop-rockization" of Popular Music', in Hesmondhalgh, David and Keith Negus (eds), *Popular Music Studies*, New York: Oxford University, pp. 251–64.

Reid, Graham (2001), review of *The Mojo Collection*, *NZ Herald*, 3 March.

Reynolds, Simon (1990), *Blissed Out: The Raptures of Rock*, London: Serpent's Tail.

—— (1989), 'Against Health and Efficiency', in McRobbie, Angela (ed.), *Zoot Suits and Second Hand Dresses*, Basingstoke: Macmillan, pp. 244–55.

—— (1985), 'New Pop and its Aftermath', in Frith, Simon and Andrew Goodwin (eds), *On Record: Rock, Pop and the Written Word*, New York, Pantheon, pp. 466–71.

Reynolds, Simon and Press, Joy (1995), *The Sex Revolts: Gender, Rebellion and Rock'n'roll*, London: Serpent's Tail.

Rius (1994), *Marx for Beginners*, Cambridge: Icon.

Robertson, Craig (1991), 'It's OK, It's All Right, Oh Yeah: The "Dunedin Sound"? An Aspect of Alternative Music in New Zealand 1979–85', unpublished dissertation, University of Otago.

Robertson, John (1988), *The Jesus and Mary Chain: A Musical Biography*, London: Omnibus.

Rogan, Johnny (1992), *Morrissey & Marr: The Severed Alliance: The Definitive Story of the Smiths*, ed. Chris Charlesworth, London: Omnibus.

Rollins, Henry (1997), *The Portable Henry Rollins*, London: Phoenix House.

Rosaldo, Renato (1993), 'After Objectivism', in During, Simon (ed.), *The Cultural Studies Reader*, London: Routledge, pp. 104–17.

Ross, Andrew (1989), *No Respect: Intellectuals & Popular Culture*, New York: Routledge.

Rubin, Gayle (1975), 'The Traffic in Women: Notes Towards a Political Economy of Sex', in Reiter, Rayna (ed.), *Towards an Anthropology of Women*, New York: Monthly Review, pp. 157–210.

Rushkoff, Douglas (1994), 'Introduction: Us, By Us', in Rushkoff, Douglas (ed.), *The GenX Reader*, New York: Ballantine, pp. 3–8.

Rutherford, Jonathan (1988), 'Who's That Man?', in Chapman, Rowena and Jonathan Rutherford (eds), *Male Order: Unwrapping Masculinity*, London: Lawrence & Wishart, pp. 21–67.

Rutherford, Jonathan and Rowena Chapman (1988), 'The Forward March of Men Halted', in Chapman, Rowena and Jonathan Rutherford (eds), *Male Order: Unwrapping Masculinity*, London: Lawrence & Wishart, pp. 9–18.

Sadie, Stanley (ed.) (2001), *The New Grove Dictionary of Music and Musicians*, executive editor John Tyrrell, London: Macmillan.

Sargeant, Jack (2002), 'Voyeurism, Sadism and Transgression: Screen Notes and Observations on Warhol's "Blow Job" and "I, a Man"', in Mendik Xavier and Steven Jay Schneider (eds), *Underground U.S.A: Filmmaking Beyond the Hollywood Canon*, London: Wallflower.

Savage, Jon (1997), *Time Travel – From the Sex Pistols to Nirvana: Pop, Media and Sexuality*, London: Vintage.

—— (1993), *England's Dreaming: Anarchy, Sex Pistols, Punk Rock, and Beyond*, New York: St. Martin's Press.

Savran, David (1998), *Taking It Like a Man: White Masculinity, Masochism, and Contemporary American Culture*, Princeton, NJ: Princeton University Press.

—— (1996), 'The Sadomasochist in the Closet: White Masculinity and the Culture of Victimisation', *Differences*, 8 (2), 127–52.

Scott, Alex (2002), 'Merleau-Ponty's *Phenomenology of Perception*', http://www.angelfire.com/md2/timewarp/merleauponty.html, accessed 22 July 2004.

Sedgwick, Eve Kosofsky (1996), 'Queer Performativity: Warhol's Shyness/Warhol's Whiteness', in Doyle, Jennifer, Jonathan Flatley and Jose Esteban Munoz (eds), *Pop Out: Queer Warhol*, Durham, NC and London: Duke University Press, pp. 134–43.

—— (1990), *Epistemology of the Closet*, Hemel Hempstead: Harvester Wheatsheaf.

—— (1985), *Between Men: English Literature and Male Homosocial Desire*, New York: Columbia University Press.

Segal, Lynne (1990), *Slow Motion: Changing Masculinities, Changing Men*, New Brunswick, NJ: Rutgers University Press.

Seidler, Victor J. (ed.) (1991), *Achilles Heel Reader: Men, Sexual Politics, and Socialism*, London and New York: Routledge.

—— (1989), *Rediscovering Masculinity: Reason, Language, and Sexuality*, London and New York: Routledge.

—— (1988), 'Fathering, Authority and Masculinity', in Chapman, Rowena and Jonathan Rutherford (eds), *Male Order: Unwrapping Masculinity*, London: Lawrence & Wishart, pp. 272–302.

Shepherd, Roger (1998), Sleevenotes for *God Save the Clean: A Tribute to The Clean*, Flying Nun.

Shuker, Roy (1998), *Key Concepts in Popular Music*, London: Routledge.

—— (1994), *Understanding Popular Music*, London: Routledge.

Shumway, David (2001), conference address, IASPM 2001, Turku, Finland, 6 July.

Siegal, Jules (1997), 'The Religious Conversion of Brian Wilson', in Abbott, Kingsley (ed.), *Back to the Beach: A Brian Wilson and The Beach Boys Reader*, London: Helter Skelter, pp. 51–63.

Silverman, Kaja (1992), *Male Subjectivity at the Margins*, New York: Routledge.

Slacker review, http://www.rollingstone.com/reviews/movie/_/id/5948975, accessed 2 January 2005.

Small, Christopher (1987), 'Performance as Ritual', in White, Avron Levine (ed.), *Lost in Music: Culture, Style and the Musical Event*, London: Routledge & Kegan Paul, pp. 6–33.

Smith, Giles (1995), *Lost in Music: A Pop Odyssey*, London: Picador.

Smith, Patrick S. (1988), *Warhol: Conversations about the Artist*, Ann Arbor, Mich.: UMI Research.

Somerson, Wendy (2004), 'White Men on the Edge: Rewriting the Borderlands in Lone Star', *Men and Masculinities*, 6 (3), 215–34.

Sørhaug, Tian (2001) 'The Semantics of Love', in Borchgrevink, Tordis and Øystein Gullvåg Holter (eds), *Labour of Love: Beyond the Self-evidence of Everyday Life*, Aldershot: Avebury, pp. 17–44.

Stadler, Gus (1995), 'Route 666', http://www.ibiblio.org/stayfree/books/route666.html, accessed 2 February 2005.

Starhawk (1987), *Truth or Dare: Encounters with Power, Authority and Mystery*, San Francisco: Harper & Row.

Stead, Oliver (1990–91), review of Flying Nun recent releases, *Music in New Zealand*, Summer, 85–87.

Straw, Will (1997a), 'Sizing Up Record Collections: Gender and Connoisseurship in Rock Music Culture', in Whiteley, Sheila (ed.), *Sexing the Groove: Popular Music and Gender*, London: Routledge, pp. 3–16.

—— (1997b), 'Communities and Scenes in Popular Music', in Gelder, Ken and Sarah Thornton (eds), *The Subcultures Reader*, London and New York: Routledge, pp. 494–505.

—— (1991), 'Systems of Articulation, Logics of Change: Communities and Scenes in Popular Music', *Cultural Studies*, 5 (3), 368–88.

Street, John (1986), *Rebel Rock: The Politics of Popular Music*, Oxford and New York: Blackwell.

Strong, Martin (1999), *The Great Alternative and Indie Discography*, Edinburgh: Canongate.

Stubbs, David (1999), 'I Hate Myself and Want to Die', in Clarke, Martin and Paul Woods (eds), *Kurt Cobain: The Cobain Dossier*, London, Plexus, pp. 95–103.

—— (1989), 'Fear of the Future', in McRobbie, Angela (ed.), *Zoot Suits and Second Hand Dresses*, Basingstoke: Macmillan, pp. 267–75.

Subotnik, Rose Rosengard (1976), 'Adorno's Diagnosis of Beethoven's Late Style: Early Symptom of a Fatal Condition', *Journal of the American Musicological Society*, 29 (2), 242–75.

Sutton, Terri (1997), 'The Soft Boys: The New Man in Rock', in O'Dair, Barbara (ed.), *Trouble Girls: The Rolling Stone Book of Women in Rock*, New York: Random House, pp. 527–35.

Symington, Neville (1993), *Narcissism: A New Theory*, London: Karnac.

Szemere, Anne (2001), *Up from the Underground: The Culture of Rock Music in Postsocialist Hungary*, University Park, PA: Pennsylvania State University Press.

Tamm, Eric (1995), *Brian Eno: His Music and the Vertical Colour of Sound*, New York: Da Capo.

Tawney, Richard H. (1970), 'Foreword', in Weber, Max, *Protestant Ethic and the Spirit of Capitalism*, trans. Talcott Parsons, London: Unwin University Press, pp. 1a–17.

Théberge, Pierre (1989), 'The "Sound of Music": Technological Rationalisation and the Production of Popular Music', *New Formations*, 8: 99–111.

Thomas, Bruce (1990), *The Big Wheel*, London: Penguin.

Thompson, Dave (2004), *Wall of Pain: The Phil Spector Story*, London: Sanctuary.

—— (2000), *Alternative Rock*, San Francisco: Miller Freeman.

Thompson, John B. (1995), *The Media and Modernity: A Social Theory of the Media*, Cambridge: Polity.

Thornton, Sarah (1995), *Clubcultures: Music, Media and Subcultural Capital*, Hanover and London: Wesleyan.

Thurschwell, Pamela (1999), 'Elvis Costello as Cultural Icon and Cultural Critic', in Dettmar, Kevin J.H. and William Richey (eds), *Reading Rock and Roll: Authenticity, Appropriation, Aesthetics*, New York: Columbia University Press, pp. 287–310.

'The Top 100: The Greatest Albums of the Last Twenty Years' (1987), *Rolling Stone*, 27 August, pp. 45–174.

Toynbee, Jason (2000a), *Making Popular Music: Musicians, Creativity and Institutions*, London: Arnold.

—— (2000b), 'From Slip Mats to Bones: Social Authorship in Jazz and Dance', IASPM UK Conference, 9 July 2000, University of Surrey.

Unofficial Sonic Youth Guitar Tunings List (2004), http://www.jauko.nl/tot/tab/s/sonicy/guitar.htm, accessed 2 November 2004.

Vance, Carole (1989), 'Social Constructionist Theory: Problems in the History of Sexuality', in Altman D. (ed.), *Homosexuality, Which Homosexuality?*, Amsterdam and London: Uitgeverij An Dekker, pp. 13–34.

Verster, François (1995), 'Mann, Adorno and Beethoven: Triangles in the Disappearance of the Musical', http://www.uwc.ac.za/arts/english/interaction/94fv.htm, accessed 10 October 2004.

Waksman, Steve (1999), *Instruments of Desire: The Electric Guitar and the Shaping of Musical Experience*, Cambridge, Mass.: Harvard University Press.

Wallerstein, Immanuel (1974), *The Modern World-System*, New York: Academic Press.

Walser, Robert (1993), *Running with the Devil: Power, Gender and Madness in Heavy Metal Music*, Hanover: University of New England.

Warhol, Andy (1975), *The Philosophy of Andy Warhol*, New York: Harcourt Brace Jovanovich.

Watney, Simon (1996), 'Queer Andy', in Doyle, Jennifer, Jonathan Flatley and Jose Esteban Munoz (eds), *Pop Out: Queer Warhol*, Durham, NC and London: Duke University Press, pp. 20–30.

—— (1995), '1985: This Charming Man', in Kureishi, Hanif and Jon Savage (eds), *The Faber Book of Pop*, London: Faber and Faber, pp. 595–601.

Weber, Max (1970), *Protestant Ethic and the Spirit of Capitalism*, trans. Talcott Parsons, London: Unwin University Press.

Weiner, Andrew (1972), *The Byrds*, London: Studio Vista.

Werner, Craig (2000), *A Change is Gonna Come: Music, Race and the Soul of America*, Edinburgh: Payback.

Whiteley, Sheila (1997), 'Introduction', in Whiteley, Sheila (ed.), *Sexing the Groove: Popular Music and Gender*, London: Routledge, pp. xiii–xxxvi.

Wilde, Oscar (1948), *The Works of Oscar Wilde*, ed. G.F. Maine, London: Collins.

Williams, Richard (2003), *Phil Spector: Out of his Head*, London: Omnibus.

Willis, Ellen (1996), 'Velvet Underground', in Marcus, Greil (ed.), *Stranded: Rock And Roll for a Desert Island*, New York: Da Capo, pp. 71–83.

Willis, Paul (1978), *Profane Culture*, London: Routledge.

Woods, Scott (2001), 'Gallery of Rockism', http://rockcritics.com/features/galleryofrockism.html, accessed 4 April 2005.

Wrenn, Mike (1988), *Bitch Bitch Bitch*, London: Omnibus.

Zanes, R.J. Warren (2002), 'A Fan's Notes: Identification, Desire and the Haunted Sound Barrier', in Beebe, Roger, Denise Fulbrook and Ben Saunders (eds), *Rock over the Edge*, London: Duke University Press, pp. 291–310.

—— (1999), 'Too Much Mead? Under the Influence (of Participant Observation)', in Dettmar, Kevin J.H. and William Richey (eds), *Reading Rock and Roll: Authenticity, Appropriation, Aesthetics*, New York: Columbia University Press, pp. 37–72.

Zuberi, Nabeel (2001), *Sounds English: Transnational Popular Music*, Urbana: University of Illinois Press.

Discography

Bailter Space (1988), *Tanker*, Flying Nun.

Bats, The (1987), *Daddy's Highway*, Flying Nun.

Beach Boys, The (1966), *Pet Sounds*, Capitol.

Beatles, The (1969), *Abbey Road*, Parlophone.

—— (1966), 'Strawberry Fields Forever', Parlophone.

—— (1966), 'Yellow Submarine', Parlophone.

Beck (1994), *Mellow Gold*, DGC.

Big Black (1987), *Headache*, Touch & Go.

Black Flag (1982), *Everything Went Black*, SST/Cherry Red.

—— (1981), *Damaged*, Unicorn/SST.

—— (1980), *Jealous Again*, SST.

—— (1979), *Nervous Breakdown*, SST.

Blasting Concept, The (1983), SST.

Bowie, David (1970), *Space Oddity*, Mercury.

Buckley, Tim (1971), *Star Sailor*, Elektra.
Byrds, The (1968), *Notorious Byrd Brothers*, Columbia.
—— (1967), *Younger Than Yesterday*, Columbia.
—— (1966a), *Turn! Turn! Turn!*, Columbia.
—— (1966b), *Fifth Dimension*, Columbia.
—— (1965), *Mr Tambourine Man*, Columbia.
Cave, Nick, and the Bad Seeds (1996), *Murder Ballads*, Warner Bros.
Chills, The (1990), *Submarine Bells*, Flying Nun.
—— (1987), *Brave Words*, Flying Nun.
—— (1986), *Kaleidoscope World*, Flying Nun.
—— (1985), *The Lost EP*, Flying Nun.
Clash, The (1977), *The Clash*, CBS.
Clean, The (1999), *Compilation*, Flying Nun.
—— (1983), 'Getting Older', Flying Nun.
—— (1982), *Great Sounds Great*, Flying Nun.
—— (1981), *Boodle Boodle Boodle*, Flying Nun.
—— (1981), 'Tally Ho', Flying Nun.
Cohen, Leonard (1968), *The Songs of Leonard Cohen*, Columbia.
Costello, Elvis (1976), *My Aim Is True*, Stiff.
Dinosaur Jr. (1991), *Green Mind*, Warner Bros.
—— (1989), *Bug*, SST.
—— (1987), *You're Living All over Me*, SST.
Direen, Bill (1995), CD reissue of *Split Seconds*, Flying Nun.
Dribbling Darts of Love (1993), *Present Perfect*, Flying Nun.
Dunedin Double (1982) (The Chills, Verlaines, Sneaky Feelings, The Stones), Flying Nun.
Dylan, Bob (1968), *John Wesley Harding*, Columbia.
—— (1967), *Bob Dylan's Greatest Hits*, Columbia.
—— (1966), *Blonde on Blonde*, Columbia.
—— (1965), *Bringing It All Back Home*, Columbia.
—— (1964), *Another Side of Bob Dylan*, Columbia.
Fall, The (1982), *Grotesque*, Rough Trade.
Feelies, The (1980), *Crazy Rhythms*, A&M.
Go-Betweens, The (1986), *Liberty Belle & the Black Diamond Express*, Beggars Banquet.
—— (1984), *Spring Hill Fair*, Rough Trade.
—— (1983), *Before Hollywood*, Rough Trade.
—— (1982), *Send Me a Lullabye*, Rough Trade.
Gordons, The (1981), *The Gordons*, Flying Nun.
Great Unwashed (1985), *Singles*, Flying Nun.
Hart, Grant (1989), *Intolerance*, SST.
Hendrix, Jimi (1968), *Smash Hits*, Polydor.
House of Love, The (1993), *Best of the House of Love*, Polygram.
Hüsker Dü (1986), *Candy Apple Grey*, Warner Bros.
—— (1986), 'Ticket to Ride', *New Musical Express* freebie.
—— (1985), 'Makes No Sense at All'/'Love Is All Around', SST.
—— (1985), *New Day Rising*, SST.
—— (1984), 'Eight Miles High', SST.
—— (1984), *Zen Arcade*, SST.

—— (1983), *Everything Falls Apart*, Reflex.

—— (1982), *Land Speed Record*, New Alliance.

Jean-Paul Sartre Experience (1990), *The Size of Food*, Flying Nun.

—— (1987), *Love Songs*, Flying Nun.

—— (1986), *The Jean Paul Sartre Experience*, Flying Nun.

Jesus and Mary Chain, The (1987), 'April Skies'/'Kill Surf City', Blanco y Negro.

——(1987), *Darklands*, Blanco y Negro.

—— (1985), *Psychocandy*, Blanco y Negro.

Kilgour, David (2004), *Frozen Orange*, Merge.

—— (2002), *A Feather in the Engine*, Merge.

—— (1994), *Sugar Mouth*, Flying Nun.

—— (1991), *Here Come The Cars*, Flying Nun.

Led Zeppelin (1971), *Untitled*, Atlantic.

Lennon, John (1970), *John Lennon/Plastic Ono Band*, Apple.

Love (1968), *Forever Changes*, Elektra.

Minor Threat (1989), *Complete Discography*, Dischord.

Minutemen (1984), *Double Nickels On The Dime*, SST.

Modern Lovers, The (1976), *The Modern Lovers*, Beserkley.

Morrissey (1988), *Viva Hate*, EMI.

My Bloody Valentine (1991), *Loveless*, Creation.

—— (1990), *Glider*, Sire.

Nirvana (1993), *In Utero*, Geffen.

—— (1992), *Incesticide*, Geffen.

—— (1991), *Nevermind*, Geffen.

—— (1989), *Bleach*, SubPop.

Nuggets: Original Artyfacts from the First Psychedelic Era, 1965–1968 (1998), Rhino.

Orange Juice (1982), *Rip It Up*, Polydor.

—— (1981), *You Can't Hide Your Love Forever*, Polydor.

Orbison, Roy (1976), *The All-Time Greatest Hits of Roy Orbison*, Monument (CD Sony 1990).

Pillows and Prayers (1982), Cherry Red.

Pink Floyd (1973), *Dark Side of the Moon*, EMI.

—— (1967), *The Piper at the Gates of Dawn*, EMI.

Radiohead (1993), *Pablo Honey*, Capitol.

Ramones (1977), *Rocket to Russia*, Sire.

Reed, Lou (1978), *Street Hassle*, Arista.

—— (1975), *Metal Machine Music*, RCA.

R.E.M. (1998), *Vintage Reckoning*, IRS.

—— (1989), *Green*, Warner Bros.

—— (1985), *Fables Of The Reconstruction*, IRS.

—— (1984), *Reckoning*, IRS.

—— (1983), *Murmur*, IRS.

—— (1982), *Chronic Town*, IRS.

Replacements, The (1987), *Pleased to Meet Me*, Sire.

—— (1985), *The Shit Hits the Fans*, Twin/Tone.

—— (1984), *Let It Be*, Twin/Tone.

—— (1983), *Hootenanny*, Twin/Tone.

Richman, Jonathan (1977), *Rock'n'Roll with the Modern Lovers*, Beserkley.

Rolling Stones (1972), *Exile on Main St*, Rolling Stone Records.

—— (1969), *Let it Bleed*, Decca.

Ronstadt, Linda (1974), *Linda Ronstadt's Greatest Hits*, Asylum.

Sebadoh (1991), *Gimme Indie Rock*, Homestead.

Sex Pistols (1977), *Never Mind the Bollocks Here's the Sex Pistols*, Virgin.

Smith, Patti (1975), *Horses*, Arista.

Smiths, The (1987a), *Louder than Bombs*, Rough Trade.

—— (1987b), *Strangeways Here We Come*.

—— (1986), *The Queen is Dead*, Rough Trade.

—— (1985), *Meat is Murder*, Rough Trade.

—— (1984a), *The Smiths*, Rough Trade.

—— (1984b), *Hatful of Hollow*, Rough Trade.

Snapper (1988), *Snapper*, Flying Nun.

Sneaky Feelings (1999), *Positively George Street*, Flying Nun.

—— (1991), *Getting Older 1981–1991*, Flying Nun.

—— (1989), *Hard Love Stories*, Flying Nun.

—— (1987), *Sentimental Education*, Flying Nun.

—— (1985), 'Husband House', Flying Nun.

—— (1984), *Send You*, Flying Nun.

—— (1982), *Dunedin Double*, Flying Nun.

Spector, Phil (1991), *Back to Mono, 1958–1969*, Phil Spector.

Springsteen, Bruce (1980), *The River*, CBS.

Stones, The (1983), *Another Disc Another Dollar*, Flying Nun.

Straitjacket Fits (1988), *Hail*, Flying Nun.

—— (1987), *Life in One Chord*, Flying Nun.

Supremes, The (1967), *Greatest Hits*, Motown.

Talking Heads (1979), *Fear of Music*, Sire.

—— (1977), *77*, Sire.

Tall Dwarfs (1994), *3 Eps*, Flying Nun.

—— (1983), *Canned Music*, Flying Nun.

—— (1982), *Three Songs*, Furtive.

That Petrol Emotion (1986), *Manic Pop Thrill*, Demon.

T-Rex (1972), *The Slider*, EMI.

U2 (1980), *Boy*, Island.

Velvet Underground, The (1974), *1969 Live*, Mercury.

—— (1970), *Loaded*, Cotillion.

—— (1969), *The Velvet Underground*, Vcrvc/Polygram.

—— (1968), *White Light/White Heat*, Verve/Polygram.

—— (1967), *The Velvet Underground and Nico*, Verve/Polygram.

Verlaines (1988), *Juvenilia*, Flying Nun.

—— (1987), *Bird-Dog*, Flying Nun.

—— (1986), *Hallelujah All the Way Home*, Flying Nun.

—— (1984), *10 O'clock in the Afternoon*, Flying Nun.

—— (1983), 'Death and the Maiden', Flying Nun.

Wedding Present, The (1987), *George Best*, Reception.

Who, The (1968), *Tommy*, Polydor.

Films and TV

Basic Instinct (1992), dir. Paul Verhoeven, USA: Carolco Pictures.
Blue Velvet (1986), dir. David Lynch, USA: De Laurentiis Entertainment Group.
Bugsy Malone (1976), dir. Alan Parker, UK: National Film Trustee Company.
Dancing in the Street (1996), UK: BBC.
Disclosure (1994), dir. Barry Levinson, USA: Warner Bros.
Dumb and Dumber (1994), dir. Peter Farrelly, USA: New Line Cinema.
Falling Down (1993), dir. Joel Schumaker, USA: Hexagon.
Fatal Attraction (1987), dir. Adrian Lyne, USA: Paramount.
Heavenly Pop Hits: The Flying Nun Story (2002), dir. Mitchell Hawkes, NZ: Satellite
    Media.
Henry – Portrait of a Serial Killer (1989), dir. John McNaughton, USA: Maljack Films.
High Fidelity (2000), dir. Stephen Frears, USA/UK: Touchstone.
Martin (1976), dir. George Romero, USA: Braddock Associates.
Rosemary's Baby (1968), dir. Roman Polanski, USA: Paramount.
sex, lies, and videotape (1989), dir. Steven Soderbergh, USA: Outlaw Productions.
Slacker (1991), dir. Richard Linklater, USA: Detour.
Taxi Driver (1976), dir. Martin Scorsese, USA: Columbia.
The Omen (1976), dir. Richard Donner, USA/UK: Twentieth Century Fox.
There's Something About Mary (1998), dir. Peter Farrelly, USA: Twentieth Century Fox.
This is Spinal Tap: A Rockumentary by Martin di Bergi (1983), dir. Rob Reiner, USA:
    Embassy Pictures.
Very Short Films (2004), NZ: Flying Nun.

Index